Repeating an earlier triumphant gesture, General Douglas MacArthur strides through shin-deep waters to the island of Luzon on January 9, 1945. MacArthur had fought for almost three years to fulfill his pledge to return to the Philippines. His first walk ashore had occurred on Leyte on October 20, 1944.

RETURN TO THE PHILIPPINES

TIME®
LIFE
BOOKS

Other Publications:

HISTORY
Our American Century
What Life Was Like
The American Story
Voices of the Civil War
The American Indians
Lost Civilizations
Mysteries of the Unknown
Time Frame
The Civil War
Cultural Atlas

COOKING
Weight Watchers® Smart Choice Recipe Collection
Great Taste~Low Fat
Williams-Sonoma Kitchen Library

DO IT YOURSELF
Total Golf
How to Fix It
The Time-Life Complete Gardener
Home Repair and Improvement
The Art of Woodworking

TIME-LIFE KIDS
Student Library
Library of First Questions and Answers
A Child's First Library of Learning
I Love Math
Nature Company Discoveries
Understanding Science & Nature

SCIENCE/NATURE
Voyage Through the Universe

For information on and a full description of
any of the Time-Life Books series listed above,
please call 1-800-621-7026 or write:

Reader Information
Time-Life Customer Service
P.O. Box C-32068
Richmond, Virginia 23261-2068

This volume is one of a series that chronicles
in full the events of the Second World War.

WORLD WAR II · TIME-LIFE BOOKS · ALEXANDRIA, VIRGINIA

BY RAFAEL STEINBERG
AND THE EDITORS OF TIME-LIFE BOOKS

RETURN TO THE PHILIPPINES

TIME®
LIFE
BOOKS

Time-Life Books is a division of Time Life Inc.

TIME LIFE INC.
PRESIDENT and CEO: George Artandi

TIME-LIFE BOOKS
PRESIDENT: Stephen R. Frary
PUBLISHER/MANAGING EDITOR: Neil Kagan
VICE PRESIDENT, MARKETING: Joseph A. Kuna

WORLD WAR II

DIRECTOR, NEW PRODUCT DEVELOPMENT:
Elizabeth D. Ward
DIRECTOR OF MARKETING: Pamela R. Farrell

Dust Jacket Design: Barbara M. Sheppard

Editorial Staff for *Return to the Philippines*
Editor: Gerald Simons
Picture Editor/Designer: Raymond Ripper
Picture Editor: Robin Richman
Text Editor: Henry Woodhead
Staff Writers: Dalton Delan, Malachy Duffy, Stuart Gannes,
Brian McGinn, Tyler Mathisen, Teresa M. C. R. Pruden
Chief Researcher: Oobie Gleysteen
Researchers: Marion F. Briggs, Charlie Clark, Christine Bowie
Dove, Jane Edwin, Frances R. Glennon, Frank McCoy
Copy Coordinators: Patricia Graber, Victoria Lee
Art Assistant: Mary Louise Mooney
Picture Coordinator: Alvin L. Ferrell
Editorial Assistant: Connie Strawbridge

Correspondents: Christine Hinze (London), Christina
Lieberman (New York)

Director of Finance: Christopher Hearing
Directors of Book Production: Marjann Caldwell,
Patricia Pascale
Director of Publishing Technology: Betsi McGrath
Director of Photography and Research: John Conrad Weiser
Director of Editorial Administration: Barbara Levitt
Production Manager: Carolyn Bounds
Quality Assurance Manager: James King
Chief Librarian: Louise D. Forstall

The Author: RAFAEL STEINBERG was a war correspondent in Korea for International News Service and *Time*. He spent many years in Japan as a correspondent for *Newsweek* and other publications, and later was managing editor of *Newsweek International*. His books include *Postscript from Hiroshima* (a book about the survivors of the nuclear bombings) and two volumes in the Time-Life Books' Foods of the World series, *The Cooking of Japan* and *Pacific and Southeast Asian Cooking*, as well as a volume in the Human Behavior series, *Man and the Organization*.

The Consultants: COL. JOHN R. ELTING, USA (Ret.), is a military historian and author of *The Battle of Bunker's Hill, The Battles of Saratoga* and *Military History and Atlas of the Napoleonic Wars.* He edited *Military Uniforms in America: The Era of the American Revolution, 1775-1795* and *Military Uniforms in America: Years of Growth, 1796-1851,* and was associate editor of *The West Point Atlas of American Wars.*

HENRY H. ADAMS served as captain aboard the destroyer U.S.S. *Owen* in the major campaigns of the central Pacific. A native of Ann Arbor, Michigan, he graduated from the University of Michigan and received his M.A. and Ph.D. degrees from Columbia University. After his service in World War II he was a professor at the U.S. Naval Academy in Annapolis, Maryland, and was later head of the English Department at Illinois State University. His books include *1942: The Year That Doomed the Axis, Years of Deadly Peril, Years of Expectation, Years to Victory* and *Harry Hopkins: A Biography.*

ROBERT ROSS SMITH received his B.A. and M.A. degrees from Duke University before World War II and a commission in the infantry from the Officers Candidate School, Fort Benning, in 1943. He served as a historian in General Douglas MacArthur's General Headquarters for two years during World War II. In 1947 he joined the U.S. Army Center of Military History and later became chief of the General History Branch. He also served as command historian, Headquarters, U.S. Army, Pacific, in Hawaii during the period 1963-1968. Lieutenant Colonel Smith wrote several volumes in the Army's official history of World War II including *The Approach to the Philippines, Triumph in the Philippines* and *The Riviera to the Rhine.*

Library of Congress Cataloging-in-Publication Data
Steinberg, Rafael
  Return to the Philippines.

  (World War II)
  Bibliography.
  Includes index.
  1. World War, 1939-1945—Campaigns—Philippine Islands
2. Philippine Islands—History—Japanese occupation, 1942-1945.
3. MacArthur, Douglas, 1880-1964.
I. Time-Life Books. II. Title. III Series.
D767.4.S73   940.54'26   78-21648
ISBN 0-7835-5709-4

CONTENTS

MANILA UNDER THE JAPANESE

Waving Japanese flags, Filipino members of the Japanese puppet government in Manila salute their recent conqueror, Lieut. General Masaharu Homma.

A TIME OF FEAR, HOPE AND CONFUSION

On January 2, 1942, less than a month after invading the Philippine Islands, triumphant Japanese forces occupied the capital city of Manila. The Japanese take-over ushered in a perplexing and paradoxical period for both the victor and the vanquished.

The Japanese authorities earnestly sought to enlist the cooperation of the Filipinos; a friendly populace would permit them to reap the benefits of their conquest without tying up troops needed elsewhere. They launched a showy program designed to transfer the Filipinos' loyalty from the United States to Japan. In their propaganda, the Japanese linked themselves to the Filipinos as Oriental peoples with a common enemy—the arrogant, white-skinned American exploiters. They made glowing promises; the best was a pledge to give the Philippines complete national independence three years before the U.S. had planned to do so.

The Filipinos distrusted the Japanese and feared reprisals for having fought beside the ousted Americans. But they were animated by growing national ambitions, and the talk of early self-government had great appeal.

The Japanese worked hard at winning over the Filipinos. They released captured Filipino soldiers. They organized Japanese-Filipino cultural exchanges and established the local language, Tagalog, as the official language along with Japanese. In 1943 they declared the Philippines an independent republic.

But even as the Japanese officials pressed for good relations, they revealed themselves as callous oppressors. They controlled the press, made it a capital offense to listen to foreign broadcasts, curtailed religion, and beat and tortured civilians whom they suspected of subversive activities. They overlooked the excesses of the Japanese troops and issued worthless military scrip, triggering a ruinous inflation.

By May of 1942, when the Japanese completed their conquest of the islands, the people of Manila had made up their minds about the Japanese. Hundreds of them took to the hills to fight again as guerrillas or joined clandestine intelligence units in the city.

Bringing the promise of Philippine independence, the Japanese Premier, Hideki Tojo (saluting), arrives with his staff in Manila on May 5, 1943.

Impressing the Filipinos with the strength of Japan, a propagandist plots the advances of the Imperial forces on a huge map in a crowded Manila square.

Celebrating their gift of independence to the Philippines, Japanese troops parade past Manila's Legislative Building and a specially built arch on October 14, 1943. A large crowd of citizens turned out to watch, but they came unwillingly, having wakened to the fact that they were far from independent. Their new government was not elected; President José P. Laurel was hand-picked for the job by the Japanese. Laurel welcomed his appointment and the congratulations he received (above) from the Japanese political and military administrator, General Takaji Wachi, and he proceeded to execute Japanese policy with dismaying efficiency.

Displaying concern for the Filipinos' well-being, a Japanese medic in a clinic tends to the health needs of refugees in this creased propaganda photograph. But other Filipinos suffered and sometimes died from Japanese policies. The conquerors confiscated rice crops, which caused a famine in Manila. They also cut off cloth shipments to the Philippines and left the Filipinos with not nearly enough cotton to make clothes for themselves; many citizens were reduced to wearing tatters (above).

In a show of friendliness, a Japanese soldier plays the clarinet for Filipinos at a local festival. But while there were soldiers who behaved decently toward the populace, others forced themselves on local women (right) or slapped Filipinos for not bowing in their presence.

A ubiquitous symbol of Japan's mastery, a Japanese soldier in Manila's business district stands guard at a pillbox with his bayonet pointed at Filipino passersby.

1

It took the people of the Philippine Islands until the summer of 1942 to recover from the shock of the Japanese invasion in December 1941 and the despair that followed the official surrender of the American forces on the island fortress of Corregidor on May 6. Their recovery was hastened by the Japanese, who, while making real efforts to conciliate the Filipinos, simultaneously enraged them with beatings, torture, public beheadings and humiliating orders to bow to the Japanese soldiers they passed.

In this atmosphere of escalating anger and resentment, dozens of guerrilla organizations sprang up to harass the conquerors. Every large island had at least a few budding resistance groups. No less than 11 major groups came into existence on Luzon, the largest and the most heavily populated of the 7,000 Philippine Islands. One group, which became known as Marking's guerrillas after the *nom de guerre* of its leader, Colonel Marcos Agustín, enlisted hundreds of recruits with a stirring credo: "If the least we do is fertilize the soil where we fall, then we grow a richer grain for tomorrow's stronger nation."

By the time the Americans returned to the islands in force in late October, 1944, they would be supported by approximately 250,000 guerrillas and nearly all of the 17 million citizens of the Philippines. But the beginnings of the guerrilla movement were chaotic in most areas. Bands of brigands, calling themselves guerrillas, terrorized farmers and villagers, stealing food and money. Long-smouldering feuds and antagonisms—between the Muslims and the Christians on Mindanao and between rival political factions on other islands—erupted into open fighting, with all of the factions claiming guerrilla legitimacy. On Luzon, the confusion was further compounded by the activities of the Communist Hukbalahaps, or Huks for short, who killed more Filipino "landlords" than Japanese occupation troops. It took the better part of a year before strong organizations absorbed many of the small, contentious ones and established some sort of order in the remote areas beyond the convenient reach of the Japanese garrisons.

In those hectic early days, the guerrillas had little to recommend their chances for success. Guns were scarce: one leader on the island of Negros later recalled that in most guerrilla units only 20 per cent of the men had firearms. And

ISLANDS OF RESISTANCE

ammunition was in such short supply that in order to conserve bullets some guerrilla groups executed spies by beheading. Nevertheless, the guerrillas did have certain sustaining assets.

All guerrilla groups worthy of the name were united by patriotism and a growing sense of nationalism. Paradoxically, they were also united by a feeling of friendship for the distant nation that had governed their islands since winning them in the Spanish-American War. The Filipinos admired American institutions, and even Tomas Confesor, a radical leader on the central Philippine Island of Panay, conceded that "we have been living during the last 40 years under a regime of justice and liberty." Nearly everyone believed the promise of the U.S. Congress that the Philippines would be given complete independence and self-government in 1946. Practically no one believed the Japanese, who promised independence three years earlier.

Moreover, the Filipinos were united in their trust of General Douglas MacArthur. They knew him well; his four tours of duty on the islands spanned nearly four decades. And they believed his pledge, soon beamed to them steadily by a radio station in San Francisco, that "I shall return." Recalled Vicente Raval, a guerrilla leader on Luzon: "We had total faith in the American promise to come back. We never faltered in our hope."

The guerrillas' most important asset was the geography of the Philippine archipelago. The jungled interiors of the large islands were natural strongholds: mountainous, generally roadless, with large unmapped areas—too dangerous for the Japanese to penetrate. Even on large islands with primitive roads, the conquerors had to transport most shipments of food, supplies and troops from place to place by water. It was impossible for the Japanese to keep close watch on all 11,000 miles of the Philippine coastline; the inhabitants, on the other hand, knew every cove and inlet, and they were able to move about freely in their outriggers and their sailboats.

The Japanese commanders made optimum use of the varying number of troops they had at their disposal. They held Manila strongly, concentrated large forces in key spots elsewhere on Luzon, established lesser garrisons in port towns on other islands, patrolled the roads and the major waterways. But the remainder of the Philippines—more than half of the total land area—was a guerrilla's paradise.

The best-organized guerrilla groups took shape on the skeleton of presurrender military units. Before Corregidor's fall, the Filipino-American forces defending some of the islands had been ordered to move their arms and equipment into the mountains to fight as guerrillas should the Japanese overwhelm them in the lowlands. In many places this movement was already under way when the American command on Corregidor surrendered. Under the Japanese threat that any soldiers captured would be executed, the U.S. commander ordered all units in the Philippines to surrender as well. Most of the senior officers obeyed, but many of their junior officers and thousands of troops refused to give up. Instead, they melted into the jungle, retrieved their stockpiled weapons and supplies, and set themselves up as guerrillas, usually under the leadership of a regular Army officer, American or Filipino.

One such leader was a Filipino lieutenant colonel named Macario Peralta Jr., who had been the operations officer of the Philippine Army force defending Panay. When his American superior surrendered, Peralta took command of some 7,000 Filipino holdouts and, with his authority unquestioned, quickly organized an effective guerrilla force. In the succeeding months, Peralta ordered all free Americans on Panay, civilians included, to join his forces. Most of them complied.

The northern Luzon guerrillas were also organized along strict military lines. In the early weeks of the war, several frontline units of Filipino soldiers and their American officers had been cut off by the swift Japanese advance in Luzon. Unable to join the general retreat to Bataan, they stayed on in the mountains, eventually coming under the leadership of Lieut. Colonel Russell W. Volckmann. They became the nucleus of one of the largest and most effective guerrilla outfits in the islands.

The southernmost island of Mindanao was weakly held by the conquerors and therefore presented the greatest opportunities for resistance. The Japanese did establish a strong base at the port city of Davao on the southeastern coast of the island, and they set up garrisons and small naval patrol bases along the northern coast, facing the inner waterways of the Philippines. But between these fortified enclaves lay thousands of square miles of ungarrisoned

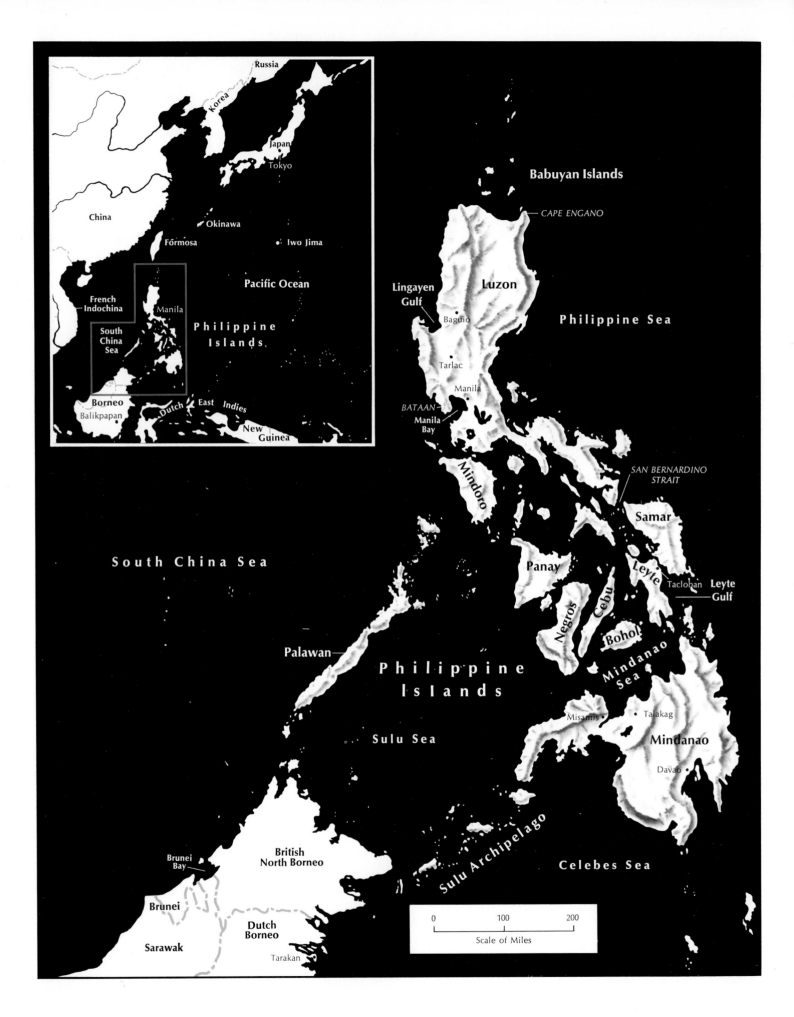

Russia
Korea
Japan
Tokyo
China
Okinawa
Formosa
Iwo Jima
Pacific Ocean
French
Indochina
Manila
South
China
Sea
Philippine
Islands
Borneo
Dutch East Indies
Balikpapan
New
Guinea

Babuyan Islands

CAPE ENGANO

Lingayen
Gulf
Luzon
Baguio
Philippine Sea

Tarlac

Manila

BATAAN
Manila
Bay

Mindoro
SAN BERNARDINO
STRAIT

Samar

Panay
Leyte

South China Sea
Negros
Cebu
Tacloban
Leyte
Gulf

Bohol
Mindanao
Sea

Palawan
Philippine
Islands

Misamis
Talakag

Sulu Sea
Mindanao

Davao

Sulu Archipelago

Brunei
Bay
British
North Borneo
Celebes Sea

Brunei
Dutch
Borneo

Sarawak
0   100   200
Tarakan
Scale of Miles

tropical wilderness, including many areas that were inhabited by belligerent Muslim Moros.

Yet another resistance movement was born on Mindanao in October 1942 in the town of Talakag. The citizens had secretly built up a small cache of rifles, hoping to make a stand against the Japanese when they gathered enough strength. But the townspeople's immediate concern was not so much the Japanese as the possibility that they might be attacked by other Filipinos. Two hostile bands of Moros were converging on Talakag to raid it, and a guerrilla unit from another area was preparing to seize the town and kill the officials who had knuckled under to the conquerors. The people of Talakag refused to call in the Japanese for protection. That decision left them with no alternative but to defend themselves.

One by one the town's leaders began sneaking out at night to discuss the problem with Major Robert Bowler and Lieutenant William McLaughlin, American Army officers who were holed up in the hills above the town. Bowler agreed to lead the citizens against the Moro attackers. But he sensed that Talakag would not be content to fight only in self-defense.

"The situation became rapidly more threatening," reported Father Edward Haggerty, an American Jesuit who had eluded the Japanese. Though the priest decided against taking part in the action, the townspeople trusted him and came to tell him that they wanted to resist the Japanese as well as their local enemies. A young lawyer explained his decision thus: "When the war is over, my boys will ask me what I did to help free my country. I cannot tell them that I had no part in it."

That day, as Father Haggerty soon learned, eight men captured the police station without firing a single shot. The policemen joined the uprising and turned over the 40 captured rifles they held. Then, giddy with success, the leading citizens of the town called another meeting and sent for Major Bowler to ask him to take charge. The town's guns, which had been hidden beneath the church, were dug up and distributed.

All night, men came to Haggerty's house, seeking advice and bringing news. "The Major is making a speech," one man reported. "He's telling the crowd their houses will be burned by the Nips, that Talakag will be bombed by the planes, that many of their families may get killed, and that maybe the United States won't come in for another year. But if they want guerrilla, then the Major says he'll lead them himself, him and McLaughlin."

At midnight, dripping with rain, Bowler himself showed up at Haggerty's place. "Well, it's here," he said. "They voted to resist the Japs . . . I guess there's no more hiding out now. We've left the woods, but only God knows for how long. I think we have about a hundred guns."

As the priest summed it up: "Sober-minded, educated civilians, fathers of families, had deliberately faced the terrors of guerrilla warfare, and in a democratic way voted to choose the dangers rather than live as conquered people. At sunrise in front of the school, Bowler raised the American and Filipino flags."

Then a transformation came over Talakag—and scores of other towns that turned guerrilla at approximately the same time. While Bowler organized and trained the men, courts functioned, farming became more intensive, and emergency money was printed to aid business transactions in the cash-short area. Doctors set up clinics, and the women of the town formed a guerrilla auxiliary to furnish clothing and supplies.

The "bamboo telegraph"—the Philippine grapevine—began bringing to isolated American soldiers and airmen who had eluded the Japanese the electrifying news that 10 or 50 or 100 miles away an American or Filipino officer had established a guerrilla organization. Most of those hiding out were country boys who had preferred to take their chances in the jungle rather than in Japanese prison camps. (City-bred Americans, one American guerrilla leader later pointed out, tended to accept the structured life of a camp rather than face the jungle.) Fed, protected and often lionized by poor farmers and villagers they periodically encountered, these men had wandered the remote areas hoping only to evade the Japanese until the American Army came back in force. Now, guided by hill folk and lowlanders, they slowly made their way to the headquarters of men like Major Bowler and reported for duty.

Filipino recruits flocked in by the thousands. Many were former soldiers who had avoided capture or escaped from the Japanese and "gone bush." Others had surrendered on

The Philippine archipelago—more than 7,000 islands stretching 1,000 miles south from Luzon to Mindanao—became the most important land and sea battleground in the Pacific war because of its strategic location off the coast of Southeast Asia (inset). Japan needed to keep the islands to protect the shipping lanes to their sources of raw materials in the Dutch East Indies and Southeast Asia. The Allies wanted to retake the Philippines to establish air bases and staging areas for an invasion of Japan.

orders and had later been released when the Japanese realized they could not offer liberation in return for Filipino cooperation and at the same time keep Filipinos interned as prisoners of war.

But this turnaround came too late for the Japanese. The Filipino soldiers had experienced Japanese brutality at first hand, and as soon as they heard of a guerrilla unit being formed in the vicinity they joined up. In every part of the Philippines, and even in those resistance units that were led by Americans, almost all the men with rifles and bolos were Filipinos.

For months, nothing of this groundswell of popular resistance was known to General MacArthur. "I was certain," he wrote later, "that a great number of those indomitable defenders of Bataan and Corregidor had escaped into the mountains and jungle, and that they were already at work against the enemy. Unfortunately, for some time I could learn nothing of these activities. A deep, black pall of silence settled over the whole archipelago."

Then, in the summer of 1942, radio messages started filtering in to San Francisco and Australia. From Luzon, Lieut. Colonel Guillermo Nakar radioed MacArthur, "Your victorious return is the nightly subject of prayers in every Filipino home." But Nakar's radio was located and destroyed by the Japanese, and he was captured, tortured and beheaded.

Colonel Peralta on Panay got through with a report to MacArthur that he had assumed command of 8,000 guerril-las and that he controlled the whole interior of the island and the west coast as well, provincial capitals excepted. "Civilians and officials 99 percent loyal," Peralta radioed. "Supplies could be dropped anywhere away from towns, and subs could make coast anywhere more than 20 miles distant from capitals." He later added: "Humblest soldier has blind faith in you."

And from northern Luzon an American captain, Ralph Praeger, radioed: "Military and civil authorities in perfect accord. If I may be permitted I can organize 5,000 able-bodied trainees, ROTCs and intelligence men provided we would be furnished arms and ammunitions."

Peralta, Praeger and others were answered promptly because they used the codes given them before the surrender for the express purpose of establishing communications. But such was not the case with one squawking message, broadcast on the wrong frequency, in a discontinued code, by an apparent American guerrilla who called himself General Wendell Fertig.

The sender was Lieut. Colonel Wendell W. Fertig, an Army engineer who had been sent to Mindanao before the surrender. In the course of his wanderings in search of a resistance group to join, he came upon competing and sometimes warring guerrilla bands, but few American servicemen and no organized commands. Acting on the supposition that he was the highest-ranking American military man still free, Fertig had put on the silver stars of a brigadier general (fashioned for him by a Moro smith) to impress rank-conscious Filipinos and thus to exercise some con-

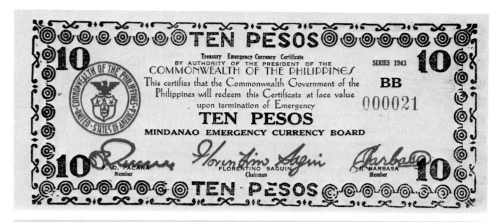

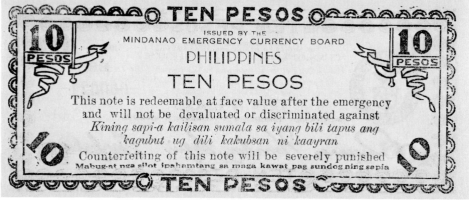

A 10-peso note, issued by Colonel Fertig's guerrillas on Mindanao to ease the shortage of legitimate Philippine money, served as a model for other unofficial currencies printed by bands of guerrillas. The Filipinos preferred the guerrilla notes, which offered the promise of postwar redemption at face value, to unsecured Japanese bills—issued in so many hundreds of millions that they became virtually worthless.

A TOUGH, PATERNAL BREED OF LEADERS

The success of the Philippine guerrillas depended to a large degree on the quality of their leadership. Though the chiefs of many resistance groups started with the advantage of Army experience, they soon found that a guerrilla command demanded much more than routine military discipline. Most guerrillas were untrained and many were unruly, and the leader needed an iron hand.

Colonel Marcos Agustín, the famous Luzon leader, believed in more than just bluster; if need be, he backed up his commands with his fists. But he was also kind, doing all he could to ensure his men's well-being. For both his compassion and his sternness, Agustín's guerrillas thought of him as a father.

To maintain the respect of the men and women under their command, the guerrilla leaders had to share the normal risks of combat—and the much greater risk of capture. For a chief who fell into enemy hands, torture was certain; if he did not remain silent, he could cause the deaths of thousands of followers. They proceeded, therefore, very cautiously; Colonel Ruperto Kangleon reportedly made no move unless he knew "every time a Jap sneezed." Luzon leader Ferdinand Marcos was caught and endured eight days of torture; he escaped by persuading his captors to follow him into an ambush.

Inevitably, the mettle of these men—and the power and experience that they gained in patriotic service—gave them a large say in their country's future. Many successful guerrilla leaders later served in important posts in the Philippine government, and two—Raymon Magsaysay and Ferdinand Marcos—were elected President of the Philippine Republic.

Ruperto Kangleon (right), highly respected by MacArthur's staff, greets an American aide.

Ferdinand Marcos led some 8,000 guerrillas on Luzon.

American Colonel Fertig, sporting a Moro hat, was a mining engineer when the War began.

Guillermo Nakar, Luzon, was one of the first guerrilla leaders killed resisting the Japanese.

Marcos Agustín, a former bus driver, and Yay Panlilio, a journalist, led 100,000 guerrillas.

trol over the contentious guerrilla factions on the island.

The several years that Fertig had spent in the Philippines and his understanding of the people and the country fitted him for his role. "I feel that I am indeed a Man of Destiny, that my course is charted," wrote Fertig in his diary. Acting swiftly to become commander in fact as well as in name, Fertig picked up assorted followers and established a relatively secure base of operation near the town of Misamis in the northwestern part of Mindanao. The entire province of Misamis Occidental was of so little strategic value that the Japanese had not even inspected the area for months. Unmolested, policed by guerrilla soldiers under Fertig's command, the citizens of Misamis resumed their prewar activities. Responsible officials were persuaded by Fertig to conduct the civil administration. The market was busy, a factory produced coconut oil, printing presses ran off currency, electric lights burned at night and some of the telephones worked.

Fertig's proclamation that he had assumed command and desired all organized resistance units to serve under him was carried by runner to the other guerrilla leaders on Mindanao, Robert Bowler among them, and the bamboo telegraph did the rest. Soon emissaries from all over Mindanao were arriving at his headquarters. Individual recruits, including civilians and American enlisted men who had been hiding in the jungle, were amazed when guards on the trails halted them and asked to see their travel passes. They were even more impressed with Misamis and its guerrilla activity: professional soldiers drilled raw recruits, technicians fashioned new springs for old rifle bolts, and women auxiliaries made uniforms, bandages and bullets. Fertig drove around in a car, and two powerboats provided coastal transportation. From Misamis, guerrilla messengers traveled by trail and boat carrying Fertig's typewritten orders to guerrilla leaders elsewhere on Mindanao.

Although some of the guerrilla chieftains, particularly the Moros, accepted Fertig's preeminence in name only and refused to take orders from him, others cooperated fully. Furthermore, Fertig was able to enlist the personal support of some influential local Filipino civilians, and through these *ilustrados* he extended his influence and even managed to make contacts with a high-level espionage network that was operating within the Japanese puppet government in Manila. But Fertig was in desperate need of arms and supplies for his men and official confirmation of his command. Until General MacArthur sent him both, his authority was fragile indeed.

Day after day, Fertig tried to raise MacArthur's headquarters with a transmitter made out of scrounged materials by a young Filipino who had learned all he knew about radios through a correspondence course. Weeks after his first transmission in late December, a return signal came —using call letters Fertig had prearranged with a friend, Charles Smith, whom he had helped to escape from Mindanao. Fertig himself had forgotten to use the letters MSF (for Mindanao Smith Fertig); he never believed that Smith would get through. Now here it was, from Station KFS in San Francisco: "KFS CALLING MSF KFS CALLING MSF."

But Fertig had to fret some more, for KFS merely asked him to send a new message using as code-key words the name of his daughter and the city she lived in—identifying information that the Japanese would scarcely have bothered to try to obtain from a prisoner. Not until the middle of February 1943 did the San Francisco station concede that Fertig was the man he said he was and inform him that his next radio message would come from MacArthur's headquarters in Australia.

After another frustrating delay, MacArthur's message arrived. It read: "LT COL W W FERTIG IS DESIGNATED TO COMMAND THE TENTH MIL DISTRICT (ISLANDS OF MINDANAO AND SULU) XXX HE WILL PERFECT INTELLIGENCE NET COVERING NINTH MIL DISTRICT (SAMAR-LEYTE) XXX NO OFFICER OF RANK OF GENERAL WILL BE DESIGNATED AT PRESENT XXX."

Fertig was disappointed not to receive a promotion, or any promise of aid or the authority to organize an attack with his guerrillas. In fact, MacArthur was anxious to prevent premature guerrilla attacks that would accomplish little and bring down Japanese reprisals on Filipino citizens. He began issuing "lie-low" orders to forestall guerrilla raids. But he had begun a new phase of operations, in which Fertig would play a large role.

What MacArthur needed from the Philippines was accurate and reliable information: about the guerrillas, about the mood of the civilians, and especially about Japanese military movements and strengths. For that kind of intelligence he could not depend solely on the self-made resistance leaders, many of whom were less known to the Americans than Fertig. MacArthur therefore decided to send in his own trained and trusted espionage agents of the Allied Intelligence Bureau.

Early in January of 1943, the U.S. submarine *Gudgeon* deposited the first penetration team on the island of Negros in the central Philippines. The team was led by Major Jesus Villamor, a pilot whose daring deeds had made him a Philippine hero in the early weeks of the war. Villamor's mission was to establish an espionage network throughout the islands. He and his five Filipino companions had been thoroughly trained in radio, codes, maps, jungle survival,

boat handling, aircraft and ship recognition; they had even been made to chop wood and plow land until their hands were grimy and cracked like a peasant's. Despite all the careful planning, however, one important fact had been overlooked: Villamor was a famous war hero, and his photograph had appeared so often in the newspapers that Filipinos immediately recognized him.

Forced to hide from his own people as well as from the Japanese, Villamor established a remote headquarters on Negros and developed his intelligence network from there. His agents, convincingly disguised as farmers or fishermen, made contact with Peralta and other trusted leaders. They carried high-grade cipher systems on microfilm concealed

American prisoners of war struggle to emplace a gun under the stern supervision of their Japanese guards on Corregidor. The punishing labor and the brutal treatment meted out by the Japanese expressed the contempt they felt for any soldier who surrendered instead of fighting to the death. A Japanese propaganda booklet published in 1943 called the American prisoners "foul water flowing down from the sewerage of a country that has been formed upon impure foundations."

A SECRET RADIO NETWORK THAT LINKED THE ISLANDS TO THE OUTSIDE WORLD

One of the most dangerous jobs in the Philippines during the Japanese occupation was operating the clandestine radios that sent information to the Allied forces about Japanese shipping and troop movements, and weather. The Japanese, using radio direction finders, often succeeded in pinpointing the locations of the jungle stations and would send troops to wipe out the guerrillas and American intelligence agents who ran them.

Radios on Luzon, Mindoro and other islands were destroyed, and many operators and headquarters personnel, including at least three prominent guerrilla leaders, were killed. But the underground radiomen persisted, moving their stations often to escape pursuit. They eventually built a network of 169 transmitters, and by January 1945, when the U.S. operations were in full swing, they were sending MacArthur's headquarters 3,700 reports a month.

A radioman monitors signals in a Mindanao station, later destroyed by the Japanese.

Carefully concealed behind trees and shrubbery, a new radio hut on Mindanao replaces an earlier station bombed by the Japanese in May 1944.

in their shoes or under a dental plate. They even smuggled radios into Manila.

Within a few weeks Villamor was recruiting new agents and exchanging radio messages with Australia. His enthusiastic reports convinced MacArthur that the guerrillas could indeed be relied on for intelligence, and that they therefore should be encouraged and supplied.

Consequently, the next American submarine mission to the islands was designated as a guerrilla supply run. As Mindanao was closest to Australia—and also considered the likeliest place for a future American invasion—Wendell Fertig was chosen to be the first recipient. And the man who came ashore from the submarine *Tambor* with her four tons of supplies was an old friend of Fertig's from Manila days: Lieut. Commander Charles "Chick" Parsons of the United States Navy.

Parsons had lived in the Philippines for 20 years before war broke out. A charming, brash and resourceful man, he had worked for a number of companies, traveled extensively throughout the islands, married a Philippine-born American of mixed parentage, played polo and joined the Naval reserve, taking active duty whenever he could. When war came, Parsons was manager of the Luzon Stevedoring Company in Manila and also served as a substitute for the absent consul for Panama. As the Japanese entered Manila, he burned his Navy uniform, got out his official Panamanian seals and ran up a Panamanian flag in front of his house. Although he was not entitled to diplomatic immunity (only career consuls were), Parsons managed to talk the Japanese into recognizing him as a Panamanian neutral and repatriating his family in exchange for Japanese nationals in Latin America. After taking his family home to North Carolina, he went to Washington, D.C., and volunteered to become MacArthur's emissary to the Philippine guerrillas. When MacArthur learned of his offer, he cabled: "SEND PARSONS IMMEDIATELY."

Chick Parsons' second-in-command was another friend of Fertig's, Army Captain Charles Smith, whom the guerrilla leader had helped to escape and who was the first to give headquarters an eyewitness account of the beginnings of Fertig's operation.

The supplies brought by Parsons and Smith dazzled the Mindanao guerrillas. There were guns, ammunition and grenades, medicines and bandages and surgical kits, radio transmitters, batteries, tools and spare parts, soap, chocolate, cigarettes and socks, a high-grade code for Fertig, and for the local priests a can of wheat flour for making communion wafers. Propaganda had not been forgotten either: every package contained small gift items *(box, page 31)* that were emblazoned with MacArthur's now-famous vow, "I shall return." And there was a stack of recent newspapers and copies of TIME, LIFE and *Newsweek* with photographs of sinking Japanese ships and stories of Allied victories. All of these American gifts confirmed Fertig's authority in the eyes of his guerrillas, and he was enormously grateful.

But Fertig was less happy with a message his two friends also brought him. "You might as well know it, Wendell," Smith told him, "we're supposed to find out whether you're competent to command. You didn't do yourself any good at Headquarters when you set yourself up as a brigadier general." Furthermore, MacArthur's representatives reminded Fertig that his primary mission was not to bushwhack Japanese patrols but to gather information. The radios delivered to Fertig, which he had hoped to distribute to scattered guerrilla commanders, were to be used instead to set up a chain of coastwatcher stations on Mindanao and Leyte to report on Japanese ship movements. Only if the stations provided the necessary information would Fertig be sent additional aid.

Parsons and Smith dutifully inspected Fertig's headquarters, interviewed his men throughout the province, asked questions, probed, observed, took notes—and then recommended to MacArthur in Australia that he be allowed to keep his command.

Late in June 1943, when Parsons and Smith had completed their survey of guerrilla operations and set up the first coastwatching stations, the American submarine *Thresher* was dispatched from Australia to pick them up near Fertig's Misamis post and return them to MacArthur's headquarters. But only a few days before the *Thresher* was due, a large force of Japanese troops, backed up by cruisers and planes, swarmed ashore near Misamis at half a dozen beaches—including the submarine rendezvous spot. The Japanese had located Fertig's transmitter with radio direction finders, and they were determined to close it down, capture Fertig and wipe out his guerrilla operation.

Many of Fertig's inexperienced guerrillas panicked and ran. His main transmitter went off the air as his radiomen hastily dismantled it and carried it to a new location. The Japanese shelling had knocked out the Misamis telephone system, and since the new radios that Parsons had brought had been sent to coastwatcher stations and not to subordinate guerrilla commanders, Fertig was forced to rely on runners for news of what was happening. Nearly encircled by the enemy, his command in disarray, Fertig abandoned his headquarters. He sent some of his administrative records to an evacuation site, buried others in tin cans, and fled into the wilds with his codes and intelligence data crammed into a trick brief case that Parsons had given him. The brief case would explode upon being opened unless a hidden switch was pushed.

Meanwhile, the *Thresher* was en route to a rendezvous site that was swarming with Japanese, and until Fertig's transmitter could be reassembled, he had no means by which to warn off the submarine. The transmitter, when he caught up with it, needed repair. On the fourth day of the Japanese assault, only hours before the rendezvous was scheduled to take place, the transmitter started working again and a message in Parsons' code crackled into headquarters in Brisbane, Australia: "WARN SUB COMMANDER SITES ONE AND TWO FOR MEETING NORTH COAST IN HANDS ENEMY. SITE THREE NOT FEASIBLE."

The *Thresher* was warned off in time, and a further exchange of messages set up a more secure rendezvous. Parsons and Smith, guided by guerrillas and accompanied by three American officers who had escaped from a Japanese prisoner-of-war camp, scrambled through the jungles and over mountains for six days before reaching the new meeting place. Finally, weary and famished, the five Americans boarded the *Thresher*.

With Parsons and Smith on their way, Fertig reestablished control over his disorganized forces and set up improvised headquarters in a straw hut and a scattering of lean-tos. But his new camp did not last very long; word came to him one night that a Japanese patrol had taken over a nearby schoolhouse, where a guerrilla company had been living. The Filipinos had fled, leaving behind records that could ruin the guerrillas' operations and mean death for their families.

Fertig and 12 men surrounded the schoolhouse in the moonlight. When all were in position, one man fired a shot at the rear of the building. The Japanese rushed out the front door, straight into automatic-rifle fire from Fertig and two men at his side. Two of the Japanese were killed; the survivors ducked back inside and spilled out through the back way, where they were mowed down by other guerrillas. All the Japanese were dead, and the records were found intact. Fertig, realizing that the discovery of the bodies would bring down a large search force, made haste to shift his headquarters again.

From then on, Fertig and his radio were almost continually on the go. He moved eastward from his original base, stopping periodically at the headquarters of his subordinate commanders, keeping in touch with other guerrilla units and with MacArthur's headquarters. Again and again the Japanese attempted to track him down, but Mindanao was simply too big, and Fertig and his men were just too nimble. Whenever headquarters gave them permission to attack, they staged ambushes and harassing raids on the Japanese throughout the province.

Chick Parsons continued to serve as a main link between the Philippine underground movement and MacArthur's headquarters. Following up on his preliminary survey, he made five more clandestine trips to the Philippines before the American Army returned in force. Although the Japanese knew his name and put a huge price on his head, Parsons always moved about unarmed and undisguised, counting on mobility and the aid of friendly Filipinos to keep him safe. Time and again he came close to disaster, but he was never caught.

Villamor's espionage net continued to expand, and in July of 1943 the major welcomed a new agent deposited on the island of Negros by the *Thresher*. His name was Dr. Emigdio Cruz, and he was the personal physician to the Philippine president-in-exile, Manuel Quezon; he had fled from Corregidor with MacArthur and Quezon.

Cruz had been given a mission of the utmost importance: he was to make his way to Manila to contact Manuel Roxas, a leading Filipino politician who was publicly collaborating with the puppet government but who was—as Fertig had told Parsons—quietly passing intelligence to the underground. President Quezon wanted information from Roxas about the loyalty of the Manila elite, and Cruz was to bring it back. But Cruz had no experience or training in clandestine activities. He arrived with all the pocket litter of a peacetime civilian, including a late-model American fountain pen, whose discovery by the Japanese could have been fatal to him and his mission.

Cruz was not only unprepared, he was dangerously naïve. Instead of lying low until Villamor could send him north, he insisted on treating the sick Filipinos he saw all around him. Word of the doctor and his medicines spread rapidly on the bamboo telegraph, bringing patients—and a spy—flocking to the area. Several days later the Japanese arrived in force. Villamor lost most of his supplies, his radio had to go off the air for several days and his entire operation came close to being wiped out.

Villamor blamed Cruz's carelessness for the near debacle and refused to put the dangerous doctor in contact with any of his agents. So, unaided and without papers, Cruz set off alone on an extraordinary odyssey.

Posing as a peddler with a stock of dried fish and chickens, he made his way toward Luzon in a small boat. Japanese boat patrols stopped and questioned him; but Cruz, skillful in many of the 87 dialects of the Philippines, insisted in the local tongue that he was but a simple peddler.

On reaching a Luzon port, he somehow managed to purchase documents that identified him as a trader, found a Chinese partner to accompany him and sailed serenely into a Japanese patrol-boat base to sell a new cargo of lumber.

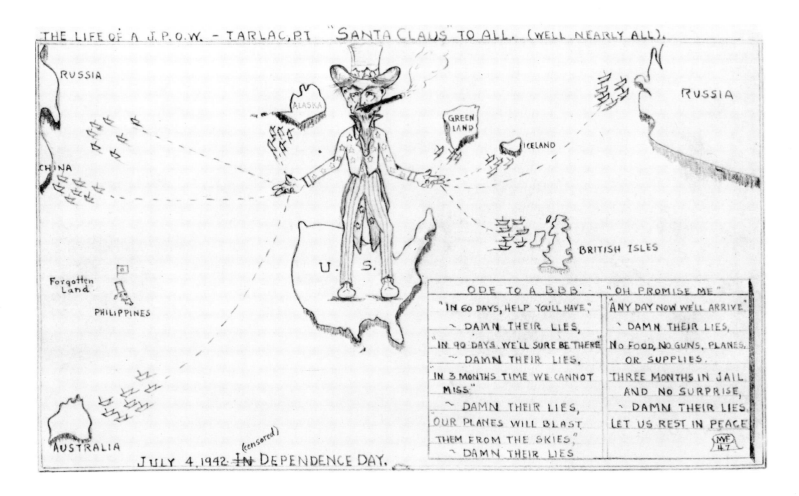

This bitter cartoon, drawn on the Fourth of July, 1942, by an American prisoner of war in the camp at Tarlac on Luzon, condemns Uncle Sam for failing to get troops and supplies to the Philippines while generously aiding other countries. The artist, Colonel Malcolm Fortier, said: "Our first Independence Day as a P.O.W. made us feel like the forgotten men."

Then, suddenly, all seemed lost: two soldiers with fixed bayonets confronted Cruz and his companion and ordered them to march into town. Prodded on, they marched.

Cruz wondered, at first, why the townspeople were waving Philippine and Japanese flags. Then he remembered what day it was: October 14, 1943, independence day for Japan's puppet Philippine republic. The two fake traders were herded onto a crowded public platform, where—much to their amazement—the soldiers left them standing, free to cheer and bow with the obedient crowd and then go their way. Apparently, their only crime had been their failure to join in the independence-day observance.

In the street afterward they were pursued by a man on a bicycle who jumped off and shouted: "Cruz! Cruz! I am delighted to see you, my old friend. And they told me you were dead." It was a former classmate. Hastily, Cruz pulled him around a corner and discreetly explained his mission.

Back on his trading boat with the Chinese, Cruz was again hailed by a patrol launch, and he had a hunch that this time he was in real trouble. So he quickly fished out a packet of Quezon's letters that he had carried all the way from Washington, weighted the lot with stones and threw it into the sea. It was a lucky move, for the Japanese came aboard, searched the boat thoroughly and questioned him insistently about a reported secret agent. In the end, disarmed by the innocent-looking traders, they gave Cruz a letter of introduction to Japanese officers in the next town—from which Cruz rode into Manila on a train.

Cruz's wife, who had remained in the capital after his departure, collapsed at the sight of him. When she recovered, she helped to arrange a succession of contacts that brought him to Roxas and other high-ranking Filipinos who were working secretly against the Japanese. Cruz stayed in Manila for a week, gathering information. Dozens of people knew of his presence and mission; no one betrayed him.

After leaving Manila, Cruz spent three months making his way to a point from which he could be picked up by submarine. But his report, listing the loyal Manila leaders and describing their underground activities, had long since been sent by courier to Colonel Peralta on Panay and radioed to Brisbane and Washington.

Thousands of other Filipino civilians were courageously fighting the secret war and getting their information to Brisbane through a variety of channels. Japanese-occupied Manila was riddled with underground operatives on various levels, some working for Villamor, some in contact with Fertig, and others with links to guerrilla bands in the Luzon mountains. A Manila radio announcer, working with a Japanese censor beside him, managed to broadcast coded information about the tonnage of ships in Manila Harbor. Employees of the Manila Hotel even smuggled out copies of the hotel's guest list, which at one point included the information that Field Marshal Count Hisaichi Terauchi, the supreme commander of the Japanese Southern Army, was ensconced in MacArthur's prewar penthouse suite.

Army officer Ferdinand Marcos worked with his long-time friend Primitivo San Agustín in the Manila underground. Each had at least one set of false identity papers and, stashed away in a safe place, a phony certificate registering his death. San Agustín even arranged to have a headstone inscribed with his real name placed in a Manila cemetery. From time to time he would pay a visit and put some flowers on his grave.

But several people knew Marcos was alive, and they all posed a constant threat even if they were utterly loyal. This Marcos learned again when he fell deathly ill. "I was sick of black water fever," he recalled. "Oozing with blood from all the orifices of my body, I was brought to the Philippine General Hospital." Marcos' mother was told that he was in the hospital, and she visited him, trailed by the Japanese secret police.

"I would have been apprehended," Marcos later said, "but my former commanding general, General Capinpin, was in touch with President Laurel"—José P. Laurel of the puppet government—"and sent me a message saying that Laurel had asked him to warn me." Marcos' comrades hurried him to safety. "Therefore I realized that Laurel's sympathies were with us, the underground, just as the sympathies of Roxas were." Most Filipinos felt—as Marcos did—that the question of loyalty was a complex one, and that some of the "collaborators" were buffers rather than traitors.

One of the most daring and successful agents in the Manila area was a young architect who made drawings for the Japanese planning department. He wangled a studio in the headquarters building of the Japanese military police,

MacArthur's patrician features dominate the cover of a news magazine sent to guerrillas.

THE "I SHALL RETURN" ADVERTISING CAMPAIGN

In August 1943, Colonel Courtney Whitney, an aide to General MacArthur in Australia, got a bright idea for using his commander in chief's famous pledge, "I shall return," to counteract Japanese propaganda. In a memo to his boss, Whitney asked, "Does the C-in-C have any objection to advantage being taken of his immense personal popularity among the Filipino people through using a short quotation?"

"No objection," replied MacArthur. "I *shall* return."

MacArthur's promise of liberation was printed on a variety of eye-catching items that were added to the shipments of vital supplies for Filipino guerrillas. The giveaways, smuggled ashore by U.S. subs, were extensively distributed. Whitney's advertising campaign was so successful that many Filipinos who knew no English could repeat the three thrilling words.

A propaganda button repeats MacArthur's vow.

On a cigarette pack, the American and Philippine flags stress the countries' historic ties.

Matchbooks display the promise of liberation.

amused the guards by his attempts to learn their language, and soon was able to pass in and out at will without being searched. When he heard rumors about the underground ammunition and fuel dumps the Japanese were constructing at nearby Nichols Field, the architect got a part-time job there, carrying water to the laborers on the back of a water buffalo. While resting on the broad back of the beast, as is the custom of Filipino farm hands, he surreptitiously made rough sketches of the installations. Back at his studio he turned these into finished drawings, rolled up the sheets, stuck them in his hip pocket and coolly carried them out past the guards. Guerrilla couriers took the drawings to a submarine rendezvous. The later bombing of Nichols Field was so accurate that a Japanese communiqué claimed the Americans had developed a new bomb that was attracted by concentrations of ammunition and fuel.

Many an agent paid the price for his daring, and so did many an innocent Filipino. From the beginning of the occupation, the Japanese military dealt harshly—often sadistically—with any islanders suspected of underground activities or of consorting with guerrillas. In some areas local commanders executed 10 Filipinos at random for every Japanese soldier killed by guerrillas. To get information, some interrogators beat prisoners systematically, forced their stomachs full of water and then jumped on their bellies, stabbed them with bayonets, made them lie for days in the tropic sun. One popular technique was to hold a prisoner's head underwater until he nearly drowned, let him up, repeat the question, then dunk him again. Other prisoners had their teeth or fingernails pulled out. Some of the victims caved in and talked, usually to save their families from torture. Many held out—and died horribly.

Trinidad Diaz was one of many victims. A cashier at a cement factory on the shores of a large inland lake in Luzon, she started her resistance activities by collecting food and clothing for a nearby guerrilla band. But then, on her own, she elected combat, and persuaded six of the factory work-ers to join her. Together they killed five Japanese officials on the factory wharf, dumped their bodies into the cement, sent the guerrilla commander the Japanese uniforms and hid their launch for guerrilla use. Some time later, Japanese investigators came to question her. She refused to say anything. They hung her by her heels, lashed her, burned her with cigarette butts; tied her to a tree and left her there for 24 hours at a stretch. She endured for 32 days, admitting nothing, denying all knowledge of the guerrilla band. Then she was too weak to answer at all, and just hung limply in her ropes until she was taken away and put to death.

Despite such brutality, the underground network continued to grow. A vast amount of intelligence flowed into MacArthur's headquarters by courier and radio. Much vital shipping information was gathered by the radio-equipped coastwatcher net initiated by Parsons, Smith and Villamor. The radio reports were flashed to American submarines, which torpedoed many of the enemy ships as they emerged from the archipelago into the open sea.

A dramatic series of messages coming into Fertig's radio center for relay to Australia told the story of one such episode. From the island of Mindoro, just south of Luzon, came a morning report: "Twenty-five ships, heavily loaded, moving south." At noon, Panay reported the same convoy; and in the evening, Negros. Next day a coastwatcher on the southwest tip of Mindanao reported the 25 ships "moving east near Malanipa Island." Two days later came a radioed message from a guerrilla commander on the coast east of Malanipa, rounding off the saga: "Have many Jap survivors from some sunken ships. What will I do with them?"

A coastwatching station that Charlie Smith had set up in the hills near Davao reported regularly on Japanese shipping coming in and out of the port. As Davao was a major assembly point supplying the Japanese troops fighting Mac-Arthur's advancing divisions in New Guinea, that information was crucial. Perhaps the most significant coastwatcher report of all was radioed from a station on San Bernardino

Strait, between Samar and southeast Luzon, in June 1944. The message, from an astonished observer named Gerald Chapman who did not know that the American invasion of the Marianas was about to begin, read: "Jap naval fleet consisting of eleven destroyers, ten cruisers, three battleships, nine aircraft carriers from west . . . last ship passed longitude one two four degrees nine minutes latitude one two degrees three four minutes at sixteen two nine now proceeding east with aerial escort. . . ." What Chapman had seen was the cream of the Imperial Japanese Navy, setting out to do battle with the American fleet off the coast of the Marianas. Thanks to Chapman's report, together with intelligence from other sources, the U.S. Navy adjusted its dispositions and scored one of its biggest victories in the Battle of the Philippine Sea a few days later.

The guerrillas and spotters reaped a harvest from the skies as well as from the seas. Downed American airmen were picked up and returned to their units; crashed Japanese planes were searched for documents. One Japanese plane wrecked in northern Luzon carried papers reporting on a high-level Japanese Army conference at which changes in the defense plan for the island had been discussed; the papers were found by guerrillas and the information sent to MacArthur's headquarters.

Like the coastwatchers, most of the guerrillas spent the long years of the occupation collecting and transmitting information: locations of fuel dumps and field guns, garrison strengths, names and movements of army units. There was little large-scale fighting, for ammunition and lives were too precious to be spent until General MacArthur's return to the Philippines, when all the resistance workers—Filipino and American guerrillas, intelligence teams, saboteurs—would join the uniformed forces of the United States in one great strike. When the guerrillas did get into a shoot-out with the Japanese, it was usually to protect a bivouac, village or radio installation, to wipe out an isolated patrol or occasionally to seize Japanese supplies and arms.

But the shadow war was gradually increasing in tempo. By the spring of 1944 the Navy's biggest submarines, capable of carrying 50 tons of supplies, were shuttling in and out of Philippine waters, making their rendezvous with guerrilla leaders and undercover operatives almost as a matter of routine. More than 150 coastwatching stations were now in operation on the islands. Internal guerrilla communications systems reached deep into Luzon, where Japanese forces were heavily concentrated. Infiltrated radio experts, liaison agents and demolition instructors moved freely through the underground, going wherever they were needed.

In September of 1944, American planes returned to Philippine skies. It was then that the guerrillas saw the first fruits of their work, as bombs blew up camouflaged Japanese ammunition dumps and air bases and destroyed the ordinary-looking houses that were Japanese headquarters—all targets disclosed by underground intelligence.

As the American invasion forces drew close to the Philippines in the autumn of 1944, guerrilla radios crackled with the attack orders they had long been awaiting: commence demolition of bridges, passes and culverts; destroy enemy wire communications; blow up supply dumps and planes; unleash "maximum violence against the enemy." Guerrillas harassed Japanese bases, seized airfields and captured key bridges and road junctions. Guerrilla units took up assigned positions to coordinate their postinvasion operations with American forces. They helped rescue prisoners of war and civilian internees. In some places they were already in such firm control that their main task consisted of repairing roads and bridges so that the American Army could use them.

Nearly all of the guerrillas were surprised when the invasion finally came on October 20, 1944. The target area was not, as they had long expected, Mindanao. A chain of unexpected events—and miscalculations on both sides—had moved the invasion site north to Leyte, in the central Philippines.

A MAN OF TWO COUNTRIES

General Douglas MacArthur and his assistant, Major Dwight D. Eisenhower, doff their skimmers at a ceremony marking MacArthur's arrival in Manila in 1935.

DOUGLAS MACARTHUR'S PURSUIT OF GREATNESS

When the Philippine Islands fell to the Japanese on May 6, 1942, their normal ties to the United States were broken. But a strong human link remained in the person of General Douglas MacArthur. He was brilliant and dramatic, and everything he said and did turned American eyes from the battlefields of Europe to his beloved lost islands in the Far East. MacArthur would not—could not—allow the Philippines to stay lost. He considered the islands and their people an American trust, and he had long since appointed himself guardian of that trust.

MacArthur's attachment to the Philippines was passed on to him by his father. General Arthur MacArthur fought there in the Spanish-American War and helped win the islands as a U.S. possession. Soon thereafter, he served as military governor and instituted legal and educational reforms that helped win friendship for America among the Filipinos.

Young Douglas, growing up in the American Southwest, prepared to follow in his father's footsteps, but in a manner powerfully shaped by his domineering mother, Mary. She instilled in him her conviction that he was destined for greatness and a life of service to others. By the time he entered West Point, Douglas was self-confident and self-willed to the point of arrogance. When an admiring young woman asked him if he was the famous general's son, he replied, "General MacArthur has that proud distinction."

After graduating at the head of his class in 1903, Second Lieutenant MacArthur was sent to the Philippines. Recalling his first glimpse of the islands, he said they "fastened me with a grip that has never relaxed." At a Manila dinner party he met lawyer Manuel Quezon, the man who sealed his commitment to the Philippines. Quezon was a fiery nationalist who had fought the U.S. as a guerrilla, surrendered to Douglas' father and then turned to politics. MacArthur and Quezon did not agree on the timing of national independence for the Philippines. But their personal ambitions dovetailed, and they soon became fast friends—"brothers," Quezon's wife called them. In MacArthur's four tours of duty in the Philippines, they rose to power together.

General Arthur MacArthur (left) leads soldiers of the U.S. 2nd Division in pursuit of anti-American guerrillas in the Philippine Islands in 1899.

Two ambitious young men whose friendship changed the course of Philippine history, Manuel Quezon (in his guerrilla uniform) and Second Lieutenant Douglas MacArthur met at a Manila dinner party. Years later, MacArthur suggested that if they had foreseen their future that night "the party might not have been so gay—or would it have been gayer?"

Three MacArthur boosters—General Wood (center), Independence Party leaders Quezon (far left) and Sergio Osmeña (far right)—meet in the 1920s.

Henry Stimson, appointed governor general in 1927, greets MacArthur in Manila. Both of them were strong advocates of military preparedness.

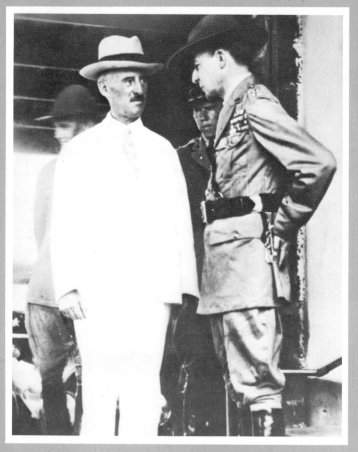

POLITICKING FOR ADVANCEMENT AND POWER

Returning to the Philippines after distinguished service as a division commander in Europe during World War I, General MacArthur spared no effort to advance his career and establish a power base in the islands. On the job, he was backed by two old friends *(above)*, who served successive terms as his superior in the post of governor general: General Leonard Wood and Henry Stimson, both of whom MacArthur had known since 1912 when he was an assistant in the office of Wood, then the U.S. Chief of Staff.

At the same time, MacArthur cultivated the friendships of wealthy and important Filipinos. Besides Manuel Quezon, his intimates included the sugar magnate Joaquin Elizalde; Carlos Romulo, the editor of the Manila *Herald;* and the political leader Manuel Roxas. MacArthur himself was a dutiful friend. Many years later, after Roxas had served in the Japanese puppet government, MacArthur remained convinced

Manuel Quezon, President of the Philippines, and MacArthur, his old friend and recently appointed military adviser, review Manila's 1936 Fourth of July parade.

of his underlying loyalty and maneuvered successfully for Roxas' exoneration.

In 1930 MacArthur reached out to take a coveted professional prize. The incumbent U.S. Chief of Staff was nearing the end of his four-year term and MacArthur politicked for the top Army post by sending an unabashedly flattering letter to Secretary of War Patrick Hurley just before Hurley was due to recommend a new chief to President Herbert Hoover. MacArthur lavishly praised Hurley's recent, ill-informed statement on independence for the Philippine Islands, expressing his "unbounded admiration" for Hurley's "comprehensive and statesmanlike paper," marveling at how it had "clarified issues which have perplexed and embarrassed statesmen for the last thirty years" and concluding with "my heartiest congratulations."

MacArthur was appointed Chief of Staff. And by a remarkable coincidence, Quezon was elected the President of the Philippine Commonwealth the same year that MacArthur's term as Chief of Staff ended. Quezon offered his old friend the post of military adviser, and MacArthur accepted.

MacArthur's palatial Manila Hotel apartment (top floor with arched windows) overlooked the pool. The $1,500-per-month rent was waived when MacArthur

The penthouse dining room was a sumptuous setting for small dinner parties. Normally, the general consumed a hearty dinner but ate light, low-calorie breakfasts and lunches to watch his waistline.

became chairman of the Manila Hotel Corporation.

MacArthur's library, where he spent much of his leisure time, contained some 8,000 volumes, many of them inherited from his father. He particularly enjoyed biographies of Confederate generals.

A LORDLY NEW HOME FOR THE GENERAL

MacArthur accepted the post of Philippine military adviser on the condition that he would receive the then-handsome salary of $18,000 and the same perquisites as the governor general. "The Governor General has, for his private residence, Malacañan Palace," MacArthur remarked to Quezon.

"We cannot build another Malacañan Palace," said Quezon. "But perhaps we can give you comparable accommodation."

Quezon met both demands. A huge, air-conditioned penthouse with breathtaking views was built atop a wing of the luxurious Manila Hotel. MacArthur was so delighted with his elegant new home that, as one aide observed, "he conducted almost as much business while walking up and down the terrace as he did at his office."

The sugar magnate Joaquin Elizalde, who was a close friend of the MacArthurs, escorts Mrs. MacArthur to a premiere game of jai alai, played in the Philippines in October of 1940. The general follows close behind.

The MacArthurs greet friends at a reception at the

A PRIVATE MAN IN THE PUBLIC EYE

Riding the crest of his Philippines power and popularity in the late 1930s, MacArthur constantly got invitations to Manila's elaborate social and civic events. He was often accompanied by vivacious Jean Faircloth, who became his wife in 1937.

At these functions MacArthur was often more of a spectator than a participant. The general never danced, but he encouraged Jean to join in. At banquets he spoke with the diners to either side and he invariably charmed them with his courtly manner and conversation. But he disliked large parties and idle chitchat, and, said an aide, "he doesn't enjoy meeting people merely for the sake of making new acquaintances." Often the MacArthurs said their goodbyes early and slipped away to see a movie.

The general and his lady did not entertain often. When they did, MacArthur preferred elegant dinners and quiet evenings with a small group of friends or staff members. He seemed to enjoy the company of his Filipino friends, and with them he had animated talks on serious subjects—principally politics and the growing threat of Japanese expansion. Yet even with his closest friends MacArthur maintained a certain formality—a reserve bordering on aloofness. Few men called him Douglas.

residence of the U.S. high commissioner in 1937. The couple addressed each other formally in public: he called her "Ma'am" and she called him "General."

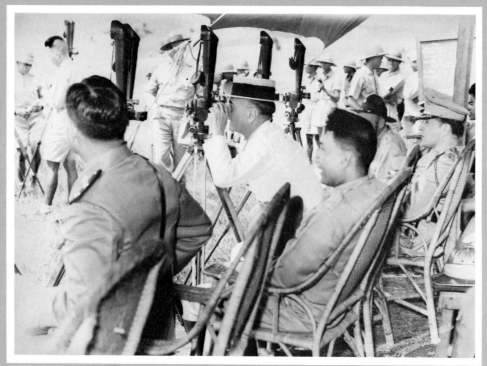

General MacArthur (right) puffs on his cigar while President Manuel Quezon, eyes glued to a periscope, avidly watches the maneuvers of Philippine Army trainees at Fort Stotsenburg in May 1939.

Stepping smartly in cadence, fully outfitted Filipino soldiers take part in a celebration marking the fourth anniversary of the Philippine Commonwealth. MacArthur watched from the reviewing stand.

LOFTY DEFENSE PLANS, DEEP DISAPPOINTMENTS

MacArthur planned to defend the Philippines with a large reserve army of trained civilians led by professional soldiers. He predicted that by 1946, the year that the U.S. promised to grant independence to the Philippines, "the nation would have a trained military force of forty divisions, comprising about 400,000 men."

But from the start, the program ran into money problems. MacArthur's assistant, Major Eisenhower, estimated that the eight million dollars allocated by the Philippine government would yield only a "skeleton force that some day might have flesh put on its bones."

Even so, MacArthur's enthusiasm for the plan led him to retire from the U.S. Army to avoid reassignment; it also misled him into taking too optimistic a view of his army's progress. The defenses developed slowly, and in 1941 the Philippines were ripe for plucking by the Japanese.

In a seemingly impressive display of power, planes

of the U.S. 4th Composite Group line up on Clark Field on the island of Luzon in 1939. But by then MacArthur's B-10 bombers and P-26 fighters were obsolescent.

Manuel Quezon congratulates MacArthur on his return to active duty in the Army as commander of U.S. Army Forces in the Far East in July 1941.

A RELUCTANT FLIGHT AND A VOW TO COME BACK

When the Japanese attacked the Philippines on December 8, 1941, the assault smashed MacArthur's flimsy defenses and sent his American and Philippine forces in confused retreat to the Bataan Peninsula. MacArthur set up his headquarters on the nearby island fortress of Corregidor and struggled to organize an effective defense. But supplies were short, especially food.

Promises of reinforcements poured in from Washington but the troops never arrived. MacArthur considered this a betrayal of the Philippine people.

On March 12, 1942, under orders from President Roosevelt, the general reluctantly boarded a PT boat and left Corregidor for Australia. Two months later, after a gallant resistance, Corregidor fell.

The Corregidor ordeal, said MacArthur, was "an inspiration to carry on the struggle until the Allies should fight their way back." For MacArthur, that fight was an inevitable, unrelenting personal crusade.

MacArthur and his chief of staff, Major General Richard K. Sutherland, await

developments in their oft-bombarded underground headquarters on Corregidor. MacArthur's long stay in the tunnel inspired critics to dub him "Dugout Doug."

2

When American forces in the Philippines surrendered in May 1942, General MacArthur's pledge to return seemed at best a valiant dream. "The road back," MacArthur himself acknowledged, "looked long and difficult." But the general's will became a driving force, and within two and a half years the Americans were ready to return. First they would have to fight the greatest naval battle of all time to guarantee that they would stay in the Philippines. No less than 282 warships would be involved in active combat, and the enormous conflict would be fought out in an expanse of water larger than France.

MacArthur's drive toward the Philippine Islands, which had brought his Southwest Pacific Area forces westward along the coast of New Guinea, was the southern prong of an enormous pincers movement. The northern prong, involving the Pacific Ocean Areas forces under Admiral Chester W. Nimitz, had thrust through Japanese-held island groups—the Solomons, Gilberts, Marshalls and Marianas—and crippled the air arm of the Japanese Navy. By September 1944, both great forces were poised some 300 miles from the southernmost Philippine island, Mindanao.

The invasion now about to take place had long been the subject of debate. MacArthur and Nimitz, coequal commanders who each took orders only from the U.S. Joint Chiefs in Washington, had cooperated effectively in their converging drives toward the Philippines, but they had disagreed on the next phase of the campaign. Nimitz did not share MacArthur's emotional commitment to liberating the Philippines. He was interested in the islands mainly as steppingstones to another objective: Formosa, 200 miles north of the Philippines and roughly 600 miles south of Japan itself. Formosa's capture would cut Japan off from its southern sources of raw materials and permit the Allies to land on the China coast around Hong Kong, where they would be able to build air bases from which to bomb the Japanese into submission.

MacArthur rebutted that if the Philippines were recaptured first, the invasion of Formosa would be easier—and perhaps unnecessary. He even proposed to liberate Luzon, the largest Philippine island.

In an effort to settle the debate, President Franklin D. Roosevelt journeyed all the way to Hawaii in July 1944. There MacArthur presented his views with his usual elo-

THE GREATEST SEA BATTLE

quence. He argued that Luzon could be taken more cheaply than Formosa and that it would serve much the same strategic purpose. He insisted that American honor and prestige in the Far East demanded that the U.S. liberate its own territory, and that it would be easier to do that than to invade Formosa because the Filipinos' loyalty and the help of the guerrillas would make it unnecessary for the U.S. to tie up large occupation forces. Though several of the participants in the conference thought MacArthur had won his case, the Luzon-Formosa issue remained unresolved.

In early September the Joint Chiefs ordered an invasion of Mindanao to take place on the 15th of November, to be followed by an invasion of Leyte on the 20th of December. Mindanao was seen as a steppingstone to Leyte, and Leyte as a convenient base for the next major offensive, whether against Formosa or Luzon.

The debate was finally settled by accident during the second week of September. At that time Admiral William F. "Bull" Halsey, commander of the Third Fleet under Nimitz, launched a series of air raids on the Philippines as a preliminary to taking the Palau Islands, 550 miles to the east of Mindanao. Vice Admiral Marc Mitscher, commander of the Third Fleet's Task Force 38, executed the attacks, and planes from his fast carriers battered Japanese airfields and naval bases on Mindanao and in the central Philippines. Returning pilots reported that they had destroyed 478 planes, most of them on the ground, and had sunk 59 ships. There was little opposition.

To Admiral Halsey this was "unbelievable and fantastic," and he jumped to the conclusion that the Japanese position in the Philippines was "a hollow shell with weak defenses and skimpy facilities." He became convinced that the whole invasion timetable could be accelerated and he proposed a speed-up. "Such a recommendation," he later wrote, "in addition to being none of my business, would upset a great many applecarts, possibly all the way up to Mr. Roosevelt and Mr. Churchill. On the other hand, it looked sound, it ought to save thousands of lives, and it might cut months off the war. . . . I sent for my aides and told them, 'I'm going to stick my neck out.' " Halsey then radioed Nimitz and suggested that the invasions of Mindanao and other islands be canceled in favor of an immediate attack on Leyte, which, Halsey noted, was "wide open."

Nimitz generally approved Halsey's suggestion and on September 13 passed it on to Washington and to Quebec, where the Joint Chiefs happened to be conferring with Roosevelt and Churchill. MacArthur's opinion was requested the same day, and approval arrived in Quebec during dinner the next evening. The Joint Chiefs excused themselves from the table and within 90 minutes had flashed new orders to MacArthur and Nimitz. The Mindanao invasion and most preliminary operations were canceled, and the Leyte invasion was moved up by two months to October 20. Halsey's Third Fleet with Mitscher's carriers was to cover the invasion, making up for air support that bases on Mindanao would have supplied.

The advancing of the timetable removed Formosa as a logical successor to the Leyte operation. Since Formosa was roughly twice as far away as Luzon, the extra distance meant that an invasion attempt would take a disproportionately longer period of time to mount. MacArthur clinched the matter by promising the Joint Chiefs that under the new schedule he would be ready to invade Luzon before the end of the year, two months earlier than any landings on Formosa could be attempted. On October 3 the Joint Chiefs made it official: the invasion of Luzon would follow the campaign for Leyte.

The decision to invade Leyte made good military sense, but it was based on a misconception. Though the Japanese in the Philippines were weak, they were not nearly so helpless as Admiral Halsey had thought.

Unbeknownst to the Americans, after the fall of the Marianas, Imperial General Headquarters had issued a defense plan designed to conserve all Japanese forces for a single decisive battle. This radical scheme, called the Sho-Go (Victory Operation), divided Japan's Pacific sphere into four huge defense zones, each with its own plan for handling an Allied attack. Every local commander was forbidden to commit his troops or planes until Tokyo activated the Sho plan for his zone. Thus the failure of Japanese aircraft to oppose Halsey's carrier-plane attacks was nothing more than a reflection of the commanders' obedience to their standing Sho orders. In fact, Imperial Headquarters had decided that Sho-1, the defense plan for the Philippines, would not be triggered until the Americans invaded Luzon, which the Japanese considered the most important island in the sprawling archipelago.

According to *Sho-1*, the Fourteenth Area Army, responsible for the defense of the Philippines, was to build impregnable defenses well inland on Luzon. Japanese troops on other islands were to fend for themselves without air or naval support if the Americans landed there first, and the Air Army was to hold off until the Luzon landings began.

The Japanese revamped their naval tactics to make the most of their great strength in battleships and cruisers. The pride of the fleet were the 68,000-ton *Yamato* and *Musashi;* they were the largest battleships afloat and possessed the biggest guns as well—18 inches. The *Sho-1* plan called for these mighty vessels and their accompanying ships, backed up by land-based planes, to sink the American invasion fleet. Four Japanese carriers were to serve as bait to lure Halsey's fast carriers away from Leyte Gulf. It did not matter if the American carriers sank the decoys and returned to the invasion area, for by then the Japanese battleships would have destroyed the American transports and battered the landing forces—and the decisive battle would be won.

As the carrier strikes on the islands increased, the Japanese became convinced that the decisive battle would be fought in the Philippines, and preparations for *Sho-1* were put into effect. Airfield construction was hastened. Reinforcements were ordered from China to the Philippines. General Tomoyuki Yamashita, a formidable tactician, was appointed to command the Fourteenth Area Army.

Japanese plans were upset in mid-October when Halsey sent Mitscher and the fast carriers to raid air bases on Formosa and Okinawa in preparation for the Leyte landing.

Tokyo sent out a tentative order alerting the combined Fleet for the start-up of *Sho-2*, the defense of Formosa and the Ryukyu Islands, between Japan and Formosa. But the Japanese aircraft carriers were then in home waters, too far away to reach Formosa in time to be of help. So the carriers were stripped of most of their aircraft; the planes were sent to land bases on Formosa and Okinawa in the Ryukyus in the belief that *Sho-2* had actually begun. This turned out to be a devastating mistake.

On Formosa the carrier aircraft came under the control of Vice Admiral Shigeru Fukudome, commander of the Second Air Fleet. On the morning of October 12, Japanese radar operators reported a "great formation" of planes approaching Formosa, and Fukudome sent all of his fighters aloft, including the "Tojos" and "Zekes" from the carriers—a total of 230 planes. Although he knew his pilots had only sketchy training—some of them had learned all they knew about aerial combat by watching films—Fukudome was confident. His planes would outnumber the Americans' and would therefore have the edge.

The great formation on the Japanese radar screens was a fighter sweep from Mitscher's carriers, the first wave of the 1,378 sorties flown that day. The Americans' mission was to knock out Fukudome's air defenses.

Commander Fred Bakutis, leading a first-wave group of six Grumman F6F Hellcats from the carrier *Enterprise*, spotted a long column of Tojos 7,000 feet below and climbing fast to intercept. As the six Grummans plummeted down in formation, Bakutis went for the leading plane; a single burst from his six .50-caliber machine guns set the Tojo ablaze. Ensign Douglas Baker came in from behind and hit a Tojo at

Amassed for the Philippines invasion, U.S. Seventh Fleet warships lie at anchor in Seeadler Harbor in the Admiralty Islands, some 1,400 miles from the targeted beachheads on Leyte. Together with the U.S. Third Fleet, the Seventh formed an immense armada of 17 fleet and 18 escort carriers, 12 battleships, 28 cruisers, 150 destroyers and hundreds of amphibious vessels of all types and their supporting units.

such close range that he had to swerve violently to avoid colliding with the flying wreckage. As he swerved, Baker saw another Tojo dead ahead and he got that one too. Then Baker rolled into a dive and immediately hit a third Tojo. In just 10 seconds, Bakutis' group had shot down five Japanese planes. The rest of the Tojos scattered.

Far below, Fukudome had eagerly stepped out of his command post to watch. "Our interceptors swooped down in great force at the invading enemy planes," he wrote later. "One after the other, planes were seen falling down, enveloped in flames. 'Well done! Well done! A tremendous success!' I clapped my hands. Alas! To my sudden disappointment, a closer watch revealed that all those shot down were our fighters, and all those proudly circling above our heads were enemy planes! In a brief, one-sided encounter, the combat terminated in our total defeat."

The first-wave attack alone cost Fukudome about one third of his fighters and did so much damage to hangars and ground installations that only about 60 Japanese interceptors rose to meet the second American strike a few hours later. By the time the third wave came in during the afternoon there were no Japanese defenders in the air, and American planes roamed over the island at will, attacking harbors, fuel dumps and airfields. For two more days the attacks continued, and when they ended close to 600 Japanese Navy and Air Army planes had been destroyed. Thus, on the eve of the Leyte invasion Japan lost a large part of her surviving aircraft.

During the American strikes, Fukudome had sent several squadrons of torpedo bombers to attack the ships of the Third Fleet at night. Although most of these planes were shot down too, they succeeded in damaging the cruisers *Canberra* and *Houston* so badly that the ships had to be towed away to safety. The inexperienced Japanese pilots—apparently mistaking the flames of their downed planes for burning ships—came back with such enthusiastic claims of success that even cynical Japanese commanders thought that Halsey's force had been severely crippled. The alleged victory was soon inflated even more. Japanese newspapers headlined a "Second Pearl Harbor," and the Emperor ordered celebrations.

The national euphoria affected the judgment of Imperial Headquarters. When an American invasion fleet appeared in Leyte Gulf a few days later, the new confidence of the Tokyo planners prompted them to question their earlier decision to fight the decisive battle on Luzon. General Yamashita saw no reason to shift the plan from Luzon, where most of his troops stood ready in prepared defenses. But his superior, Field Marshal Terauchi, argued that *Sho-1* should go into effect whenever the first Philippine island was invaded. He won over Imperial Headquarters to his view; Tokyo believed that at least half of the Third Fleet had been sunk off Formosa and that the Americans were recklessly attempting an invasion of Leyte with reduced forces. Presumably, the weakened U.S. carrier-plane force would be unable to prevent a massive movement of Japanese troops and supplies to Leyte.

On October 18 the decision was made: the climactic battle would be fought on Leyte. The order was carried by liaison officers who did not arrive in Manila until October 20. By that time, the invasion of Leyte was under way.

To retake the island, the separate commands of General MacArthur and Admiral Nimitz had converged on Leyte Gulf and the island's east coast. Nimitz' Third Fleet, under Halsey, contained Mitscher's force of 16 fast carriers, plus six fast new battleships and 81 cruisers and destroyers. Almost everything else came under MacArthur's control, adding up to a staggering command: Lieut. General Walter Krueger's Sixth Army, with six divisions totaling 200,000 men; Lieut. General George C. Kenney's Fifth Air Force based on five Pacific islands; and "MacArthur's Navy," Vice Admiral Thomas C. Kinkaid's U.S. Seventh Fleet, which was to support the beachhead with its small escort carriers and slow old battleships. All these units arrived unopposed, and Krueger's assault forces met with only light resistance as they went ashore on Leyte's east coast on the morning of October 20. The Americans assumed that enemy warships were closing in around them, but they had no inkling of what the Japanese battle plan might be.

Admiral Soemu Toyoda, the commander of the Combined Fleet, was deliberately risking the destruction of the Japanese Navy. If the Americans took the Philippines, he reasoned, U.S. planes would cut off the Navy wherever it was and prevent it from moving north or south. If isolated to the south of the Philippines, the Navy could receive no ammunition from Japan; if trapped to the north, it would be denied oil from the East Indies. "In the end," said Toyoda, "even if you had a fleet, it would have been a white elephant." For the Japanese Navy, the Battle for Leyte Gulf would be the last real chance to survive—and the last real chance to stem the enemy tide.

Toyoda's fleet (map, page 67) was divided into three forces. The most powerful of these was Vice Admiral Takeo Kurita's Center Force, which included the mammoth battleships *Musashi* and *Yamato*. Kurita, approaching from Singapore via Borneo, planned to steam eastward through the middle of the Philippine archipelago, transit San Bernardino Strait between Luzon and Samar and emerge into the open sea. Then he would come roaring down from the north upon the American invasion forces in Leyte Gulf at dawn on October 25.

At the same time, Vice Admiral Shoji Nishimura's Southern Force was to enter Leyte Gulf from the south through Surigao Strait with a fleet of seven older, slower warships. Nishimura's force was the second arm of the pincers movement that Toyoda hoped would wipe out the American invasion fleet. Behind Nishimura, serving as a sort of rear guard for his ships, would come Vice Admiral Kiyohide Shima with seven cruisers and destroyers.

The third segment of the divided fleet, the Northern Force, was weak but indispensable to Toyoda's hopes. It consisted of four aircraft carriers, which had put out from Japan in the company of two battleships with small flight decks, and 11 light cruisers and destroyers. This force, under the command of Vice Admiral Jisaburo Ozawa, had sailed from Japanese home waters with only 116 planes aboard. But Ozawa needed no planes to fulfill his mission; he was to be a decoy and his only function was to lure the Third Fleet carriers north, away from Leyte Gulf, so that Kurita, Nishimura and Shima could strike unopposed.

The Japanese plan began to unravel almost at once. On the morning of October 23, Kurita's approaching Center Force was spotted by two American submarines (opposite), and they radioed a warning to the Third Fleet, giving Halsey his first news of what the Japanese were up to. Alerted for action, the Third Fleet carriers swung east of the Philippines and dispatched scout planes to search for Kurita's ships.

The next morning, October 24, a search plane from the U.S. carrier *Intrepid* found Kurita's Center Force steaming through the Sibuyan Sea; another plane from the *Enterprise* located Nishimura's Southern Force in the Sulu Sea west of Mindanao; and a Fifth Air Force patrol bomber observed Shima's Southern Force heading toward the Mindanao Sea. With mounting excitement, Admiral Halsey assumed direct tactical command of Mitscher's carrier planes by personally ordering them to attack the big target, Kurita's Center Force.

American radar picked up several large groups of Japanese planes headed for the American Third Fleet. These were the remains of Admiral Fukudome's air forces based on Luzon and Formosa, about 200 planes in all, and they represented the aerial punch of the *Sho* operation. But the Americans were ready for them. Hellcat fighters destroyed about 70 of the Japanese aircraft and prevented all but one of them from getting near the American ships. However, that one Japanese plane dropped a bomb on the carrier *Princeton*, turning her into an inferno (page 58).

Yet the sinking of the *Princeton* cost the Japanese dearly. In concentrating all planes in the vicinity on one of Halsey's carrier groups, Fukudome had left Admiral Kurita's Center Force with practically no air cover.

Two of the Third Fleet carrier groups had launched planes for a massive attack on Kurita's powerful force as it came steaming in broad daylight through the Sibuyan Sea toward San Bernardino Strait. Without fighter protection, Kurita had to rely on his vessels' antiaircraft firepower. Each battleship carried 120 antiaircraft guns, each cruiser 90. Kurita also had a unique secret weapon: the huge 18-inch guns aboard his superbattleships, the *Musashi* and the *Yamato*, could be elevated to fire at aircraft with a special type of shell known as *sanshikidon,* each of which would spray 6,000 steel pellets in shotgun style over the sky.

With all antiaircraft guns pointed skyward, Kurita's battleships looked like giant porcupines when the American airplanes struck. The first wave of 21 fighters, 12 dive bombers and 12 torpedo bombers from the carriers *Intrepid* and *Cabot* flung themselves against a wall of flak at 10:30 a.m. Several of the planes were hit, but many got through. The U.S. fighters strafed the decks of the warships and forced the gunners to take cover as the torpedo bombers skimmed in to drop their missiles. One torpedo hit the cruiser *Myoko*,

A SUBMARINE PATROL THAT BLUNTED A JAPANESE ATTACK

The U.S. Darter, abandoned by her crew, lies stranded on a coral reef west of Palawan Island. Attempts by both the Americans and the Japanese to destroy the sub were unsuccessful.

Japan's Center Force, captured in a rare snapshot, steams toward its encounter with the Darter and the Dace. The second and third vessels in line are the Musashi and the Yamato, then the largest battleships in the world.

At exactly 1:16 a.m. on October 23, 1944, the U.S. submarine *Darter* made a radar contact that played a key role in the Battle for Leyte Gulf. While the sub was patrolling dangerous waters in the western Philippines, her radar screens were suddenly covered with a mass of blips—the Japanese Navy's Center Force, whose whereabouts had been a worrisome mystery for four days. This powerful arm of the Japanese fleet, commanded by Vice Admiral Takeo Kurita, was heading north from Borneo to launch an attack on American Naval units supporting the invasion of Leyte.

Commander David McClintock of the *Darter* radioed an alert to the Third Fleet. Then the *Darter,* joined by another sub, the nearby *Dace,* closed in on the Japanese fleet. McClintock found—to his delight—that Kurita had not deployed his force to defend against submarine attacks.

McClintock pumped four torpedoes into a cruiser, and 18 minutes later he saw "the sight of a lifetime"—the great ship going under. Meanwhile, the *Dace* sank a second cruiser and the *Darter* crippled a third.

The men of the *Darter* later made an error in navigation and ran aground on a reef. They were forced to escape in the *Dace.* Nevertheless, the U.S. had won the first round of the Leyte Gulf battle.

which lost speed and had to retire. A bomb and a torpedo hit the *Musashi,* but the great ship was protected by armor plate 16 inches thick, and she just shuddered at the blows and steamed serenely on.

Shortly after noon a second attack wave struck. Hits were scored on Kurita's flagship, the *Yamato,* and four more torpedoes shook the *Musashi.* Three of those torpedoes struck the *Musashi's* port bow, where her armor was relatively thin, and the explosion peeled back the outer plates. The jagged rip slowed the ship down, and Kurita ordered the entire fleet to reduce speed to 22 knots so that the *Musashi* could keep up. Now a worried man, Kurita radioed Ozawa and Manila headquarters: "We are being subjected to repeated enemy carrier-based air attacks. Advise immediately of contacts and attacks made by you on the enemy."

Less than an hour later another group of planes, from the *Lexington* and the *Essex,* swarmed over the groggy Japanese fleet. The *Musashi's* damaged bow kept spewing a great geyser of water into the air as the battleship plowed along, making her plight obvious to all the American fliers, who swooped in for the kill. Four more torpedoes ripped into the *Musashi.* As her damaged bow sank lower in the water, the battleship began to fall behind the rest of the fleet.

Until early afternoon the captain of the *Musashi,* Rear Admiral Toshihira Inoguchi, refused to fire his main battery's *sanshiki-don* at the attacking planes. Those special shells could damage a gun's bore and Inoguchi wanted to save his barrels for the 3,220-pound shells he still expected to fire at surface targets in Leyte Gulf the next day. But now he knew all too well that the *Musashi* was in trouble, and he gave his gunnery officer the go-ahead. The three great turrets—three guns each—swung toward the east and the massive 180-ton, 70-foot barrels were pointed skyward.

When another wave of American carrier planes appeared in the distance at 2:30 p.m., the guns fired with an enormous concussive roar. The men on deck were deafened for a while, and those below felt as though a spread of torpedoes had smashed into the ship's hull. The gunnery officer peered through the smoke and noted with dismay that the planes were still advancing.

The oncoming pilots, launched from the *Enterprise* and the *Franklin,* noted that the antiaircraft barrage was the heaviest they had encountered in the War. But the Japanese marksmanship was surprisingly poor: the shellbursts always trailed behind the planes. Commander Daniel F. Smith, leading the planes from the *Enterprise,* discovered why. When his flight passed through a thin cirrus cloud, the antiaircraft fire from the entire fleet stopped, "and when we emerged from the clouds they opened up again like the hammers of hell." Clearly, the Japanese gunners were aiming not by radar but by sight.

While the *Franklin's* planes concentrated on the *Yamato,* Smith and his *Enterprise* cohorts attacked the *Musashi.* To blind the antiaircraft gunners below, Commander Smith led his flight around the Japanese force until the sun was directly behind him. Then, one by one, his nine Helldivers, each carrying a double load of two 1,000-pound armor-piercing bombs, nosed over and screamed down at the *Musashi.* The bomber pilots had never seen such an inviting target: big, steady and slow-moving. They stayed late in their dives, released both bombs and pulled away, scooting out of danger to the north.

Then the *Enterprise's* eight Avenger torpedo bombers spread out and came in low on each side of the *Musashi,* aiming for the damaged bow. Just as the last Helldiver released its bombs, the Avengers dropped their torpedoes into the water and swerved away. Wrote one *Enterprise* officer later: "The big battlewagon was momentarily lost under the towering fountains of near misses and torpedo hits, soaring puffs of white smoke from bomb hits and streaming black smoke from resultant fires. Then the long, dark bow slid out of the caldron, slowing. *Musashi* stopped, down by the head, and burning."

One bomb had hit the battleship's bridge, and for a few moments no one was in charge of the vessel. Below the bridge in an open signal booth, Petty Officer Second Class Shiro Hosoya watched in horror as torpedo tracks closed in on the ship, and he was knocked down by the explosions. Then he heard the voice of his commanding officer, Admiral Inoguchi, coming to him on the speaking tube from the observation tower high above: "First bridge, all killed. Captain will take command from the second bridge." More explosions followed, and then: "Captain is wounded. Executive Officer, take command."

From the second bridge the executive officer leaned out

to the signal booth and handed Hosoya a message for transmittal to Admiral Kurita on the *Yamato*. There was no electricity for the signal light, so Hosoya had to use semaphore flags. "*Musashi* capable of cruising at 15 knots," he wigwagged. "Listing to port about 15 degrees."

The message had scarcely been sent when planes from the *Intrepid*, *Essex* and *Cabot* joined those from the *Franklin* and *Enterprise* and swarmed over Kurita's ships at 3:10 p.m. Several more torpedoes hit the *Musashi*, knocking out two of her four propellers and forcing damage-control personnel to flood three of her four engine rooms to prevent the ship from capsizing. Hosoya signaled a more plaintive message: "Speed six knots. Capable of operation. Damage great. What shall we do?"

Kurita ordered Inoguchi to return to base, but the *Musashi* was rapidly taking on water, and her list had increased, forcing her to move in a circle. Later, Kurita ordered: "*Musashi* go forward or backward at top speed and ground on nearest island and become a land battery." Even this ignominious mission was too much for the *Musashi*.

The great ship started to go under. A sailor played the national anthem on a trumpet. To save the *Musashi*'s flag, sailors lowered it and wrapped it around the waist of a strong swimmer. The executive officer shouted, "All crew abandon ship. You're on your own." Some men placed their shoes and leggings neatly on the deck before diving into the water, as if they planned to return.

The ship rolled over onto her side, baring her barnacle-encrusted bottom. Water rushed through gaping torpedo holes, pulling swimming men back into the ship. Hosoya, still aboard, sprinted and scrambled along the ship's bottom, his bare feet lacerated and bleeding. Reaching the bow, which now dragged at water level, he stepped into the sea and started swimming. When he looked back he saw the *Musashi*'s stern pointing straight up, silhouetted against the setting sun, with several men clinging to it. Then the great ship plunged beneath the sea with loud suckings and rumblings and underwater explosions. Four hours later destroyers picked up Hosoya and several hundred other survivors, but 1,023 officers and sailors, almost half the *Musashi*'s crew, had perished with the ship.

In addition to sinking the *Musashi* and crippling the cruiser *Myoko*, the day-long attacks had damaged the *Yamato*

and two other battleships. The damaged ships could still fight, but Kurita had to slow down his fleet to prevent them from falling out of formation. Estimating that enemy planes could make up to three more strikes on his slow-moving fleet before sunset, Kurita prudently reversed course in order to delay his transit of the narrow and dangerous San Bernardino Strait until after dark.

The westward turn was noted by Halsey's fliers, and it influenced the admiral's next decision. His pilots reported that four of Kurita's battleships had been severely damaged, that nine cruisers and destroyers had been sunk or heavily damaged, and that the remains of the armada were retreating westward. Halsey assumed that the Center Force was no longer a threat, and he turned his attention to what he thought was bigger game.

All day his planes had been searching for the carriers he felt sure must be part of this massive Japanese naval operation. Finally, at about 5:30 in the afternoon, one spotted the carriers of Admiral Ozawa's Northern Force 300 miles to the north of San Bernardino Strait. Now, Halsey reckoned, he had "all the pieces of the puzzle."

Halsey regarded the Northern Force as the major threat; if its air strength was combined with the other enemy forces, it could jeopardize MacArthur's landing operations in Leyte Gulf. Halsey did not know, of course, that Ozawa's four carriers had only a few planes left on board. Lacking that intelligence, the Third Fleet commander considered three courses of action; he could keep his fleet where it was, in position to guard against attacks by both the Northern and Center Forces; he could send his carriers after the Northern Force and leave his battleships behind to guard San Bernardino Strait, through which the Center Force would have to pass to reach Leyte Gulf; or he could rush north with his entire armada to destroy the Japanese carriers.

Characteristically, Halsey opted for the all-out attack. Leaving not even a destroyer patrol to give warning if Kurita emerged from San Bernardino Strait, Halsey ordered the Third Fleet north. He had swallowed Ozawa's bait.

In choosing to chase after Ozawa, Halsey had made a decision that would come back to haunt him. MacArthur and his Seventh Fleet commander, Kinkaid, believed that Halsey's first duty was to protect the invasion convoy and the troops ashore. But Halsey was responsible only to Nimitz, who had clearly instructed him that his "primary task" was the destruction of the enemy whenever he had the chance. Besides, Halsey was willing to risk condemnation for almost anything but lack of aggressive spirit.

In any case, the lack of a unified command now led to a misunderstanding that nearly proved disastrous for the American forces in Leyte Gulf. Halsey realized that Kurita's Center Force, battered though it was, might yet attempt to enter the gulf. Even before sighting Ozawa's carriers, he had transmitted to his Third Fleet commanders a stand-by battle plan that set up a separate detachment of fast battleships, cruisers and destroyers to confront Kurita. This group of warships would, if so ordered, form Task Force 34 under Vice Admiral Willis Lee and "engage decisively at long ranges." Halsey's radioed plan was simply an alert, not an operational order for immediate action. To make sure that none of his subordinates misunderstood, Halsey called them on short-range radio and said: "If the enemy sorties, Task Force 34 will be formed *when directed by me.*"

Although Halsey's original stand-by plan to set up the new task force was not addressed to him, Admiral Kinkaid of the Seventh Fleet received a copy of the radioed message—but not the clarifying amendment. He assumed that Lee and Task Force 34 were being sent to guard San Bernardino Strait immediately. Halsey, who did not realize that Kinkaid even knew about Lee's unborn task force, assumed that planes from Kinkaid's escort carriers would keep an eye on the strait. Halsey also assumed that the Seventh Fleet was strong enough to defeat both the weakened Center Force and the two sections of the Southern Force. Such was the danger of divided command: San Bernardino Strait was unguarded and no one knew it.

And Kurita was coming back. As Halsey and all his ships raced north through the night in pursuit of Ozawa's decoy carriers, Kurita, who had turned his battered but still-potent Center Force around again, was once more threading his way through the interior waterways toward San Bernardino, heading for the open sea and Leyte Gulf. At the same time, the second arm of the Japanese pincers, Admiral Nishimura's Southern Force, was approaching Surigao Strait, the southern entrance to Leyte Gulf. Although he knew that

Kurita had been delayed and would not be able to keep the dawn rendezvous in Leyte Gulf, Nishimura steamed ahead on schedule, relishing the prospect of engaging the Seventh Fleet in a night battle.

Nishimura's wish was realized in the predawn hours of October 25, when his warships plunged into a brief but one-sided battle in the darkness of Surigao Strait. Search planes and coastwatchers had kept the Seventh Fleet informed of the Southern Force's movements, and Vice Admiral Jesse B. Oldendorf, commanding Kinkaid's fighting ships, was waiting for Nishimura.

Oldendorf's six battleships were old and slow. Three had been damaged and two had been sunk at Pearl Harbor; they had been raised or reconditioned and put back into service. Nishimura's ships were even more ancient; his two battleships were of World War I vintage and had been relegated to training assignments for most of the War. Nishimura also had one cruiser and four old destroyers, while Oldendorf deployed eight cruisers, 28 destroyers and 39 PT boats. Furthermore, the American battleships were equipped with fire-control radar, and the Japanese ships were not.

As Nishimura's force steamed single file into the southern approaches of Surigao Strait, it was ambushed by several groups of American PT boats, which had been lying motionless in the water so as not to leave wakes that would give away their positions. The PTs waited until the ships came within range and then darted in to launch their torpedoes. Though none scored hits, they were able to radio back to Oldendorf precise information about Nishimura's course, location and speed.

A few miles farther north the Japanese entered a more effective prearranged trap: a gauntlet of American and Australian destroyers. As Nishimura's force filed up the center of the strait, the destroyers raced down both sides of it in formations of two or three, firing half salvos of torpedoes at ranges of about four miles, and then turning and speeding away before the Japanese guns could find them.

Lieutenant Leonard H. Hudson of the destroyer *Remey* made the first of the torpedo runs. He later recounted, "When the target was less than five miles the Captain radioed to ships astern: 'Follow me.' Then came the rapid orders: 'Stand by to fire torpedoes! Fire torpedoes! Torpedoes away!' About that time the Jap radar picked us up.

They quickly turned on their searchlights and they were right on target. I felt like my picture was being taken with a flash bulb camera. We were in so close that they shot over us with their AA guns. They shot in front of us, behind us and straddled us, but we got out without a scratch."

Zigzagging and throwing up smoke screens, the destroyers escaped. Then, eight minutes after firing, the crew heard explosions; two of the Japanese ships were hit by the first salvo of torpedoes, and other torpedoes were already in the water from the far side of the strait. Another two-sided attack followed, and then a third. The results were devastating. The battleship *Fuso* blew up and split in two; Nishimura's flagship, the battleship *Yamashiro*, took hits, and two of his destroyers were sunk.

But still Nishimura came on, and Oldendorf prepared to cross the enemy's "T"—a classic maneuver in which one fleet cuts in front of the enemy column in a single-file

formation, or battle line. Crossing the "T" had the advantage of allowing every ship in the battle line to fire broadside at the enemy ships, while they could only return fire with their forward guns. With the advent of aircraft carriers, the maneuver had been rendered practically obsolete, since the battle line could not be formed or held under air attack. The absence of aircraft and the darkness of Surigao Strait gave Oldendorf the chance to use the tactic one last time. "We were in the ideal position," said his flagship commander, "a position dreamed of, studied and plotted in War College maneuvers and never hoped to be attained."

Thus, Oldendorf's battleships and cruisers steamed directly across Nishimura's path, blocking his passage from Surigao Strait to Leyte Gulf. On every U.S. ship, men studied their radar scopes; fire-control personnel tracked the range and bearing of the enemy ships and fed a steady stream of aiming data to the men standing by their guns. As the battle line marched across the mouth of the strait, every turret slowly turned.

Oldendorf, on the flag bridge of the cruiser *Louisville*, held his fire until Nishimura's lead ship closed the range to 15,600 yards. Then, shortly before 4 a.m., he gave the order to fire. The *Louisville*'s captain spoke the order into a radio circuit and his voice crackled out from squawk boxes on every ship. "Upon giving the order to 'open fire'" Oldendorf recalled, "it seemed as if every ship opened at once, and there was a semicircle of fire which landed squarely on one point, which was the leading battleship."

For Captain Roland N. Smoot, whose destroyer squadron was steaming south between the U.S. battle line and the Japanese ships, the opening barrage was "the most beautiful sight I have ever witnessed. The arched line of tracers in the darkness looked like a continual stream of lighted railroad cars going over a hill. No target could be observed at first, then shortly there would be fires and explosions, and another enemy ship would be accounted for."

Within 18 minutes, the battleships *West Virginia*, *California*, *Tennessee*, *Maryland* and *Mississippi* fired some 270 shells at Nishimura's vessels from their 14- and 16-inch guns. During that same period, cruisers fired more than 4,000 rounds of 6- and 8-inch shells, and Smoot's destroyer squadron launched torpedoes at the burning Japanese ships. After taking several hits, the battleship *Yamashiro*

Admiral William F. Halsey, commander of the U.S. Third Fleet during the Battle for Leyte Gulf, won the admiration and affection of his men for his aggressive leadership, considerate treatment and plain good humor. One of his sailors voiced the general opinion to a fellow seaman on board the admiral's flagship: "I'd go through hell for that old son-of-a-bitch." Halsey, unseen but close enough to overhear the remark, confronted the sailor and said with mock severity, "Young man, I'm not so old!"

Nosing dangerously close to the burning Princeton, the ill-starred cruiser Birmingham drenches the carrier with her hoses but fails to put out the fires.

THE FATAL ORDEAL OF A FAST CARRIER

On the morning of October 24, 1944, the fast carrier *Princeton* was prowling the rain-swept waters east of Luzon, searching for Japanese warships reportedly en route to Leyte Gulf. The *Princeton's* Hellcat fighters had shot down 36 Japanese planes with only a single loss, and the elated crewmen scented victory in the coming battle for the gulf. Then at 9:38, a lone Japanese "Judy" bomber swooped out of thick clouds, evaded the *Princeton's* antiaircraft barrage and dropped a 550-pound bomb on the flight deck.

Without exploding, the bomb crashed through the steel plate down to the hangar deck. "When the bomb hit," Captain William H. Buracker of the *Princeton* remarked, "I felt no immediate concern. I saw the hole, which was small, and visualized slapping on a patch in a hurry and

resuming operations." But in seconds the bomb detonated in the middle of six torpedo planes on the hangar deck. Soon a chain reaction of exploding torpedoes sent flame and smoke racing through the ship. Many crewmen were wounded and trapped. Buracker ordered all but the essential personnel to abandon ship.

Several of the *Princeton's* companion vessels drew close to the burning carrier and turned on fire hoses. The destroyer *Irwin* came alongside and, said a *Princeton* officer, "Many men jumped or went down lines from the flight deck into the water, and swam the narrow gap to the cargo nets hanging from the destroyer's side." Some sailors drowned in the turbulent strip of water, but 600 climbed safely aboard the *Irwin*. Other ships picked up more survivors.

By early afternoon, the fires on the *Princeton* seemed to be controlled, and the light cruiser *Birmingham* approached the stricken carrier and prepared to take

her in tow. Then, at 3:23, a finger of flame reached a bomb and torpedo magazine. A tremendous explosion blew off most of the carrier's stern, and killed or wounded almost everyone still aboard.

The *Birmingham* was hit even harder by the explosion. Hot chunks of flying metal raked her decks, mowing down sailors, gunners and fire fighters in what a survivor called "a grisly scene of human fragmentation." Another noted that "men with legs off, with arms off, with gaping wounds in their sides" insisted that they were all right and that the doctors treat the even more badly wounded.

The double disaster took a heavy toll. On the *Birmingham*, 229 men lay dead or dying, another 420 were wounded. The *Princeton* lost 108 men—and was lost herself. Despite terrible wounds, the ship was still afloat, and Buracker still wanted to save her. But orders came to scuttle the carrier. At dusk the flaming hulk was finally sent to the bottom.

exploded, then quickly capsized and sank. All but one of Nishimura's vessels, a destroyer, had been crippled or sunk. No American ships were lost, although one of Captain Smoot's destroyers, the *Albert W. Grant,* was severely damaged when she got caught in a cross fire of Japanese and American shells and took hits from American guns. To prevent any further mishaps, Oldendorf gave the order to cease firing until all his ships had identified themselves.

Meanwhile, Admiral Shima's rear-guard section of the Southern Force had passed into Surigao Strait as the battle was ending. To his dismay, Shima found only dense smoke and the burning hulks of Japanese ships. He retreated before Oldendorf's guns could get him too; his only contribution to the Japanese effort was to let Kurita know that there would be no Southern Force to meet him in Leyte Gulf.

Some 200 miles to the north, Kurita's still-formidable Center Force was taking full advantage of its good fortune—the American mix-up that had left San Bernardino Strait unguarded. In a display of superior seamanship, Kurita had maneuvered his fleet through the narrow channel at 20 knots. His lookouts and his crews at battle stations were sure they had been detected and thought they would have to fight their way out of the channel into the open sea.

Meanwhile, Admiral Halsey and his Third Fleet hurried northward in pursuit of Ozawa's Northern Force. Admiral Lee, the commander of the still-unactivated Task Force 34, doubted the wisdom of the chase; twice he suggested to Halsey that the Northern Force was just a decoy and that the big Japanese effort would be aimed through San Bernardino at the Seventh Fleet. Halsey ignored him.

The last attempt to rectify the error came after a predawn staff meeting on Kinkaid's command ship, the *Wasatch.* Commander Richard Cruzen, Kinkaid's operations officer, turned to his commanding officer and said: "Admiral, I can think of only one thing. We've never asked Halsey directly if Task Force 34 is guarding San Bernardino Strait." Kinkaid replied: "All right. Send it." The query was dispatched, but because of a backlog of radio transmissions Halsey did not receive the message for two and a half hours.

By that time, Kurita had emerged unopposed from the strait and was racing southward along the coast of Samar Island heading for Leyte Gulf. At daybreak on October 25,

Princeton survivors aboard a raft await an approaching rescue ship.

Hit by three torpedoes, the sinking carrier spouts a geyser of flame.

American carriers were sighted on the horizon. "Several masts came in sight about 30 kilometers to the southeast," wrote Kurita's chief of staff, Admiral Tomiji Koyanagi, "and presently we could see planes being launched. This was indeed a miracle. Think of a surface fleet coming up on an enemy carrier group. Nothing is more vulnerable than an aircraft carrier in a surface engagement."

Kurita thought he had caught Halsey's fast carriers with most of their planes down. He judged the ships ahead to be a "gigantic enemy task force, including six or seven carriers accompanied by many cruisers and destroyers." In fact, Halsey and his fast carriers were 300 miles to the north, and 180 of his planes were taking off to attack Ozawa's Northern Force. Ozawa radioed Kurita that he was under attack by the big American carriers, but Kurita never received the message. If he had, he would have realized that only a thin screen of puny ships stood between him and Leyte Gulf.

What Kurita had come upon was Rear Admiral Clifton A. F. Sprague's Taffy 3, one of three groups of escort carriers from Kinkaid's Seventh Fleet assigned to provide air cover and antisubmarine patrol for the Leyte landings. These vessels, condescendingly nicknamed "jeep" carriers or "baby flattops," were actually merchant ships fitted with short flight decks. The six escort carriers of Taffy 3 carried only about 28 planes each; they could attain a top speed of only 17 knots (half the speed of Kurita's battleships), had virtually no armor plate and were equipped with only 5-inch guns. The group was protected by three destroyers and four destroyer escorts. Altogether, the 13 ships of Sprague's little fleet had only 29 guns, none of them capable of even denting the thick armor plate of Kurita's battlewagons. Furthermore, Sprague's pilots were trained to provide tactical support for ground troops, not to attack enemy warships.

Sprague's first warning of Kurita's force came just after 6:45 a.m., when Ensign Hans Jensen, flying an Avenger torpedo bomber on a routine antisubmarine patrol off Samar, radioed that an enemy force of battleships, cruisers and destroyers was approaching at high speed. Assuming that the pilot had mistaken a Third Fleet unit for an enemy force, Sprague angrily yelled at the radio operator on his flagship: "Air plot, tell him to check his identification." From his Avenger, pilot Jensen took another look at the unmistakable superstructure of the Japanese battleships and then radioed back: "Identification of enemy forces

Framed by a porthole of his flagship, the Fanshaw Bay, Rear Admiral Clifton A. F. Sprague peers seaward during the Leyte Gulf battle between his small Taffy 3 task unit and the mighty Japanese Center Force. The Americans' daring attacks confused the Japanese and hit them, Sprague later said, "with everything in the armory—including the doorknobs."

confirmed. Ships have pagoda masts." By this time, the lookouts on Sprague's own ship had caught the first glimpse of the pagoda-shaped enemy masts as they appeared on the northern horizon.

Sprague wasted no time. He swung his carriers east into the wind at top speed and launched every operational plane—including his fighters. He instructed all ships to throw up smoke screens, alerted his destroyers for an attack and radioed for help.

Within minutes, the 18-inch guns of the *Yamato* and the 14-inch guns of the other Japanese battleships were dropping salvos all around the American ships. These sent up huge fountains of colored water—red, green, yellow and purple; each shell contained a distinctive dye that helped gunners adjust their fire. "They're shooting at us in technicolor," quipped one American seaman. Near misses rocked Taffy 3's carriers, hurling men to the decks and showering them with shrapnel. The barrage was close, and getting closer; to Sprague "it did not appear that any of our ships could survive another five minutes of the heavy-caliber fire being received." Then Providence intervened; a rain squall appeared, and Taffy 3 ducked into it.

As the last flights of Taffy 3's planes took off to hit the enemy, Sprague changed course, heading south toward the two other Seventh Fleet Taffy groups, whose planes were already on their way to aid him. But the nearest group, Taffy 2, was more than 60 miles away; Taffy 1 was some 130 miles distant. And Oldendorf's battleships, whose big guns were what Sprague needed most, were still in Surigao Strait and could not reach Samar for at least three or four hours.

For the next three hours, while Taffy 3 broadcast repeated calls for help and Kinkaid frantically radioed Halsey to return south to take on the Japanese fleet, Sprague eased south with his carriers in a series of brilliant evasive maneuvers. The counterattacks by his aircraft and seven fighting ships were so fierce, so concentrated and so effective that the Japanese continued to believe they were engaging a much bigger force. All the planes that could fly were kept aloft almost continuously; flight-deck crews refueled and rearmed them when they bounced down on the decks. Once the carriers' small stock of torpedoes was exhausted, the torpedo planes were loaded with bombs; when the bombs were gone the pilots dropped depth charges or

made dry runs to trick the Japanese into twisting and dodging off course. Fighters strafed the decks and bridges, sending the gun crews and bridge officers diving for cover. One fighter pilot made 20 attacks—half of them without any ammunition.

Under the shaky cover of the planes, Sprague's destroyers and destroyer escorts recklessly threw themselves in front of their carriers. Following zigzag courses and laying great clouds of black and white smoke, they plunged into the midst of Kurita's force in an attempt to get close enough to bring their small guns within range. The destroyers and the destroyer escorts kept firing torpedoes, and though few of the missiles found their marks, the misses served to delay and distract the faster Japanese ships.

The destroyer *Johnston* was in the thick of the hectic fight all morning. She fired her last torpedoes just before being hit by three 14-inch shells. "It was like a puppy being smacked by a truck," one officer later reported. Then three smaller shells tore into the hull. A rain squall covered the destroyer while her crew made emergency repairs, but she had to be steered manually with her speed cut in half. When the *Johnston* emerged from a cloud of smoke, she found herself bow to bow with a Japanese battleship. Firing as she went, she ducked back into the smoke and soon came upon the crippled American carrier *Gambier Bay*, which was under attack by a Japanese cruiser. Realizing that the carrier was damaged too severely to flee, the *Johnston's* captain, Commander Ernest Evans, rushed in with guns blazing to draw off the cruiser. But the Japanese, intent on larger prey, ignored the *Johnston*.

At this point a line of five Japanese warships bore down upon the *Gambier Bay* and her companion carriers. The *Johnston* turned again and Evans fired at the Japanese column. He hit a light cruiser, and his ship took hits in return. Then, as the Japanese destroyers turned away, Kurita's fast cruisers began to close in on Sprague's carriers. The *Gambier Bay* was beginning to sink, but she continued to blaze away with her single 5-inch gun.

Tracking the enemy aboard his flagship, the *Fanshaw Bay*, Admiral Sprague barked out an order to his destroyers: "Intercept enemy cruiser coming in on my port quarter." Moments later he gave a more urgent command: "Intercept enemy heavy cruiser coming in on port quarter. EXPEDITE!"

Commander Amos T. Hathaway of the destroyer *Heermann* realized that the wounded *Johnston* could not make speed and hastened to carry out the order. But he faced a serious problem. As he said later: "A destroyer can't very well intercept a cruiser without torpedoes, and we had none, since we had used all of ours earlier. . . . Anything we could do now would have to be mostly bluff."

Breaking out of the smoke, Hathaway saw four Japanese cruisers bearing down on a carrier and rushed to the attack. "We were opposed by a total of thirty-eight 8-inch guns and about twenty 5-inch. Our entire strength on the *Heermann* consisted of five 5-inchers. I had one thing in my favor: a splendid range. Those cruisers made beautiful targets for our little guns at 12,000 yards; we made a difficult target for their big ones. . . . The enemy splashes were consistently close, but not too close. . . . Then all at once a red salvo landed 1,000 yards short. The next red salvo was 100 yards closer. Thus they walked up in steady 100-yard steps until they hit us squarely. Even then, the Nips didn't have sense enough to know they'd found the range. The next salvo landed over us, and we were never hit again."

One shell that did hit the *Heermann* tore a hole in her bow, flooding the forward magazines. Her bow began to go down, and "the ship felt as though, racing full speed, she were about to dive headfirst beneath the surface," recalled Hathaway. "We were so far down by the head that our anchors were dragging in the bow wave, throwing torrents of water on the deck. Yet we were still firing." Hathaway kept plowing along. And the *Heermann* survived.

But Evans' *Johnston* did not survive. "The ship was being hit with disconcerting frequency during this period," her action report stated. "Finally, about 0930 we found ourselves with two cruisers dead ahead of us, several Jap destroyers on our starboard quarter and two cruisers on our port quarter. The battleships were well astern of us. At this fateful time, numerous Japanese units had us under fire. . . . An avalanche of shells knocked out our lone remaining engine and fire room. Director and plot lost power. All communications were lost throughout the ship. All guns—except number four, which was in local control and still shooting—were out. As the ship went dead in the water, its fate long since inevitable, the Captain gave the order to abandon ship." Still under fire, the destroyer went down. Only 141 of the 327 men aboard survived, and Evans was not among them.

In the meantime, 300 miles to the north Halsey was attacking Ozawa's decoy Northern Force. From eight in the morning until five in the afternoon on October 25, full deckloads of dive bombers and torpedo bombers from three different carrier groups flew repeated sorties against the Japanese flattops. As many as 200 U.S. planes were in the air at the same time. By 10 o'clock one enemy carrier had been sunk and three more damaged.

By this time Admiral Lee's Task Force 34 had been activated, but not to fight Kurita as had been originally planned. Instead, the battleships and cruisers of Task Force 34 were sent ahead of the Third Fleet carriers to finish off the Japanese carriers as soon as the planes had done their work. "If the enemy held his course and speed, he would be under our guns before noon," Halsey wrote later. "I rubbed my hands at the prospect of blasting the cripples that our planes were setting up for us."

But Halsey was not to have that satisfaction. All morning he had been receiving frantic messages from Kinkaid, reporting on Taffy 3's ordeal and requesting assistance. "Urgently need fast battleships Leyte Gulf at once," said one message. The summons surprised Halsey because "it was not my job to protect the Seventh Fleet. My job was offensive." Halsey replied that he was busy engaging enemy carriers and pointed out to Kinkaid that the Third Fleet was already too far away to be of much help. Nevertheless, he ordered his fourth carrier group, which had been refueling far to the east, to hurry to Sprague's assistance. Still Halsey felt he could not break off his own engagement with Ozawa just as he was on the verge of victory. When Kinkaid sent his next dispatch to Halsey, he was so desperate that he wasted no time putting it into code: "Where is Lee? Send Lee."

At the same time, around 10 a.m., Halsey received an even more remarkable radiogram. This one was from Admiral Nimitz, who had been monitoring the battle from Pearl Harbor and who had received a copy of Halsey's original stand-by order for Task Force 34. Nimitz' message was handed to Halsey on the bridge of the battleship *New Jersey*. It read: "WHERE IS RPT WHERE IS TASK FORCE 34 RR

THE WORLD WONDERS." Halsey took the message as a sarcastic comment on his tactics. According to one of his officers, "the 'Old Man' was fit to be tied."

Nimitz had not intended to criticize Halsey. For a while he had been misled by the earlier Task Force 34 message, but by now he had guessed that the fast battleships were still with the Third Fleet. Aware of Kinkaid's increasingly urgent cries for help, Nimitz had meant merely to nudge Halsey into reconsidering his position. The phrase, "the world wonders," which especially infuriated Halsey, was part of the nonsense padding routinely added to secret dispatches by coding officers to befuddle enemy cryptographers. But it was not quite nonsensical enough; it fooled Halsey's decoders, who thought it was part of the message and left it in, and it drove Halsey himself, already uneasy because of Kinkaid's appeals, to change his course. Halsey, as he put it, "turned my back on the opportunity I had dreamed of since my days as a cadet." Leaving Admiral Mitscher to finish off Ozawa with two carrier groups, he swung Lee's fast battleships—including his own flagship—toward the south in a race against time.

As Task Force 34 sped southward, the battle between Kurita and Taffy 3 took an unexpected turn. The Japanese clearly held the upper hand—though they still did not know it. Disorganized, running out of fuel, slowed down by the bold assaults of the Americans and still convinced that the retreating ships were fast Third Fleet carriers, Kurita made another mistake. As he later explained: "That day I had been badly battered. Nishimura had been wiped out. I had started out for Leyte Gulf but then I realized that I could not make it through according to my original plan and still have fuel to get back to my base. . . . Then I intercepted a message that help would come to the American force in two hours. . . . So after two hours I reassembled my force and withdrew before I could be caught between the two American forces." Kurita's ships began to retire the way they had come; they would safely transit San Bernardino Strait three hours before Task Force 34 could stop them.

The sight of Kurita's departing force left Sprague dumfounded. "I could not believe my eyes," he said afterward. "It took a whole series of reports from circling planes to convince me. I could not get the fact to soak into my battle-numbed brain." The reaction of his chief quartermaster epitomized the fighting spirit of the battered Taffy 3. "My God, Admiral," he exclaimed, "they're going to get away."

Taffy 3, incredibly, had outfought and outlasted an overwhelmingly superior enemy—and, in doing so, had kept the heavy guns of the Japanese fleet off the American troop transports and MacArthur's beachhead on Leyte. Admiral Sprague credited Taffy 3's survival to "our successful smoke screen, our torpedo counterattack, continuous harassment of enemy by bomb, torpedo and strafing air attacks, timely maneuvers and the definite partiality of Almighty God."

The biggest, fastest battleships of the U.S. fleet had spent the entire climactic day of the immense naval battle racing fruitlessly north and south without firing a shot. Yet even without the help of Halsey's surface ships, Mitscher's carrier planes demolished all four carriers of Ozawa's Northern Force. Kurita's premature withdrawal had canceled out the initial American mistake of leaving the San Bernardino Strait unguarded. And with Kurita's retreat, the Battle for Leyte Gulf was over. The U.S. now controlled the seas around the Philippines, and the Sixth Army was safely ashore on Leyte.

It was a tremendous victory for the U.S. Navy. All told, in the four major engagements of the battle, the Americans had lost only one fast carrier, two escort carriers, two destroyers, one destroyer escort and fewer than 3,000 men. The Japanese had lost four of their remaining carriers, three battleships, six heavy cruisers, four light cruisers, nine destroyers and about 10,000 lives. Their Navy was shattered—knocked out of the War for good.

But a significant epilogue to the battle came on October 25, the day of victory. The Japanese assaulted the Seventh Fleet with a new weapon—Kamikaze suicide pilots. Eleven volunteers took off from bases on Luzon to crash-dive their bomb-bearing planes on Kinkaid's escort carriers. The St. Lo was sunk by Kamikazes that day and four other carriers were damaged. These human sacrifices—frightening and incomprehensible to Americans—would claim many more ships and hundreds of lives before the U.S. Navy worked out new tactics to meet the threat.

While MacArthur's Seventh Fleet was battling the Kamikazes, his Sixth Army on Leyte was having troubles of its own. And they were troubles that close air support would have helped—the easy invasion was turning into a knockdown, drag-out affair.

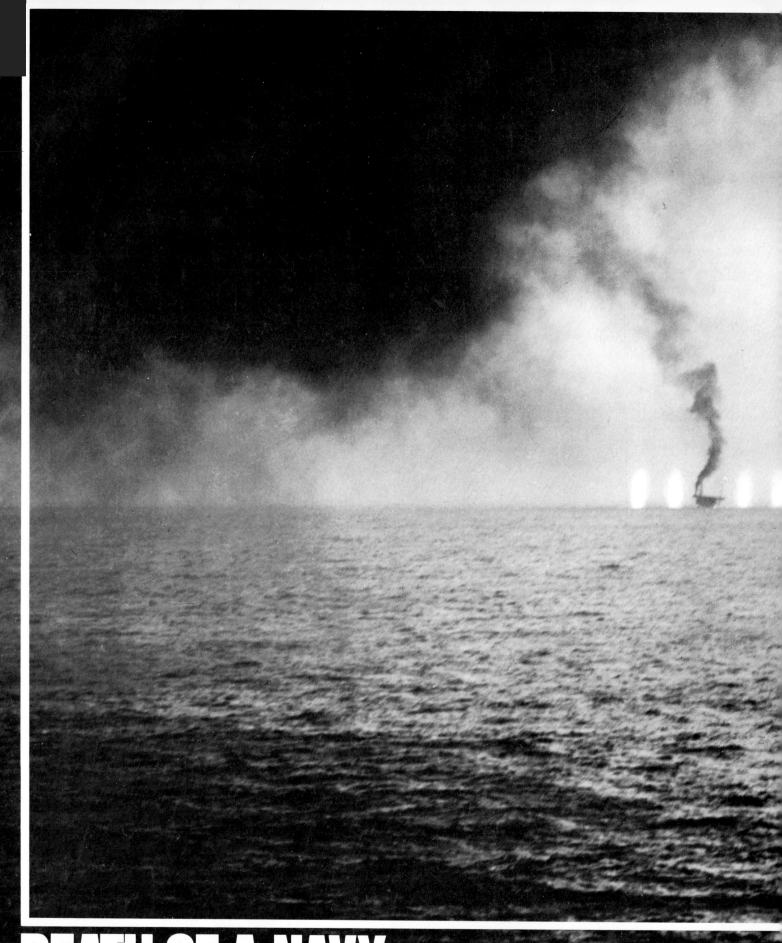

DEATH OF A NAVY

A DESPERATE GAMBLE TO PROTECT JAPAN

Admiral Toyoda, the mastermind of his Navy's desperate plan to halt the U.S. invasion of the Philippines, stands stiffly aboard the cruiser Oyoda.

Admiral Soemu Toyoda, the commanding officer of Japan's Combined Fleet, made up his mind on October 18, 1944, to send his three separate naval forces to destroy the two U.S. fleets and an immense invasion convoy heading for Leyte. The decision, he said, was "as difficult as swallowing molten iron"—and for good reason. The admiral's battle plan, outlined on the map shown at right, was designed to neutralize the air superiority of the American Third Fleet whose 800 carrier-based planes outnumbered all of the Japanese aircraft within range of Leyte Gulf. Toyoda knew that even if the plan was successful, it would probably cost him half of his warships.

But with the security of the home islands at stake, Toyoda's admirals welcomed the mission. Vice Admiral Takeo Kurita, commanding the main force of battleships and cruisers, felt that the fleet had "the suicide spirit." Vice Admiral Shoji Nishimura, whose only son had recently been killed in action, was eager to join him in patriotic death. Vice Admiral Jisaburo Ozawa volunteered to sacrifice his entire force to lure the Third Fleet away from Leyte Gulf.

As Toyoda's forces steamed out to do battle, nearly everything went wrong. Radio failures disrupted the admirals efforts to coordinate their attacks, and they were betrayed by their inferior radar equipment. Human error exacted an even heavier toll: the veteran commanders, their judgment impaired by exhaustion and mounting losses, made blunders that hastened their downfall. Toyoda himself was responsible for many of the reverses that were suffered by his forces. He tried unwisely to direct the battle from his underground headquarters located in a Tokyo suburb, and he contributed to the destruction of the Southern Force by permitting its two sections to go into action without a single overall commander.

The far-flung struggle ebbed and flowed for three days with clashes taking place as much as 500 miles apart. When the battle ended, the Japanese Navy had lost 26 of its 64 participating warships. Never again would it engage the enemy as an integral fighting force.

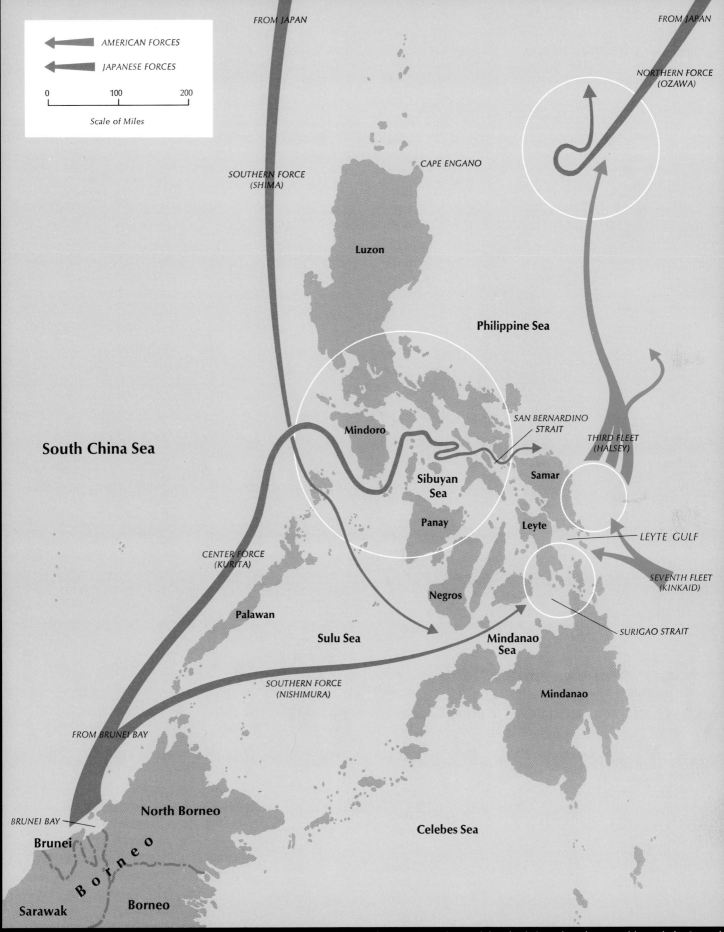

FROM JAPAN

FROM JAPAN

NORTHERN FORCE
(OZAWA)

SOUTHERN FORCE
(SHIMA)

CAPE ENGANO

AMERICAN FORCES

JAPANESE FORCES

| 0 | 100 | 200 |

Scale of Miles

Luzon

Philippine Sea

South China Sea

Mindoro

SAN BERNARDINO
STRAIT

THIRD FLEET
(HALSEY)

Sibuyan
Sea

Samar

Panay

Leyte

LEYTE GULF

CENTER FORCE
(KURITA)

SEVENTH FLEET
(KINKAID)

Negros

Palawan

Sulu Sea

Mindanao
Sea

SURIGAO STRAIT

SOUTHERN FORCE
(NISHIMURA)

Mindanao

FROM BRUNEI BAY

BRUNEI BAY

North Borneo

Celebes Sea

Brunei

B o r n e o

Sarawak

Borneo

Toyoda's plan called for his forces (red) to converge on the U.S. fleets (blue). While one force decoyed the Third Fleet, the others would attack the Seventh.

Vice Admiral Takeo Kurita

Admiral Kurita had reason to feel confident about his 27-ship Center Force: it contained the world's two largest battleships, the *Musashi* and the *Yamato*. And no one could have felt more sure of success than the *Musashi's* commanding officer, Rear Admiral Toshihira Inoguchi, a strong advocate of large battleships even at a time when the trend was toward aircraft carriers.

But then the planes came—those frequent and terrible flights of U.S. carrier-based aircraft. In five hours, 259 American planes attacked the *Musashi*, and not even she could withstand the direct hits of 17 torpedoes and 19 bombs. The *Musashi* started to go down.

Inoguchi, wounded and with his arm in a sling, then proceeded to do what honor demanded. He wrote a last testament apologizing to the Emperor for backing big battleships. He gathered his officers and ordered them to save the Emperor's portrait and "to avenge today's battle." Then, just before he went down with his ship, he said, "Thank you for your service. Do your best to the end." Of the 2,400-man crew, only half survived.

The Musashi (foreground) succumbs to U.S. air attacks in the Sibuyan Sea, where Kurita's Center Force lost three other warships. After retreating briefly (map) to escape further damage, the Center Force turned east again and slipped through the unguarded San Bernardino Strait in the dark.

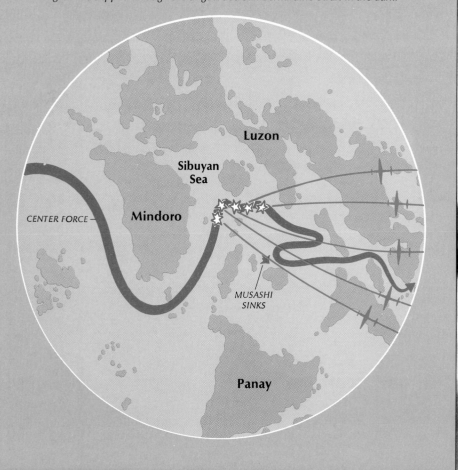

AN INVINCIBLE SHIP HAS ITS DAY OF COMEUPPANCE

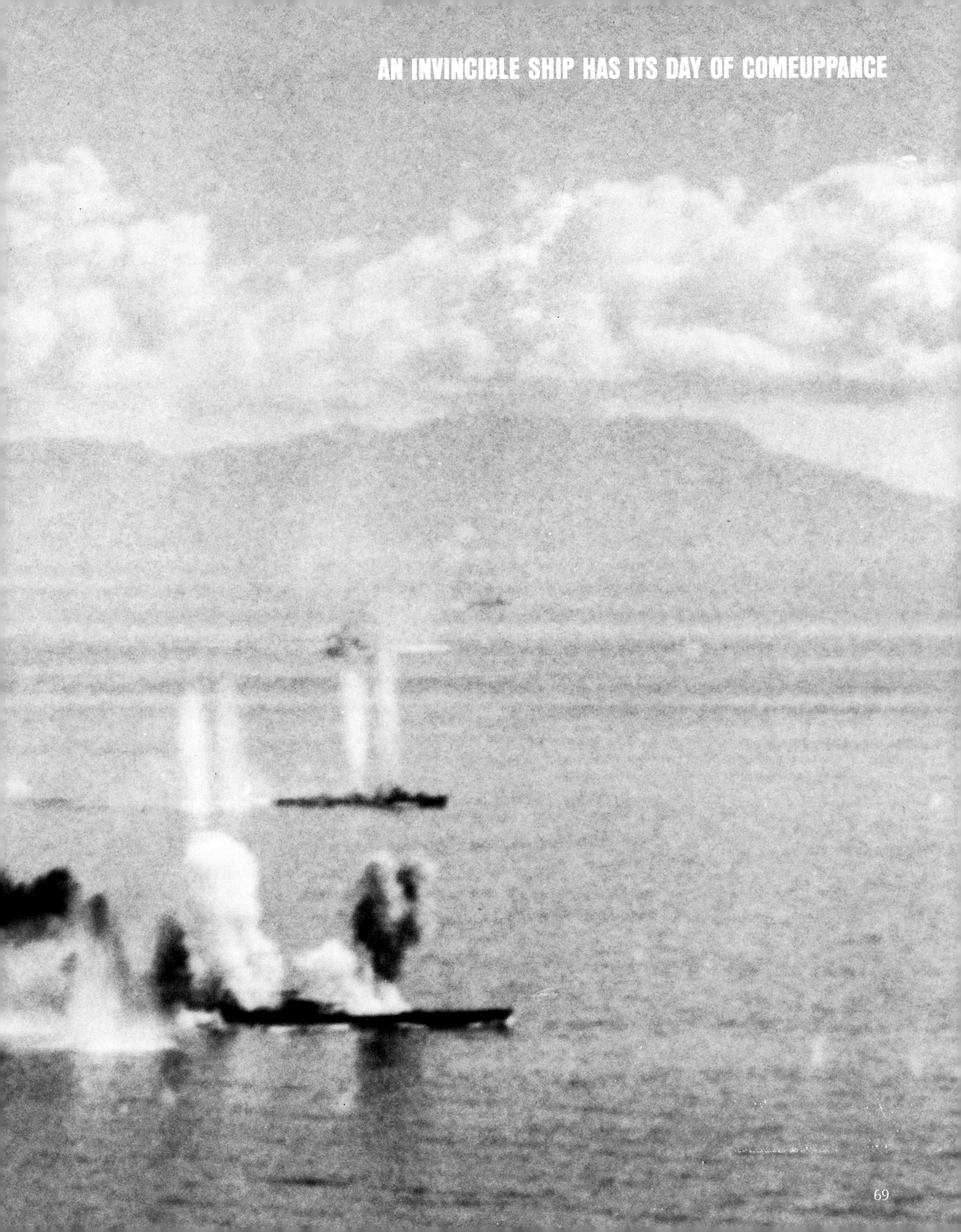

Vice Admirals Kiyohide Shima
(top) and Shoji Nishimura

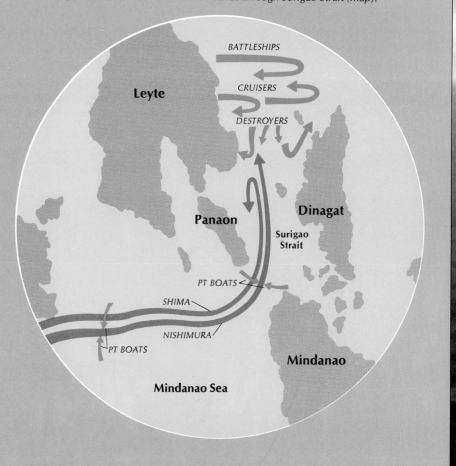

A deadly barrage from U.S. warships (foreground flashes, far right) lights up the night sky and scores hits on the battleship Yamashiro and the cruiser Mogami (background flashes). The action took place on October 25, as Nishimura led the Southern Force through Surigao Strait (map).

Even before it entered battle, the divided Southern Force had lost any chance of success, because one of its two commanders harbored an old grudge against the other. Admiral Nishimura, who had risen in the ranks through duty at sea, resented the success of Vice Admiral Kiyohide Shima, who had forged ahead of him by politicking on shore. Because Shima was his senior in rank and would take command if they cooperated in the Leyte Gulf attack, Nishimura refused to communicate with him. Thus, the two men sailed into battle totally ignorant of each other's attack plan.

Nishimura's 12 vessels quickly met with disaster in Surigao Strait (map). American warships sank two of his destroyers and two battleships and set fire to the cruiser Mogami. Shima arrived at the hectic battle scene two hours later and stayed just long enough—five minutes—for his cruiser, the Nachi, to collide with the burning Mogami. By the time Shima retreated behind a smoke screen, Nishimura had gone down with his flagship, the Yamashiro. Some of Nishimura's associates later said his death was fortunate: it spared him the need to answer for the debacle.

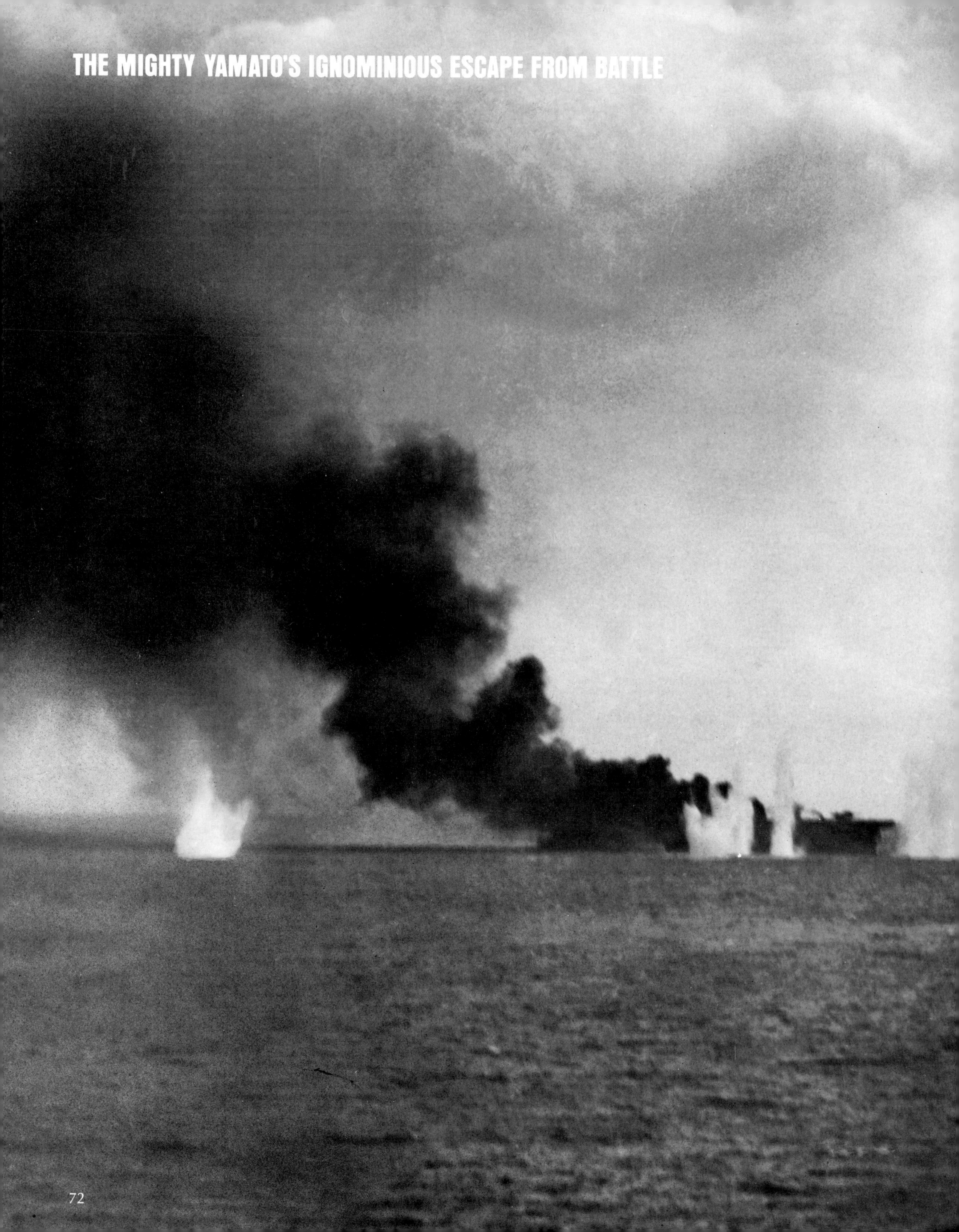

On October 25, the day after the giant *Musashi* was sunk, her sister ship, the *Yamato*, failed ignominiously in a running battle that brought the mission of Kurita's Center Force to a futile end.

The *Yamato*'s commanding officer, Rear Admiral Nobuei Morishita, was pursuing some U.S. carriers off the island of Samar when he spotted a spread of torpedoes heading his way. Morishita swiftly maneuvered his ponderous battleship to present the smallest target possible. But, instead of turning toward the torpedoes in order to let them pass by, he turned away from them. Now the *Yamato* was flanked and pursued by the oncoming spread, unable to slow down or change course. Morishita could only keep ahead of the torpedoes—steaming away from the battle.

The torpedoes ran out of fuel in just 10 minutes, though "it seemed like a month," a Japanese officer said. But by then it was too late. The *Yamato* was so far behind the fleeing U.S. carriers that she never got back into the fight.

During the three-hour battle, five warships of the Center Force were sunk or crippled. Kurita, the man who had boasted of the fleet's "suicide spirit," lost that spirit himself. Overcome with a desire to salvage his remaining ships, Kurita called off the helter-skelter chase and quit the Battle for Leyte Gulf.

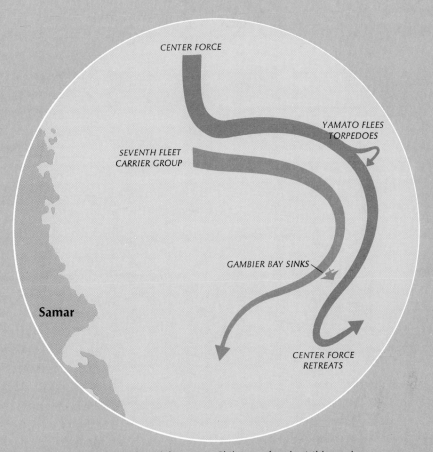

CENTER FORCE

YAMATO FLEES TORPEDOES

SEVENTH FLEET CARRIER GROUP

GAMBIER BAY SINKS

Samar

CENTER FORCE RETREATS

Japanese gunners aboard the cruiser Chikuma—barely visible on the horizon line (below)—finish off the U.S. carrier Gambier Bay, wreathed in black smoke at left. It was the Center Force's only major victory in its vain pursuit (map) of U.S. Seventh Fleet escort carriers and destroyers.

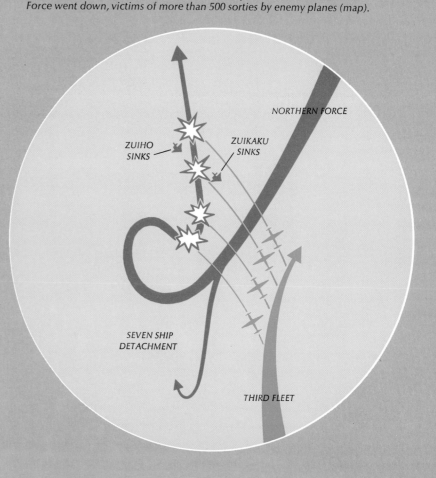

Vice Admiral Jisaburo Ozawa

The burning carrier Zuiho, her planeless flight deck camouflaged to resemble a battleship, swerves to escape U.S. attacks during the battle off Cape Engaño. But the Zuiho and four other ships of Ozawa's Northern Force went down, victims of more than 500 sorties by enemy planes (map).

By October 24, Admiral Ozawa was a worried man: his efforts to lure the U.S. Third Fleet north from Leyte Gulf had gone unnoticed. So Ozawa took desperate measures to attract the Americans' attention. He first attempted to broadcast uncoded messages, and when that failed because of a faulty transmitter, he ordered seven of his 17 ships to hurry south and to flaunt themselves before the big enemy carriers.

To Ozawa's great relief, this worked. The next morning his Northern Force was hit with a 180-plane raid. No matter that his last 13 planes were quickly shot down, nor that one ship after another was sunk by continuing American air attacks. He had tied up the Third Fleet, and thus executed his assignment successfully—the only Japanese commander to do so.

During the nine hours of American attacks, Ozawa's flagship, the *Zuikaku*, was dealt mortal blows, and he prepared to go down with the carrier (pages 76-77). But his devoted officers dragged him to safety aboard an undamaged cruiser. Ozawa was later appointed commander in chief of the Imperial Navy—a navy that, after Leyte Gulf, scarcely existed any longer.

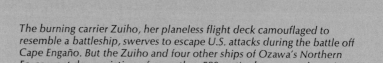

NORTHERN FORCE

ZUIHO SINKS

ZUIKAKU SINKS

SEVEN SHIP DETACHMENT

THIRD FLEET

Japanese crewmen on the sinking carrier Zuikaku raise their arms and voices in a farewell banzai cheer. Almost half the 1,700-man crew went down with the ship.

3

On the morning of October 20, 1944, General MacArthur watched with satisfaction from the bridge of the cruiser *Nashville* as men of the Sixth Army stormed ashore virtually unopposed on Leyte's east coast. Having redeemed his long-standing pledge to return to the Philippines, he was prepared to make the most of the occasion. He donned a fresh, starched uniform, pocketed a revolver as a precaution against being captured alive and boarded a landing craft for the trip to the beach. Light fighting was going on a half mile inland, and as MacArthur's boat neared the beachhead, he and his party—his generals, newsmen and Philippine President Sergio Osmeña—could hear sporadic rifle and mortar fire.

The landing craft went aground in shallow water 35 yards from shore and the harried beachmaster, with hundreds of landing craft unloading and snipers' bullets spitting from nearby groves, had no time to provide a smaller craft for transfer. "Let 'em walk!" the beachmaster snapped to one of the general's aides—and went about his business.

MacArthur and his party had to wade through water that came up to their knees, an event that the cameramen present recorded in detail. "It took me only 30 or 40 long strides to reach dry land," MacArthur later wrote, "but that was one of the most meaningful walks I ever took." After greeting his shore commanders, he stepped before a Signal Corps microphone on the beach and broadcast a sermon-like two-minute speech. "People of the Philippines, I have returned," the general began, his hands shaking and his voice quavering with emotion. "By the grace of Almighty God our forces stand again on Philippine soil. . . . The hour of your redemption is here. Your patriots have demonstrated an unswerving and resolute devotion to the principles of freedom. . . . Rally to me. Let the indomitable spirit of Bataan and Corregidor lead on. As the lines of battle roll forward to bring you within the zone of operations, rise and strike. . . . For future generations of your sons and daughters, strike! In the name of your sacred dead, strike! Let no heart be faint. Let every arm be steeled."

As MacArthur spoke, the Sixth Army's X Corps was sweeping toward its first major objectives, Tacloban, the provincial capital, and its adjacent airfield, just north of the beachhead. When the soldiers arrived at the field shortly before nightfall, they found it abandoned by the Japanese. In a

THE FIGHT FOR LEYTE

separate landing a little more than 14 miles to the south, the XXIV Corps had had similar good fortune and quickly captured the town of Dulag. By nighttime the men were dug in at the edge of another vital airstrip.

It had been an altogether successful day for the Americans, an auspicious beginning for their Leyte campaign. But in fact, the Sixth Army had met only small rear-guard enemy forces; the bulk of the 10,500-man Japanese 16th Division, along with 11,000 other troops, had retreated inland to escape the preinvasion naval and aerial bombardment of the coast. The real fight was yet to come.

In the next two days, the two American beachheads expanded steadily inland to the west, and on October 23 MacArthur presided over another ceremony. He and President Osmeña, as well as all the senior officers of the Sixth Army, assembled on the steps of the capital building in Tacloban. As a dirty and tired guard of honor from the 1st Cavalry Division stood at attention, the Philippine and American flags were raised and an officer read a proclamation from President Roosevelt restoring the civil government of the Philippines. Three days later MacArthur transferred his headquarters from the cruiser *Nashville* to Tacloban and moved into a large mansion built by an American businessman before the War and used as an officers' club by the Japanese. From here he would direct the campaign for Leyte.

The campaign's prime objective was to secure Leyte Valley, a broad plain stretching from the east-coast landing beaches to the rugged spine of jungled mountains running up the center of the island. This great flatland boasted several towns, a road network, five airfields and a friendly population. It was here that MacArthur intended to establish a complex of air bases, supply dumps and troop staging areas. From these bases American planes would be able to strike at Japanese forces anywhere in the Philippines, and could even range as far as Formosa and the China coast. They would also be able to cut Japan's lifeline to Southeast Asia, with its oil and other raw materials.

These grand expectations were spelled out in MacArthur's directives to General Krueger, the Sixth Army commander. Within five days of the landing, Krueger was to establish air-base facilities for two fighter groups, one night-fighter squadron, one medium-bomber group, and patrol and reconnaissance squadrons. By the end of a month it was expected that Leyte would be supporting an additional fighter squadron, two light-bomber groups and an air-sea rescue squadron. And by early December heavy bombers were scheduled to begin operating from the island.

This ambitious timetable was soon set back by the terrain of Leyte Valley as well as by the failure of the weather to cooperate. In planning the operation, MacArthur's staff had taken a calculated risk, hoping that the ground would be dry enough to support the weight of heavy aircraft. But typhoons and an abnormally heavy monsoon dumped 35 inches of rainfall on the valley, slowing down the development of the captured airstrips at Tacloban and Dulag and transforming MacArthur's proposed airfield complex into a vast quagmire.

Until the planned air bases could be put into operation, MacArthur and his forces faced an unaccustomed problem: they did not have control of the air. All through the War the general had tried to avoid launching an invasion beyond the range of his own land-based airplanes. He had made an exception at Leyte on the assumption that naval carrier planes would provide continued support in the initial stages of the operation. But then the Seventh Fleet's escort carriers had to be withdrawn from Philippine waters because of crew exhaustion and damage sustained during the Battle for Leyte Gulf. And Halsey's Third Fleet fliers were too busy attacking Japanese convoys and bombing Japanese bases in Luzon to supply the close air support MacArthur desired for his ground forces.

The Japanese used the unexpected shortage of American planes to good advantage. From the moment they settled on Leyte as the place to stage their decisive battle for the islands, both Admiral Fukudome and Lieut. General Kyoji Tominaga had been shifting their few precious aircraft from Formosa and northern Luzon to bases within range of Leyte. Whenever the weather cleared, large and small flights of planes struck at the American shipping in the gulf, the beachheads and MacArthur's headquarters in Tacloban— one bomb exploding within a block of his mansion. The Tacloban airstrip was bombed continuously: one raid destroyed 27 U.S. planes on the ground. Not since the air attacks on Corregidor at the beginning of the War had the

Japanese air forces sent such powerful and sustained raids against American positions.

At the same time, General Yamashita, the Japanese Army commander in the Philippines, swung into action. Though he would have preferred to fight for Luzon, Yamashita reluctantly reinforced Leyte by sending in fresh troops from Luzon and other islands. About 2,000 landed at Ormoc, a port town on Leyte's west coast, while the Battle for Leyte Gulf was under way; by mid-November at least 25,000 more troops, including the 1st Division from Manchuria, would arrive on the island. Even though heavy American attacks on convoys in the Visayan Sea cut up many units and forced others to land without weapons and supplies, Yamashita was able to double the size of his Leyte forces within two weeks. All told he would add some 45,000 soldiers to his Leyte command.

These reinforcements came as a surprise to MacArthur's intelligence officers, who had estimated that only 12,000 Japanese would be sent to Leyte after the American landings. The heavy influx of enemy troops, the scarcity of U.S. planes, the soggy Leyte terrain—all would combine to make the campaign longer and more bloody than the Americans had anticipated.

Still the advantage did not shift to the Japanese. Yamashita's reinforcements, landing on the west coast, were too far away from Lieut. General Shiro Makino's 16th Division to be of any immediate help as it withdrew across Leyte Valley into the island's central mountain range. By the end of October, General Krueger was able to join his two separate footholds into one beachhead about 15 miles deep, clearing Makino's soldiers out of most of the valley and capturing the five airstrips there.

The Americans continued to press forward. The XXIV Corps, advancing on Krueger's left flank, sent elements of its 7th Division south along the coast on a narrow, winding road through the mountains; the Japanese, judging the road impassable, had left it undefended. A few days later, advance patrols of the 7th crossed the island and reached the west coast. In the center of the beachhead, the XXIV Corps's 96th Division and the X Corps's 24th Division pushed inland to the edge of the mountains, where Makino had set up his main defensive position. In the X Corps's northern sector, elements of the 1st Cavalry Division made an amphibious end run around the mountainous northeastern tip of Leyte and landed near the fishing port of Carigara.

Carigara loomed as a tactical keystone of the campaign. The Americans and Japanese needed it for the same reason: the town commanded a road that looped around the central mountains, swinging southwest to the main Japanese base at Ormoc and southeast to the main American base at Tacloban. The army that held Carigara would have the upper hand, whether for defensive or offensive purposes.

Major General Franklin C. Sibert, commander of the X Corps, expected a stiff battle for Carigara, and after a squadron of the 1st Cavalry Division landed nearby, its vanguard approached the town gingerly. On October 28, patrols met with increasing opposition. Believing a guerrilla report that several thousand Japanese were in the town, Sibert ordered the 1st Cavalry to halt until the 24th Division could move up overland from the south to join in a coordinated attack

A Japanese bomb explodes on the Tacloban waterfront, just missing a Liberty ship. Japanese bombers hit the captured port for six weeks, destroying fuel tanks and supply dumps.

American LSTs moored to hastily built jetties near Tacloban spew ashore tons of equipment needed for the construction of the airfield at rear. So supplied, Army engineers laid a 2,500-foot runway of steel matting in just two days.

with the full weight of the X Corps's artillery. The delay would prove costly.

At that time, Japanese reinforcements were on their way north from Ormoc to Carigara, with the vanguard regiment under orders to link up with General Makino's 16th Division south of the town. On reaching the area, the reinforcements turned south as ordered, but instead of linking up with Makino they tangled with Americans of the advancing 24th Division. Meanwhile, the main body of the Japanese relief force began arriving in Carigara in a long column and found the 1st Cavalry poised on the eastern outskirts of town. Many of the Japanese troops had lost supplies and weapons in American air raids on the convoys that brought them to Leyte; most were not marching in battle formation and were unprepared for a fight. Things might have been disastrous for the Japanese had not Major Chuji Kaneko, a staff officer bearing orders from Ormoc for the troop commanders in the area, arrived on the scene on November 1.

Kaneko's orders called for the four battalions in the Carigara area to establish a defense line east of the town. But the American 1st Cavalry was already in position there, and it was soon joined by the 24th Division. Since Kaneko had no radio contact with headquarters and no time to waste, he scrapped his orders and, in effect, took command of the disorganized troops. He advised the local commanders to evacuate Carigara and set up a defense line on the heights to the southwest.

The Japanese abandoned the town just in time. The next morning, November 2, the Americans laid down a heavy artillery barrage, and then General Sibert's two divisions entered Carigara. "The assault companies marching through the deserted streets were ready for anything that might happen," wrote Jan Valtin, a combat reporter with the 24th. "But the streets were empty and the houses were silent hulks and there was only the distant boom of the surf."

The Americans could not quite account for their uncontested victory. A Sixth Army report contended that the enemy, by "clever deception as to his strength and intentions," had deluded the X Corps into believing that a nonexistent major force had been in the town. As it turned out, the man credited with this master deception, Lieut. General Sosaku Suzuki, the Thirty-fifth Army commander in charge of the central and southern Philippines, was in the dark himself. Suzuki arrived in Ormoc from Cebu, a neighboring island, the day Carigara fell, and he issued a grandiose —and impossible—counterattack plan: "Upon completion of the assembly of the 1st Division in the Carigara area, the Army will begin an offensive in the direction of Tacloban and will destroy the enemy." Not until November 3 did Major Kaneko's courier bring Suzuki the bad news. The general immediately approved Kaneko's dispositions and revised his plans.

That same morning, as the unsuspecting advance guard of the Japanese 1st Division was approaching Carigara, it suddenly came face to face with a battalion of the American 24th Division. The battle that had failed to materialize at Carigara would now be fought out instead along a few miles of mountain road west of the town.

Although the Japanese soldiers were outnumbered and outgunned, they coolly deployed along a stream bed and

halted the American advance for 24 hours. In that period American planes bombed and strafed the main body of the 1st Division strung out along the mountain road, killing hundreds of men. But when an American company attempted to outflank the Japanese troops by making another end-run amphibious landing in their rear, a regiment of the 1st Division fought them off. After dark on November 3, the Japanese again stopped the Americans advancing from Carigara and pulled back a mile or so to the point where the road from the town, turning south from the coast on the way to Ormoc, began to climb a series of steep rocky ridges near the hamlet of Limon.

Once more a cautious American commander squandered a golden opportunity by stopping the advance. General Krueger, the Sixth Army commander, had been alarmed by reconnaissance pilots' reports of the reinforcements streaming up the road from Ormoc. He judged that if the Japanese could ship so many troops into Ormoc, they could just as easily land other elements around Carigara and cut off his vanguard forces. So instead of throwing the entire X Corps into an attack on the still-disorganized Japanese, Krueger called for another pause and rearranged his troops. He directed Sibert to deploy the 1st Cavalry Division and a

considerable segment of the corps's artillery along the Carigara beaches to guard against a landing that would never come. Then, while one regiment of the battle-weary 24th Division fought to wrest the high ground southwest of Carigara from the Japanese who had evacuated the town, the 21st Regiment of the 24th Division went it alone against the Japanese in the ridges astride the road to Ormoc.

The Japanese of the 1st Division had chosen a formidable natural defense line. For three miles the road wound through hairpin turns and over convoluted ridges. Steep razor-back spurs, topped by rocky knobs, branched off in every direction, commanding almost every approach. Tall, knife-edged cogon grass covered the open slopes, and trees filled the valleys and ravines.

During the hiatus in the fighting, the Japanese dug in on the ridges and, with their usual skill at exploiting terrain, turned the position into a formidable bastion. They placed their few field guns to cover the sharpest turns in the road, dug elaborate trench systems, foxholes and firing pits, cut crisscrossing firing lanes through the tall grass, and turned wooded pockets into forts and rocky knobs into makeshift pillboxes. However formidable they may have made this complex, the Japanese regarded it not as a major defense line but merely as a place to stop while they massed their forces for a counteroffensive. To the Americans of the 24th Division it would be as strong a defense line as they were to meet, and they named the heights through which it ran "Breakneck Ridge."

The struggle for Breakneck Ridge became the toughest clash of the Leyte campaign. It lasted three weeks, the American and Japanese fighting savagely, often hand to hand on the slick, muddy heights.

As the days wore on, reinforcements poured in, beefing up both sides, leaving them evenly matched. The Americans had an edge in artillery; the terrain favored the Japanese defenses. The result was a bloody stalemate. As the struggle swirled in and around the spurs and ravines, it was often impossible to tell where the front was or who held which height. Rain fell constantly, filling foxholes and making supply trails impassable. The coastal road from Carigara was so marshy that it disintegrated completely under the double pounding of monsoon rains and heavy traffic, and not even

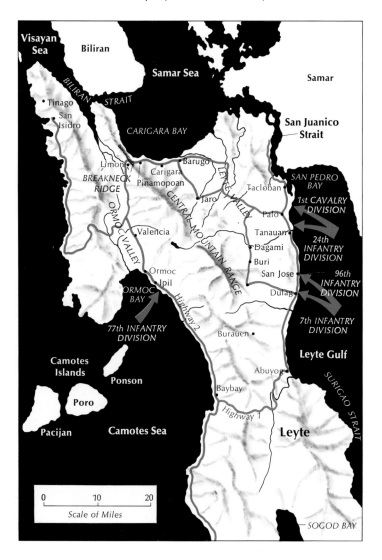

The invasion of Leyte began on October 20, 1944, when two corps of the U.S. Sixth Army came ashore at the points indicated. The XXIV Corps fought westward, following a rugged road through the island's central mountains. The X Corps battled north along the road to Carigara, and then drove across to Leyte's western coast. The two corps later converged on the Japanese headquarters, the vital port city of Ormoc. To complement this offensive, U.S. troops landed to the south of Ormoc.

night-and-day labors by thousands of engineers could keep it open. American tanks, useless on the slopes, bogged down on the road. Whenever the tanks could move, riflemen had to escort them—at any moment a Japanese might dash out from a hole to slap a mine on the treads.

The Japanese were dug into foxholes known as *takotsubo*—octopus traps. These were about four and a half feet deep and each had a man-sized cavity scooped out of its side. Huddled there, a Japanese was safe even from a shell bursting directly above or from a passing American spraying the hole with automatic rifle fire. Time and again Japanese soldiers would lay low in their *takotsubo* while American patrols searched an area; then they would crawl out and raise havoc in the Americans' rear area. Or whole platoons of Japanese would allow American patrols to pass unmolested and then open fire with rifles and machine guns when a larger formation appeared.

The Japanese fought with patriotic fervor—and died in droves. So many men died, in fact, that survivors rose rapidly in the decimated ranks. One oft-promoted survivor was Corporal Kiyoshi Kamiko, who arrived at Breakneck Ridge as a squad leader in the 57th Regiment of the 1st Division. Two days later his platoon leader was wounded while leading a premature charge into the teeth of an American attack. Kamiko managed to rally his squad and keep the eight men firing at the enemy until a few Japanese artillery rounds scattered the Americans. Then, throwing grenades, he led a successful charge to the crest of one of the spurs of Breakneck Ridge. Kamiko was horrified by the scorched, swollen and dismembered American corpses he found on the ridge, but he brought back an American carbine for his company commander and an American helmet for his battalion's commanding officer.

That night Kamiko was named platoon leader. The company commander said: "Reinforcements are sure to come. When the main force of the division arrives, it will be easy to wipe out the enemy. Until then we must defend this position to the end. I hope that each platoon leader will do his best, with resolution, despite the condition of the men."

There were 80 in the company at dawn on November 7; only 25 remained after blunting another American attack. For two more days the battle seesawed. Each time Americans rained mortar fire on the crest preparatory to an infantry attack, Kamiko ordered his men to sprint back down the hill to the *takotsubo* in a valley; from there they directed a steady stream of machine-gun fire on the height, preventing the Americans from coming over it. Then they would rush up again, hurling grenades, and be driven down to the valley again, leaving behind more dead or wounded.

That routine went on for three days in driving rain. On the fourth day, after a heavy American artillery barrage had lifted, Kamiko ordered his platoon to the crest and saw below him two full battalions of Americans swarming up the hill. Kamiko's men fled back to their *takotsubo,* but they were running out of ammunition and the promised reinforcements had not come. Frustrated, the corporal and three others floundered up the muddy slope again, lobbing grenades. Kamiko yelled "Charge!" in English, and an obedient American rushed over the crest with fixed bayonet. The two stared at each other, both too startled to fire. Then, simultaneously, they ran away.

At that moment Kamiko's company commander shouted a word that Kamiko had never expected to hear in battle.

On a soggy battlefield on Leyte, Lieut. General Walter Krueger (left), the commander of the U.S. Sixth Army, confers with Major General Franklin C. Sibert (center), the commander of the X Corps, and Major General William H. Gill, the commander of the 32nd Division. They are wearing army raincoats to keep dry in Leyte's storms and persistent drizzle.

The word was *tenshin*. Literally it meant "turn around and advance," and it was a recently coined euphemism for retreat. Kamiko knew what it meant and repeated it automatically to his platoon, adding hopefully, "we will advance later." But the men in the next platoon had never heard of *tenshin*, and they jumped from their holes ready for a final attack. The company commander, his captured American carbine in hand, rushed to turn them around. As Kamiko watched, too stunned to move, the American fire concentrated on the confused tableau and the company commander fell, blood gushing from his throat.

Corporal Kamiko was now in charge of what remained of a company. He ordered his men—just five of them—to "throw all the grenades you have left," and then he led them in pell-mell *tenshin* from the ridge. When they reached the rear, an officer congratulated them on their "great victory." Kamiko stared in silence at the officer, thinking bitterly of the promised reinforcements that had failed to show up.

By the second week of November, the 21st Regiment of the American 24th Division was approaching the central crest of Breakneck Ridge, accompanied by tanks. The road—mined and barricaded—ran over a saddle at the crest, and the Japanese held the heights on both sides. Slowly, the tanks advanced. The regiment's reconnaissance platoon flanked the tanks to protect them from Japanese demolition men who might hurl mines at them. Engineers crawled forward a few feet to probe for mines and remove log barricades while the tanks' cannon fired over their heads at the Japanese on the heights. Then the engineers rolled to the side, and the tanks again inched forward. After two days of this, gaining only 300 yards a day, the 21st Infantry finally took the crest on November 12.

A few days later, two American battalions were sent on wide flanking movements through the hills. They reached the road south of Breakneck, blocking it and forcing the Japanese to detour supply columns through the jungle. On November 16 the battered men of the 24th Division were replaced by the 32nd Division on Breakneck Ridge, and the fresh troops were able to wear down the weary Japanese defenders and finally drive them from the slopes—but only after another week of raging battle. In more than a month of fighting on the ridge and hills near it, the 24th and 32nd Divisions had suffered about 1,500 casualties, killed an estimated 5,250 Japanese and advanced just two miles.

While the battle for Breakneck Ridge was going on, the Japanese headquarters and port at Ormoc to the south were facing a threat from Major General John R. Hodge's XXIV Corps, particularly Major General Archibald V. Arnold's 7th Division. Hodge's troops had cleared Leyte Valley and were pushing into the mountains. On Hodge's southern flank, the 7th, which had earlier crossed the island by way of the road the Japanese had thought impassable, turned north toward Ormoc. But the 7th had an extended supply line and soon found itself facing a fresh Japanese division, the 26th, which fought stubbornly; the 7th's advance was slowed.

The American capture of Carigara made it painfully clear to General Yamashita that Suzuki's forces could not take Tacloban. Indeed, Yamashita was now firmly convinced that the commitment to Leyte would lead to disaster. Several times he tried to halt the wasteful flow of men and supplies to Leyte from other Philippine islands in order to conserve Japanese strength for the battle on Luzon, where he had wanted to make the decisive fight from the beginning. But Yamashita's superior, Field Marshal Terauchi, remained adamant. Even after it became clear that Suzuki's forces would never be able to retake Carigara, Terauchi refused to go against Imperial General Headquarters' edict to stake everything on the battle for Leyte. Terauchi listened politely to Yamashita's arguments and then ordered him and his Fourteenth Area Army to "continue the Leyte operation as before"—that is, by sending in more and more men. "I fully understand your intention," Yamashita replied dutifully. "I will carry it out to a successful end."

Yamashita ordered two more supply convoys to Leyte during the last week in November and asked Tominaga, the Fourth Air Army commander based in Manila, to provide them with air cover. Since the beginning of the campaign, Japanese Army and Navy aircraft reinforcements had been pouring into the Philippines from as far away as Manchuria—about 1,000 additional planes in all. But the air power of the Americans on Leyte was growing too, and the influx of U.S. planes made it increasingly difficult for Japanese ships to operate around Leyte. To protect Yamashita's convoys, therefore, Tominaga planned a large-scale air offensive against the five American-held air bases on the island.

Tominaga's plan contained a novel and daring idea. In addition to concentrated bomber raids on the U.S. airstrips at Tacloban and Dulag, near the original Leyte landing beaches, a special unit of 80 men, the Kaoru Airborne Raiding Detachment, was to crash-land in three transports on two of the three fields near Burauen, thus blocking the runways. The raiders were to blow up installations and then escape westward into the hills to join General Makino's 16th Division. This hit-and-run operation was intended to cripple the American Leyte-based air force long enough to give the Japanese temporary air superiority over the island and enable Yamashita's convoys to reach Ormoc.

General Yamashita immediately discerned even greater possibilities in Tominaga's plan. Nothing would do, as he put it, but "to annihilate the enemy's air power," thus removing the threat the Americans posed to Japan's lifeline to Southeast Asia and in particular to the oil-rich Dutch East Indies. Together, Yamashita and Tominaga drew up Operation *Wa*, an ambitious scheme for a coordinated air and ground assault on the American air bases. Heavy bombing of the fields was to be followed on the night of November 26 by the crash landing of demolition experts. Then, on the night of December 5, two regiments of paratroopers were to land on the Burauen fields, while most of General Makino's 16th Division and the freshest Japanese division on Leyte, the 26th, pushed on over the mountains to attack the fields from the west. After capturing the fields and destroying what was left of the American planes and installations, the combined force was then to advance eastward and wreak havoc at Dulag.

Operation *Wa* got off to a bad start. Preceded by two days of Kamikaze and bomber attacks on the Leyte airfields and on U.S. ships in Leyte Gulf, three transports carrying the demolition experts took off from a field in southern Luzon at 2:30 a.m. on November 27. One plane was hit by antiaircraft fire and came down on one of the Burauen strips with the loss of all men aboard.

The other two transports managed to crash-land without injuring the raiders, but they were far from any airfield. American units near both planes, confused in the darkness, mistook them for friendly aircraft. An American soldier climbed on the wing of one of the planes to assist the occupants. The Japanese piled out, tossing grenades. In the brief skirmish that followed, several Japanese were

DEVASTATING HELP FROM FLYING LEATHERNECKS

In late November of 1944, U.S. Naval Air bases on the Palaus and the Bismarck archipelago sent 87 Marine fighter-bombers to Leyte to beef up the ground-based air support of the Sixth Army. Included were 75 F4U Corsairs of Marine Aircraft Group 12 and the whole Marine Night Fighting Squadron 541, nicknamed the "Bateyes" for their radar-equipped F6F Hellcats.

The leathernecks started operations on the 3rd of December. Their principal assignment was to help the U.S. Army Air Force keep Japanese troops and supplies from reaching Leyte. The American fliers did the job thoroughly, and in five weeks of wide-ranging sorties, they downed 63 enemy planes and sank 23 ships laden with Japanese troops and supplies—a performance, said Sixth Army headquarters, that was "a major contribution to the success of the Leyte operations."

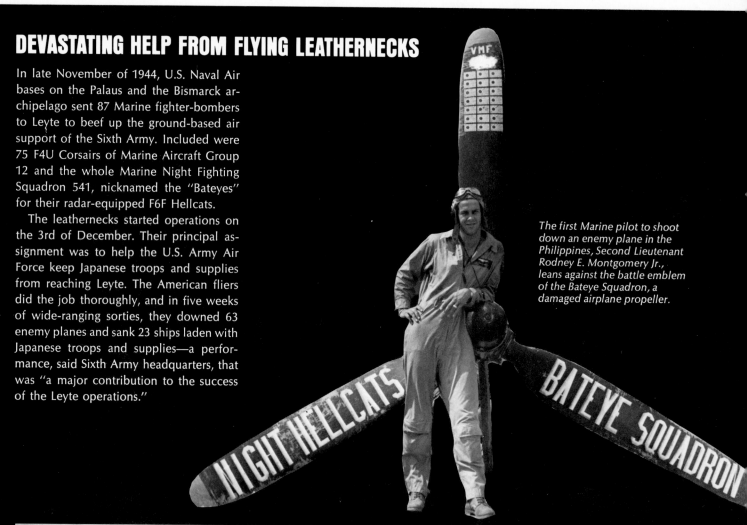

The first Marine pilot to shoot down an enemy plane in the Philippines, Second Lieutenant Rodney E. Montgomery Jr., leans against the battle emblem of the Bateye Squadron, a damaged airplane propeller.

Their propellers raising swirls of dust, Marine Corsair fighters take off from a hastily built airstrip on Leyte in December of 1944. Improvising to make

After crash-landing on a Leyte field, Major Theodore Olsen stands by as ground crewmen rush to move his damaged Corsair to clear the runway.

up for the lack of proper facilities, ground crewmen illuminated the runway for returning night-fighter pilots by lining up jeeps with their headlights on.

killed; most escaped, but they did no damage. The second plane had come down across a creek from an American antiaircraft gun. "Need any help?" the Americans called out. One of the Japanese yelled back in English, "No, everything OK." The Americans resumed their sky watch, and the Japanese slipped away in the darkness. In their haste to get away, the raiders left most of their demolition charges behind in the plane.

Rain squalls grounded most of the American aircraft on November 27, and when no enemy planes appeared over Ormoc that day, Yamashita and Tominaga concluded that the special Kaoru detachment had accomplished its mission, and they proceeded with the operation for capturing the airstrips.

The infantry units in the combined ground and air assault force were in poor shape for launching offensives. General Makino's 16th Division had been reduced to less than 2,000 demoralized men and pushed back into the central mountains by aggressive American patrols. The Japanese had abandoned their wounded, and the men, having lost their meager food supply to greedy officers, were subsisting on coconuts and bananas. Troubles of a different sort hampered the Japanese 26th Division; it suddenly found itself opposing the northward advance of the 7th Division on Leyte's west coast, and only part of it could be spared for the Burauen operation.

The paratroopers, still scheduled to drop on the Buri airfield, one of the three Burauen fields, were, unlike the men on the ground, fresh, fit and superbly outfitted. Besides being heavily armed with infantry weapons, they carried all sorts of signaling equipment, even musical instruments—harmonicas, bugles, whistles and flutes. They also had unit flags, luminous material sewed to their uniforms for identification in the dark, and plenty of rations, including some bottles of *sake*. All that was lacking were enough planes to carry all 1,400 of them at once. Since the planes were not available, they were to be dropped in three waves, separated by the time it would take for each plane to return to Luzon and bring back another contingent.

From the start, the operation was ill-fated. Radio communications had broken down, and when bad weather forced a one-day postponement of the airborne assault, General Makino never got the word. By the night of December 5 he and the remnants of his division filtered through the jungle, avoiding American patrols. At dawn Makino, believing that the paratroopers had already dropped on the strips, ordered the assault. His little force broke from the jungle and attacked the Buri airstrip, the northernmost of the three Burauen fields. Some of his soldiers overran a bivouac and bayoneted a number of service and engineer troops who lay asleep on the ground. Other Americans, shoeless and in their underwear, grabbed their weapons and began firing but had to retreat. One cook later reported that he had killed five hungry Japanese trying to loot his field kitchen.

Driving ahead on the impetus of the surprise attack, the Japanese captured half of the Buri strip before the Americans could organize their defenses. But then the Americans launched a counterattack. Makino still did not know that the paratroopers had been delayed; all that he knew was that he was not getting any help from them. As his casualties mounted, he ordered his men to fall back and dig in along the north side of the field.

The first wave of paratroopers, about 360 men, dropped from the skies that evening. They were supposed to land on Buri, where Makino was holding out, but heavy antiaircraft fire disrupted the formation and only about 60 landed on target and managed to link up with Makino's men. The rest drifted down about two miles away at San Pablo, and for the remainder of the night the airstrip there was a bedlam. The Americans, mostly headquarters personnel, Air Force ground crews and Army engineers, lacked a coordinated defense plan; they fired their weapons wildly or simply fled. The Japanese went about their tasks, setting fire to fuel and ammunition dumps and the few liaison planes parked on the strip. They shot off flares, sounded their musical instruments and raced up and down the edge of the strip screaming incessantly.

During the night the paratroopers finally realized that they were on the wrong field, and at dawn they moved on to Buri. By midmorning of December 7 the Japanese held the entire strip. Two infantry battalions of the U.S. 38th Division, which had just arrived on Leyte, were hurriedly sent to beef up the 96th Division and 11th Airborne in the Burauen area. Arriving at the eastern strip at noon, battalion officers of the 38th Division were met by Major General

Joseph M. Swing, commander of the 11th Airborne, who told them: "Glad to see you. . . . We've been having a hell of a time here. Last night approximately 75 Jap paratroopers dropped on us. Fifteen hundred yards from here is another airstrip just like this one. . . . It is now 1400. I want that strip secure by nightfall."

General Swing had gravely underestimated the enemy's strength. There were 300 Japanese on the Buri strip, and they had not only their own arms but also a stock of abandoned American carbines, rifles, grenades and machine guns to defend themselves with. Though they faced elements of three divisions backed up by tanks, heavy mortars and artillery, the Japanese clung tenaciously to the strip. They received no further reinforcements. The second wave of paratroopers was forced back by bad weather, the third was grounded in Luzon, and the detachment of the 26th Division had such trouble moving across the mountains that only one battalion came within striking distance of Burauen.

A significant breach in the Japanese positions was made at dawn on December 8. Japanese machine-gun fire had pinned down Company A of the 382nd Regiment just off the edge of the airstrip. One GI, Private First Class Warren G. Perkins, braving the enemy bullets, pinpointed the machine-gun position and called in mortar fire. A shower of shells silenced the machine guns. Seizing the moment, another GI, Private Ova A. Kelley, charged the position alone and killed eight Japanese before he was wounded. His company moved in, secured the edge of the strip and set up a perimeter. A few hours later Kelley was shot dead as he lay in a foxhole waiting to be evacuated. He was awarded the Medal of Honor posthumously.

The struggle dragged on two days more. Finally on December 10, an artillery barrage and a three-company assault cleared the airfield.

Still the Japanese were not finished. That evening a group of them eluded the surrounding infantry battalions and stormed the headquarters of the Fifth Air Force in Burauen. As the startled headquarters personnel retreated, bullets tore through the plywood walls of the house of Major General Ennis C. Whitehead, the Fifth Air Force commander. The firing sounded like American .50-caliber machine guns, and the infuriated Whitehead, unaware that the Japanese were attacking, ordered the shooting to cease.

One of his staff officers picked up a phone and called a forward unit. "You've got to stop that promiscuous firing down there immediately," he said.

"Like to, sir, but the Japs . . ."

"Japs! That can't be the Japs. That fire is coming from our fifties."

"That's right . . . and the Japs are doing the shooting."

"Where the hell did the Japs get our machine guns?"

"How the hell should I know, sir?"

"The bullets are coming right through the general's quarters."

"Tell the general to get down on the floor."

The general did just that.

The Japanese burned tents and damaged some equipment before being repulsed by the Air Force men. Twenty-three Japanese died in the final, useless skirmish of General Yamashita's bold scheme. Most of the remaining survivors died in the mountains trying to make their way back to Leyte's west coast.

It had all been for nothing. Before the Japanese attack, the Americans had stopped work on the Burauen strips

In an improvised hospital in the cathedral at Palo, a badly burned American soldier peers from a mask of bandages while a group of barefoot Filipino women pray in the background. When the fighting ended in the area, hundreds of civilians came out of hiding and volunteered to tend the wounded.

because the ground was too marshy, and a new Leyte strip, unknown to the Japanese, was under construction at Tana-uan, a town on the east coast. Moreover, by sending part of the 26th Division into the mountains to join the assault on Burauen, Yamashita and Suzuki had stripped their supply port of Ormoc of vital defenses at precisely the moment they were needed there.

General Krueger in the meantime had concocted a daring plan, and he put it into effect as the battle for the airstrips was taking place. Some weeks earlier, while the X Corps was struggling through the Breakneck Ridge area north of Ormoc and the 7th Division of the XXIV Corps was making slow progress toward Ormoc from the south, Krueger had proposed landing a division in the immediate vicinity of Ormoc. He reasoned that it would split Suzuki's forces, capture the port of entry for all the Japanese supplies and reinforcements, and wrap up the campaign in short order. The plan was strategically sound but logistically impossible. The invasion of the island of Mindoro had been set for December 5, and there were not enough ships on hand to mount both operations. Furthermore, Admiral Kinkaid felt an invasion convoy would be vulnerable to Japanese warplanes. The idea was dropped.

Ironically, on November 30, General MacArthur recognized that he lacked enough air cover to invade Mindoro on schedule and reluctantly agreed to postpone that operation for 10 days. The postponement released the shipping and naval support that could be used for a landing near Ormoc, and when Krueger brought the idea up again, MacArthur and Kinkaid agreed. They set December 7 as the day for the landing by Major General Andrew D. Bruce's 77th Division.

The Japanese on Leyte's west coast were ill prepared to withstand an American landing. The main force there was the 26th Division; part of it was strung out on the mountain trails attempting to reach the Burauen airstrips, and the rest was locked in battle with the U.S. 7th Division about seven miles south of the landing area. About 2,000 miscellaneous Japanese troops were the only forces standing between Bruce's beachhead and Ormoc.

On the morning of the landing, a Japanese convoy, bearing 5,000 of Yamashita's reinforcements, was scheduled to arrive at Ormoc, and the simultaneous presence of two naval forces—one American, one Japanese—in the Ormoc area made it a busy day for the air forces of both sides. Fifty-six P-47 fighters from Tacloban, joined by a group of recently arrived Marine fliers (pages 86-87), bombed and strafed the Japanese convoy, sinking most of the ships, while about 50 Japanese planes struck the invasion convoy. Despite the protection of two squadrons of P-38 fighters, two American destroyers were lost because of Kamikaze attacks, and several ships were severely damaged. But about two thirds of the enemy's planes were destroyed—including almost all the bombers the Japanese had left in the Philippines.

At 7:07 a.m. that day, the 77th Division landed about four miles south of Ormoc and met so little ground opposition that the entire division, with all its supplies and equipment, was ashore before 10 a.m.

General Bruce had intended to establish a secure beachhead and then wait for reinforcements before moving out toward Ormoc, but resistance was so feeble that he decided to strike at once. Bruce ordered a regiment of his 77th Division, the 307th Infantry, to spearhead an attack northward toward Ormoc.

The Japanese in the area were at first confused by the attack, but they soon mustered all available troops and placed them in hastily constructed pillboxes on little finger ridges overlooking the coastal road and along the edges of ravines and rivers. They dug well-camouflaged foxholes and machine-gun nests beneath Philippine houses raised off the ground on stilts.

The next day, resistance grew even stronger. The Japanese rounded up more miscellaneous units and threw them into the defense of Ormoc. In turn, the Americans brought up heavy mortars, self-propelled howitzers and larger artillery pieces to fire point-blank at enemy positions. In the early afternoon the Japanese tried to counterattack from a stand of woods about a mile south of Ormoc. Colonel Stephen S. Hamilton, the 307th's commander, called for mortar fire on the ridgeline to cover his right flank.

The American infantrymen pulled back, and the mortars and artillery bracketed in on Japanese gunfire from a wooded area. High-explosive shells drove the Japanese under cover and then the searing smoke of white phosphorus shells flushed them into the open again. Under such punishment the Japanese detachment scattered and gave way, and the 307th Infantry inched closer and closer to Ormoc.

That night more Japanese reinforcements dug in on other ridges that flanked the road to Ormoc. Their machine guns and camouflaged fieldpieces were set to sweep the rice paddies and grassy fields that the Americans had to cross. Japanese infantrymen hid in the tall grass and waited.

During the American advance the next day, First Lieutenant Albert J. Golia and three riflemen were scouting a route for their platoon. Suddenly, while they were crossing a grassy field, a lone Japanese soldier reared up from his hiding place in the grass 100 yards away and fired at the men. Golia killed the man with a single shot, and then—as if on cue—some 50 Japanese arose from the grass and charged the four Americans, firing sporadically and screaming, "Banzai." Golia and his men returned the fire, and the Japanese dropped into the grass and began crawling toward them. Golia ordered his men to fall back, and he covered their retreat against the advancing Japanese. Two of Golia's riflemen made it back to a low terrace where the platoon was dug in. The third stopped halfway back to cover Golia's withdrawal, and they were together when a bullet creased the lieutenant's forehead, knocking him to the ground and sending his helmet flying.

Golia refused to accept a compress for his wound. He got up and hurled two hand grenades at the Japanese. Then he and his scout dashed back to the platoon's position. Golia stood half shielded by a coconut tree and, with blood streaming into his eyes, he fired furiously at the Japanese until a burst of machine-gun fire struck him in the chest and knocked him sprawling.

Miraculously, Golia was unhurt—a bandoleer across his chest had deflected the bullets. On the ground with the wind knocked out of him, the lieutenant once more refused aid. He got up again and tossed a grenade at an approaching Japanese. Then he raced up and down the line held by his platoon, shouting encouragement to his men and firing at the enemy positions. He knocked out two enemy machine guns. Thereupon the Japanese gave up the fight, and Golia hastened their retreat with well-directed mortar fire. Only then did he allow someone to dress his wound. Later the platoon counted 35 Japanese dead in front of their position; Golia was responsible for nearly half the total.

The determination of the Americans, combined with the weight of their artillery, overcame Japanese tenacity that day, and by nightfall General Bruce was able to set up a new command post from which he could look down on Ormoc.

On the morning of December 10, after a 15-minute artillery bombardment fired by every gun in the division, amphibious tanks rumbled into Ormoc. At the same time, landing craft with rocket launchers swept into Ormoc Bay, and their high-explosive missiles smashed the center of the town. Within minutes, according to the 77th Division operations report, Ormoc had become "a blazing inferno of bursting white phosphorus shells, burning houses and exploding ammunition dumps, and over it all hung a pall of heavy smoke from burning dumps mixed with the gray dust of destroyed concrete buildings blasted by artillery, mortar and rocket fire."

Into this storm moved two of Bruce's regiments, the 307th along the coast road and the 306th on an inland sweep to block Japanese reinforcements and encircle the town.

Despite the bombardment, Japanese troops still fought doggedly from their positions underneath the houses, slowing the 307th's advance through the rubble-strewn streets. By afternoon, however, the flanking movement threatened to surround the surviving Japanese, and they withdrew to the north. Ormoc, the wellspring of Japanese resistance through the seven terrible weeks of the Leyte campaign, was finally in American hands.

A day later the 7th Division linked up with the 77th, and by Christmas the remaining Japanese forces were completely isolated without hope of further reinforcements and with little hope of escape. It would take several more weeks of bloody mopping up to wipe out pockets of resistance, especially the resolute force that had been fighting north of Ormoc around Breakneck Ridge. But the battle termed "decisive" by the Japanese was over. Approximately 60,000 Japanese soldiers had lost their lives, on Leyte or in the surrounding waters when their transports were sunk. The toll of U.S. Army casualties was 3,500 soldiers killed and 12,000 wounded.

The fall of Leyte was a resounding defeat for General Yamashita. MacArthur was later to say that it was "perhaps the greatest defeat in the military annals of the Japanese Army." But it did not spell the end of the fighting in the Philippines. Luzon lay ahead.

ASSAULT BY KAMIKAZE

Kamikaze pilots salute their commander before taking off on a training flight. A few days later they left on a suicide mission, attacking U.S. ships off Luzon.

VOLUNTEERS FOR A PATRIOTIC DEATH

In founding the Kamikaze corps, Admiral Onishi doubted that history would "justify what I have done." But the pilots' success reassured him.

On October 19, 1944, Vice Admiral Takijiro Onishi, commander of Japan's First Air Fleet, announced a shocking plan during a staff meeting on Luzon. "As you know, the war situation is grave," he said. "There is only one way of assuring that our meager strength will be effective to a maximum degree. That is to organize suicide attack units composed of Zero fighters armed with 550-pound bombs, with each plane to crash-dive into an enemy carrier."

The admiral made his proposal knowing that single suicide planes often did more damage than a whole squadron flown by men intent on surviving to fight again. Earlier, several pilots had impulsively crash-dived into enemy ships with devastating effect. What shocked the admiral's officers was the idea of making such attacks an official operation.

Nevertheless, a suicide air corps was formed that night. It was named Kamikaze, or Divine Wind, after the legendary typhoon that saved Japan from a Mongol invasion in the 13th Century. And it quickly attracted an excess of volunteers—two or three times more men than planes available. Some men showed their eagerness to join by writing their applications in blood. As a rule, expert fliers were rejected since they were needed as teachers and escort pilots; generally, the volunteers were inexperienced youths.

But what the Kamikazes lacked in training, they made up for in fervor. Some were inspired by Japanese religious and military traditions of self-sacrifice. "How I appreciate this chance to die like a man!" one such pilot wrote. Others, resigned to being killed in combat anyway, welcomed the opportunity to die magnificently sinking an important ship.

In the Philippines, 424 of these men embarked on suicide missions; they destroyed 16 ships, damaged some 80 others. For the Americans, they were not only a devastating force but a puzzle. "There was a hypnotic fascination to a sight so alien to our Western philosophy," wrote Vice Admiral Charles R. Brown. "We watched each plunging Kamikaze with the detached horror of one witnessing a terrible spectacle rather than as the intended victim. . . . And dominating it all was a strange admixture of respect and pity."

Bound for the Philippines, pilots who have volunteered to fly Kamikaze missions pray at the foot of a national monument honoring the patriotic dead.

"GODS WITHOUT EARTHLY DESIRES"

During their final days of life, the Kamikaze pilots displayed no anxiety over their impending deaths. At air bases scattered through the Philippines, they performed their military duties conscientiously and spent their free time in normal pursuits: reading, singing, playing cards, listening to records, studying aerial navigation charts. Emulating the calm of the samurai warrior, they quietly awaited the final call, which might come at any moment. Some men were called upon the day after joining the corps. Others waited for months.

Beneath their calm exterior, the Kamikaze pilots were excited, even elated. Many of them wrote poems extolling the Emperor, their heritage and Japan's heroic warriors. They spoke often of death, and some men made jokes about their future places in the Yasukuni Shrine, Japan's war memorial to its martyred dead. Their nonchalance in the face of death confirmed the statement made by Admiral Onishi to the first Kamikaze recruits: "You are already gods without earthly desires."

Indeed, the Kamikazes were treated like gods. At a time when food was in short supply, men in the ground crews gave up their meager fare to keep the fliers well fed. They often labored all night to put the pilots' obsolete planes in the best possible condition. One tireless worker even scoured and polished the cockpits so that the planes would be coffins worthy of the heroes. He did not expect the Kamikazes to notice his humble efforts, and when one pilot thanked him, he was moved to tears. In speechless gratitude, he raced alongside the plane with one hand on the wing as his hero taxied into his last takeoff.

In a dimly lighted room,

United by a fatal assignment, Kamikazes join in song around a piano. They sang patriotic, religious and childhood songs.

Kamikazes listen attentively as their instructor (left) explains the next day's mission. The pilots "displayed intense eagerness to learn," one instructor recalled.

During a farewell party in October of 1944, held in the middle of an airfield, a group of smiling Kamikaze pilots is regaled with sake, rice and special rations.

Kamikazes performed a few simple rituals before embarking on their death flights. They gave their belongings to friends and, if time permitted, drank a final toast with their commander. They wrote last letters home, sending relics to be treasured, such as fingernail clippings and locks of hair.

Their letters were often beautiful and moving. In one, 23-year-old Isao Matsuo wrote to his parents: "Please congratulate me. I have been given a splendid opportunity to die. This is my last day. The destiny of our homeland hinges on the decisive battle in the seas to the south where I shall fall like a blossom from a radiant cherry tree. . . . We are 16 warriors manning the bombers. May our death be as sudden and clean as the shattering of crystal."

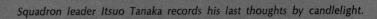

Squadron leader Itsuo Tanaka records his last thoughts by candlelight.

As a parting gesture, a commander offers his Kamikazes a cup of sake before they fly off to attack U.S. ships in Leyte Gulf.

A TRIUMPHANT MEETING WITH FATE

When takeoff time arrived, the Kamikazes were summoned to a final briefing. As they assembled, they calmly exchanged views on how best to sink an enemy ship. "Such talk," one commander recalled, "always seemed more like a discussion of a good fishing place than an analysis of a rendezvous with death."

After the briefing, the Kamikazes went to their planes. Some of them took along flags, photographs of their loved ones or magic charms. Each man was given a box of food containing such staples as bean curd and rice. Then the moment arrived when the pilots were airborne, rushing toward their patriotic destiny. Yet, in spite of their eagerness, they followed the advice in "The First Order to the Kamikazes." It counseled: "Do not be in too much of a hurry to die. If you cannot find your target, turn back; next time you may find a more favorable opportunity. Choose a death which brings about a maximum result."

Passing his cheering comrades, a pilot taxies his bomb-laden Zeke in preparation for a mission in the Leyte

campaign. The Kamikazes usually went up in groups of three, accompanied by two escort planes, which attempted to fend off American fighters.

Bent on destruction, a Kamikaze plane speeds toward the U.S.S. Essex, a large aircraft carrier sailing off the coast of Leyte on the 25th of November, 1944.

Just seconds before the crash, the plane—set afire by an antiaircraft shell—plummets toward the flight deck of the Essex. The ship was only lightly damaged.

Hit by a Kamikaze plane, the U.S. escort carrier St. Lo spews flame and smoke off Samar on October 25, 1944. The fierce fire started by the crash set off a series of

devastating explosions that ripped the St. Lo in half and sent the carrier to the bottom within half an hour. The St. Lo *was the first ship sunk by the suicide pilots.*

4

On paper, General MacArthur's plan for invading Luzon was textbook perfect. It called for an initial landing in great force at the best site: Lingayen Gulf, halfway up the west coast of the huge, strategically vital island. From there, the invading army would drive 110 miles south to its primary objective, the port and capital city of Manila, over the best route available: Luzon's broad central plain, whose roads and flat terrain favored large-scale offensive maneuvers. The planners had thus avoided tempting landing sites that were closer to Manila but would have forced the troops to advance through dangerous defensive terrain—mountain passes and narrow coastal strips. The plan was, in fact, tried and true; it generally resembled the plan for the successful Japanese invasion three years earlier.

For practical purposes, a U.S. invasion convoy faced a Hobson's choice of two well-defended routes from Leyte Gulf to Lingayen Gulf. The fleet could steam through open seas all the way around the northern tip of Luzon, braving possible rough weather and coming within range of Japanese bombers based on Formosa as well as on Luzon. Or it could sail through the less turbulent inner waterways of the Philippine archipelago, passing the island fortress of Corregidor, the Bataan Peninsula and the bay of Manila. By either route, the fleet would need protection from Japanese planes based at Clark Field on Luzon's central plain some 50 miles north of Manila. Although the Americans were building airfields on Leyte to defend the fleet and attack Clark Field, their work had been delayed by the heavy rains and soggy terrain. MacArthur decided to take the shorter route through the inner waterways and to protect the fleet by establishing air bases on Mindoro, a thinly defended mountainous island just south off Luzon.

The attack on Mindoro was launched on December 15 and, as MacArthur anticipated, the Japanese there offered only light resistance. Stiff opposition did develop, however, from another source. As soon as the Japanese commanders learned of the invasion convoy, they ordered their Kamikaze pilots into action. The suicide planes, each armed with a 550-pound bomb, continued to attack for three weeks as the Americans sent more ships with men and matériel to build the Mindoro airfields.

The Kamikazes were shot down in large numbers by the shipboard gun crews and carrier-based fighters, but always

DRIVE TO MANILA

a few got through. Flying low over the water and dodging around islands to evade radar, they crashed with sickening accuracy on the swerving vessels of the Allied fleet. One Kamikaze dived into the stern of the cruiser *Nashville,* the invasion flagship, killing 137 men. (MacArthur had planned to be aboard for the landing but at the last minute his staff talked him out of going along.) Other planes sank four landing craft, damaged four destroyers and blew up three cargo-carrying Liberty ships.

The slow, clumsy Liberty ships were highly vulnerable, especially those that carried ammunition. The *John Burke,* laden with explosives, took a Kamikaze hit and vanished in a tremendous blast. Another ammunition ship, the *Lewis L. Dyche,* blew up with such force that two PT boats a quarter of a mile away were lifted out of the water and damaged by falling debris. Unexploded shells from the *Dyche* showered down on other nearby vessels, causing additional casualties.

The assault on Mindoro surprised the field commander of the Japanese Army, General Yamashita. That tough old veteran knew that the Americans would need air bases closer to Luzon to cover the invasion, but he had assumed they would go after established bases on islands farther south rather than build new ones on Mindoro. Yamashita had underestimated the capabilities of American and Australian engineers equipped with American bulldozers. Within eight days of the December 15 landing on Mindoro, they had put two brand-new fighter strips into operation, and a few days later the Fifth Air Force was flying B-25 bombers from Mindoro. Besides protecting the Lingayen invasion convoy and attacking Japanese air bases on Luzon, planes from the new Mindoro fields helped to close Manila Bay to Japanese shipping, isolating Yamashita from his forces in the southern Philippines and blocking all further reinforcements from China and Japan.

Yamashita, being a realist, held out little hope for victory on Luzon. All branches of the Japanese war machine had suffered staggering losses in the Leyte campaign. More than half of the ships carrying reinforcements and supplies to Leyte had been sunk en route; thousands of troops had been lost, along with about 80 per cent of the consignments of foodstuffs. The Japanese air defenses were weak, with little more than 200 planes left on Luzon by mid-December. And the Navy was even worse off: in Luzon waters all the Japanese had were two subchasers, 19 PT boats, 10 midget subs and a desperate new flotilla of about 180 one-man suicide boats, many of them in Manila Bay.

Yamashita's troop strength was considerable but deceptive. He led more than 275,000 men, including one armored and six infantry divisions. However, many units were hodge-podges of survivors, convalescents and service troops, hastily organized, poorly equipped and weakly led. Another 16,000 Naval ground troops were stationed in and around Manila, but Yamashita had only limited authority over them.

Realizing he could not prevent a U.S. landing or engage the invaders in a big decisive battle on Luzon's central plain, Yamashita shrewdly ordered most of his troops to withdraw from the coastal areas and to prepare for a long delaying action in the interior. His goal was to prevent the Allies from using the island as a base to attack Japan. He sent his main force of 152,000 into several mountain strongholds in the north, from which they would harass the Americans, tying down as many of them as possible. He dispatched a second group of 80,000 to hold southern Luzon and the hills east of Manila controlling the city's water supply. A third force of 30,000 was deployed west of the plain in the mountains overlooking the giant Clark Field complex.

As for Manila, Yamashita considered it too flat and, with its sections of thatched-roof bamboo houses, too flammable to be defended; and he knew he could not feed its 700,000 citizens during an attack. He planned to evacuate all his troops, except a small contingent that would protect supply routes and blow up bridges as the Americans arrived. In effect, Yamashita wanted to make Manila an open city. But the Japanese Naval troops there had other ideas.

In spite of added air support from the new bases on Mindoro, the invasion fleet's six-day journey early in January 1945 from Leyte Gulf to Lingayen Gulf turned out to be an ordeal. The 850 ships sailed through Surigao Strait, passed Mindanao and headed north along the west coasts of Panay, Mindoro and Luzon. All along the way they ran a gauntlet of Kamikaze attacks. Fortunately for the Sixth Army soldiers, their crowded troop transports traveled three days behind Admiral Oldendorf's group of battleships, cruisers, escort carriers and destroyers. Oldendorf's official mission was to bombard the beaches, knock out Japanese defenses and support the troops after their landings; but by bearing the brunt of the Kamikaze storm, his force made a major contribution of an entirely different sort.

The first blow fell on January 4, when a twin-engined Japanese bomber lunged into the escort carrier *Ommaney Bay*, killing 97 men and damaging the ship so badly that she had to be scuttled. Late the next afternoon 16 suicide planes

battered Oldendorf's fleet 100 miles off Corregidor, hitting nine U.S. and Australian warships, including two heavy cruisers and an escort carrier. Another escort carrier, the *Savo Island,* escaped a direct hit by blinding the pilot with a searchlight in the final seconds of his suicide dive.

The fleet steamed on, and as it entered Lingayen Gulf on January 6, the desperate Japanese commanders ordered out the last big Kamikaze strike of the Philippines campaign. Dozens of young pilots in every plane available attacked Oldendorf's ships in a day-long kaleidoscope of plunging aircraft, burning ships and drowning seamen.

A flaming Kamikaze plowed into the bridge of the battleship *New Mexico*, killing 29 men, including her captain and British Lieut. General Herbert Lumsden, Winston Churchill's personal liaison officer to MacArthur. The cruiser *Louisville* was knocked out of action by a plane that exploded on her bridge and killed 32 men. Another plane plunged into Oldendorf's flagship, the *California*, but its bomb failed to explode and the battleship was able to remain on station. A Kamikaze crashed through the deck of the light cruiser *Columbia;* its bomb exploded deep within the ship, starting fires and knocking out the steering mechanism. The crew saved the ship by promptly flooding the ammunition magazines. In the worst day for the U.S. Navy in more than two years, 11 vessels had been badly damaged, one minesweeper sunk, one cruiser crippled and hundreds of American and Australian sailors killed.

At sunset on January 8, the eve of the landings, a Kamikaze maneuvered into position 6,000 feet above the escort carrier *Kitkun Bay*, nosed into a screaming dive and scored a solid hit. "There was a great explosion," reported a sailor aboard a nearby cruiser, "and the stern of the carrier looked like a big red furnace, black smoke was also coming from it. It was an awful sight. It looked like it would be impossible to save it, everything was exploding on it and with all that high octane gas and bombs on it you never knew when it would be blown sky high. They finally got it under control."

By now the Japanese were running out of aircraft and pilots to fly them. Fighter-bombers from the Third Fleet's carriers and B-25s from the Fifth Air Force's bases on Mindoro and Leyte had been plastering Clark Field, adding to the heavy toll of enemy aircraft. Some of the surviving Japanese planes were withdrawn to Formosa. The last sui-

The invasion of Luzon, the strategic prize of the Philippines, was a multiple-assault offensive aimed at liberating Manila and its superb harbor. Between January 9 and February 16, 1945, U.S. forces launched separate assaults on Luzon and nearby Corregidor at the points indicated. The Japanese resisted stubbornly at Clark Field, ZigZag Pass and other marked positions, but their main force took up defensive positions in the north.

cide planes hit two troop transports but without serious effect. By the evening of January 13, the Japanese had fewer than a dozen operational planes left in the Philippines.

Early on the morning of January 9, 1945, as Oldendorf's warships shepherded the troop transports into position in Lingayen Gulf, the admiral trained his fleet's guns on suspected enemy coastal positions. The American command had received a message from Filipino guerrillas saying that "there will be no—repeat no—opposition on the beaches." But Oldendorf had no choice in the matter: he was under orders to bombard the coast. He sent planes to drop leaflets warning the citizens of coastal towns to evacuate, and then he went ahead with his plans. The warships blasted the area, destroying many homes and public buildings and little else.

At 9:30 a.m., 68,000 men of General Krueger's Sixth Army began streaming ashore, and they quickly discovered that the guerrillas had been right: the Japanese were gone. The residents of the coastal town of Lingayen returned to their damaged homes, broke out long-hidden American flags and greeted the liberators with a joyful celebration.

In the first few days, the assault forces quickly captured the coastal towns and spread out along dusty roads to secure a 20-mile-long beachhead. The rapid advance "far exceeded the wildest dreams of those who had planned the operation," said an official report. The town of San Fabian was taken easily, and four frightened Japanese defenders won dubious fame by trying to escape disguised as women.

The rapid advance continued for the two divisions of Major General Oscar Griswold's XIV Corps, which moved steadily southward through the Luzon plain without finding any enemy to fight. On the eastern edge of the plain to the left of Griswold's troops, however, the two divisions of Major General Innis Swift's I Corps met with stiff resistance from the forward line of Yamashita's mountain stronghold. Krueger recognized the fact that unless the Japanese there were driven back into the hills, they would continue to harass the advance across the plain and might even sweep down on the Lingayen beachhead, cutting his army off from its source of supply.

Consequently, Krueger called in a reserve division and an unattached regimental combat team and sent them at once to help Swift's I Corps secure the Sixth Army's eastern flank. Meanwhile, MacArthur was urging Krueger to prod Gris-

Planes of the U.S. Fifth Air Force attack a Japanese-held railway (top) in southern Luzon, and (bottom) parachute fragmentation bombs shower a camouflaged truck convoy passing through an island town. By January of 1945, when these raids took place, the Japanese had lost so many planes in the Philippine campaign that the Americans could bomb virtually at will. They wrecked hundreds of Japanese railroad cars and trucks, and they disrupted the flow of supplies to the defenders of Luzon.

109

wold's XIV Corps on its advance toward Manila. MacArthur wanted the capital captured as quickly as possible, to obtain its port facilities and also to free the Allied prisoners there; they were starving and in danger of Japanese reprisals.

Swift's reinforced I Corps tackled the brutal job of dislodging the enemy in the eastern foothills. The Japanese positions were a formidable maze of caves, tunnels and pillboxes overlooking a major north-south highway along a 20-mile front. "A helluva lot of good that road does us," muttered a GI; "we have to crawl all over those damn hills before we can use it."

Crawl they did, up naked slopes against well-planned strong points with interlocking fields of fire. At the heart of these defenses were enemy tanks—scores of them. Most of the tanks were not used as tanks at all; since their mobility was limited by fuel shortages and American air control, the Japanese commanders had turned the vehicles into mini-pillboxes, burying them in the ground up to the turrets of their 47mm guns, surrounding each with a network of rifle pits. One such defense line of 30 dug-in tanks, 15 mobile ones and 1,000 determined Japanese stymied the advance of the I Corps's 25th Division for nearly a week.

Meanwhile, on the right flank the troops of General Griswold's XIV Corps were literally having a picnic. As the

two divisions marched south toward Manila, Filipino civilians cheered the GIs from town to town and regaled them with traditional Philippine feasts of chicken, bananas, coconuts and rice cakes. While the celebrations went on, patrols were sent out to find the elusive enemy. They found few Japanese, and of those even fewer stayed to fight.

In a week the XIV Corps pushed inland 25 miles—not nearly far enough to satisfy MacArthur. He informed Griswold and Krueger that they were proceeding too cautiously. But Krueger was reluctant to let Griswold's force range far ahead of Swift's, fearing that the Japanese might counterattack in the gap between the two corps. Krueger was further slowed by logistic problems. His supply units did not have enough trucks, Bailey bridges or other equipment to sustain a steady flow of matériel to the advancing soldiers.

MacArthur accepted no excuses; he repeatedly urged Krueger to speed up the advance. By January 17 he was so exasperated that he issued a formal order to Krueger to get his forces moving.

Krueger relayed MacArthur's orders to Griswold's XIV Corps, with mixed results. Griswold's troops hurried south, but on January 23 they ran into forward elements of the 30,000-man force that General Yamashita had ordered to hold Clark Field and the Zambales Mountains to the west.

Unaware that he had reached a major defense line, Griswold sent only two battalions of the 40th Division to clear out the heights north of Clark Field. But the Japanese there were firmly ensconced in tunnels and caves protected by machine guns and mortars. The GIs soon learned that to capture each cave they needed the help of tanks, flamethrowers and demolition men. Though hundreds of troops of the 40th Division were thrown into the battle, after four days they had taken only 2,000 yards of hillside, and most of the ridgeline remained in enemy hands.

Griswold then made a daring move. Leaving his left flank virtually unguarded and assigning only one reinforced regiment to continue down the road to Manila, he wheeled the rest of his two divisions to the right and assaulted Clark Field with what he hoped was overwhelming strength.

The Japanese had sown the airfield with mines, which slowed down American tanks. Their own tanks counterattacked repeatedly, and their infantrymen kept up a withering fire from the rubble of bombed-out installations and hidden positions between the advancing U.S. units. American casualties mounted swiftly. "The Japanese," recalled one GI, "were using their antiaircraft guns as antipersonnel and that's how I got wounded. They were using 40mm stuff, striking the trees near us, splintering the trees and the splinters dug right into us."

After close to a week of rugged combat, the superior American firepower prevailed. The Japanese, who had lost 2,000 troops, began pulling back to the hills. By the evening of January 30, Clark Field and the ridgeline to the north were clear of Japanese.

With the bulk of the XIV Corps staying behind to occupy Clark Field, the 129th Infantry Regiment of the 37th Division headed west and took Fort Stotsenburg, a prewar American Army base abutting the air base. Then the 129th started up the steep, open slopes of a 1,000-foot hill that the soldiers called "Top of the World," whose gun batteries were still shelling Clark Field and denying its runways to American planes. Japanese light artillery and mortars were zeroed in on the slopes, and the GIs took heavy losses advancing through the fields of fire. Soon the fighting was going on in such close quarters that, according to one account, "the defenders and the attackers almost reached the point of engaging in games of catch with hand grenades." By midday of February 1, after only one day, the Americans had taken Top of the World. General Griswold assigned the 40th Division to contain the remnants of the Japanese forces around Clark Field; he put the rest of the XIV Corps back on the road to Manila. But MacArthur was still unsatisfied.

As the fighting ended in the hills near Clark Field, MacArthur drove south in his jeep to check up on the progress of the regiment that Griswold had sent ahead to take Calumpit, a vital river crossing 25 miles northwest of Manila. The troops were moving along at a respectable pace but not fast enough for MacArthur. He sent Sixth Army headquarters another sharp rebuke: "There was a noticeable lack of drive and aggressive initiative today in the movement toward Calumpit." Krueger passed MacArthur's message down the chain of command. Calumpit was taken the next day.

As Clark Field and Calumpit fell, the Luzon campaign entered a new phase. MacArthur's staff had carefully planned several subsidiary operations whose ultimate purpose was to close in on Manila from all sides. The troops that were engaged in these new operations, together with Sixth Army units already in action and their reinforcements, would bring the total strength of MacArthur's forces on Luzon to 10 full divisions, plus elements of other units adding up to the equivalent of four or five divisions more—a greater commitment of manpower than the United States was making in the Italian campaign.

The first of the new operations began on January 29, when the 40,000 troops of Major General Charles P. Hall's XI Corps came ashore at San Antonio on the west coast of Luzon, just to the north of the Bataan Peninsula. The XI Corps's objectives were to capture the airfield at San Marcelino, to take the Naval base at Subic Bay and to seal off Bataan, preventing any Japanese forces from holding out on the rocky peninsula as MacArthur's forces had done in 1942. The landing was unopposed; the Japanese had pulled back from the shore and manned a defense line on mountainous terrain some three miles inland, abandoning valuable air and Naval bases.

Three days later, as the American forces pushed eastward into the foothills of the Zambales Mountains, they ran head-on into the newly established enemy positions. Dug in at key points above a narrow serpentine road known to the

Flushed with success, grinning U.S. Rangers and Filipino guerrillas return to their lines after freeing 486 American soldiers from a Japanese prison camp at Cabanatuan, located 60 miles to the north of Manila. On the night of January 30, 1945, after the Rangers had thrust through 25 miles of enemy-held territory to Cabanatuan, they crushed the 150-man garrison in just half an hour and removed the prisoners, transporting the weakest ones on their backs. As they returned to U.S. lines, they were protected by guerrillas, who held off nearly 800 Japanese troops.

Americans as ZigZag Pass, the Japanese greeted the XI Corps troops with an avalanche of mortar and artillery fire. All through the first week of February, the Americans flung themselves against the enemy—to no avail.

The Japanese had dug their positions with deadly purpose. On one hill, men of an American battalion failed to notice an underground enemy strong point until they were suddenly ambushed by point-blank fire; by then the Japanese were so close that the Americans could not fire back for fear of hitting one another. In a similar attack on enemy trenches and tunnels, a regiment suffered such heavy casualties in three days of fighting that it had to be withdrawn.

During the first days of fierce resistance at ZigZag Pass, several American unit commanders suggested to General Hall that he stop the assault until an airstrip was completed at San Marcelino less than 15 miles to the northwest, permitting planes to provide close air support. Hall refused; he ordered the infantry to press on, and when the advance stalled again, he blamed his generals and colonels. Presently, Hall relieved a division commander—without improving the situation appreciably.

The tables were turned on February 7 with the completion of the San Marcelino airfield. U.S. planes bombed, strafed and dropped heavy doses of napalm on ZigZag Pass. At the same time, artillery stepped up the pace of support fire, and ground troops made slow but steady advances. Finally, by February 15 the last enemy stronghold on ZigZag Pass was eliminated. In all, it had taken the XI Corps more than two weeks to establish a line reaching from Subic Bay to Manila Bay and seal off the Bataan Peninsula. The Japa-

nese had lost 2,400 men dead and 25 prisoners; the Americans suffered 1,400 casualties, including 250 killed. Hall's men prepared to turn their attention to the peninsula itself and to the island of Corregidor to the south.

The second new operation was launched on January 31 and brought the vanguard of Lieut. General Robert Eichelberger's Eighth Army into the Luzon campaign. About 8,000 men of that army's 11th Airborne Division, which had been fighting on Leyte, were put ashore by boat at Nasugbu Bay, 55 miles southwest of Manila. The landing was designated a reconnaissance in force, which meant that Eichelberger was authorized to pull the troops out if heavy resistance developed. But there were few Japanese in the vicinity, and the soldiers' most memorable opposition came from a resident Scotsman whose sugar mill had been damaged in the preliminary naval bombardment. "For three years I've been fighting those Japs," the Scot shouted angrily to a U.S. officer, "but even they didn't try to destroy my sugar mill."

Eichelberger then issued orders to his troops to dash up the road toward Manila and overwhelm any Japanese who might try to bar their way. The maneuver was, said Eichelberger, "a monumental bluff," and he helped it along with pure chicanery. "Our vehicles went roaring up and down the road, raising never-ending clouds of dust," the general later wrote. "By the generous use of what artillery we had, by our heavy and confident assaults, by repeated strikes from the air, we gave the enemy the impression that a force of army proportions—complete with an armored division—was invading southern Luzon. This impression was not lessened by the fact that American radio an-

Pointing out the attack targets on a model of Corregidor, Colonel George M. Jones of the 503rd Parachute Infantry briefs his officers on their hazardous airdrop. Despite careful preparation, the assault miscarried badly, as shown on the aerial photograph at right. More than half of the paratroopers drifted past their cramped drop zones, a parade ground (center) and a golf course (right). Many crashed into buildings and trees, while others floated out to sea. Although the regiment succeeded in its mission, approximately 280 of the 2,050 paratroopers were killed or injured.

nounced the news that the 'Eighth Army' had landed there."

Three days after Eichelberger's landing, the 11th Airborne Division's 511th Parachute Regiment dropped on Tagaytay Ridge, a suspected enemy stronghold and the most important tactical position south of Manila. Because of errors by pilots and overeager jumpmasters, most of the paratroopers jumped too soon and landed in disarray in a forest of banana trees an alarming distance from their assigned drop zones. Fortunately, there were no Japanese in the area.

The 511th Parachute Regiment soon linked up with the main body of the 11th Airborne, and the whole division boarded trucks and raced for Manila on a paved highway. Brushing aside small enemy units, the 11th Airborne captured two key bridges before the Japanese could blow them up. Then, on the evening of February 4, the 11th Airborne was halted at a line of camouflaged steel and concrete pillboxes on Manila's southern outskirts. The 11th Airborne could go no farther until it was reassembled and resupplied; its five-day dash had left the troops spread out dangerously along what Eichelberger called a beachhead "sixty-nine miles long and five hundred yards wide."

Another subsidiary operation involved General Swift's I Corps, advancing to the southeast after rugged fighting in the eastern foothills. Now the I Corps was ordered to seize San Jose, a crossroads town on the eastern edge of the Luzon plain, and then to drive about 35 miles to the east coast of the island. This maneuver would drive a wedge between Yamashita's northern and southern forces and permit each half to be dealt with separately. Yamashita needed to hold on to San Jose until he could finish funneling troops

and supplies from Manila and southern Luzon through San Jose to his northern mountain strongholds.

To defend the town, Yamashita sacrificed his entire 2nd Tank Division, burying nearly 150 tanks to guard the approaches to the town. When Swift's 25th and 6th Divisions ran up against these positions on February 1, they instantly became bogged down in bitter, bloody fighting. Even with air and artillery support, American tanks and infantry could make little headway. The riflemen were pinned down in foul-smelling irrigation ditches, their only cover in the flat paddy land. Japanese artillery and the 47mm guns of the dug-in tanks held up the American armor for three crucial days on two roads leading to the town.

On February 3, the tanks and troops of the 6th Infantry Division outflanked the buried Japanese tanks and closed in on San Jose from the rear. But it was too late. Next morning, the Americans entered the town and found it empty. Yamashita had succeeded in delaying the I Corps's advance long enough to remove nearly all his troops and supplies to the north. Though they had not achieved their primary objective, a few days later the soldiers of the I Corps pressed east to the shores of the Philippine Sea, severing all Japanese land communication between north and south Luzon.

The most dramatic operation in the Manila squeeze play came about largely by chance. On February 1, 1945, MacArthur visited Guimba, the assembly area of the XIV Corps's 1st Cavalry Division, newly arrived from Leyte. Only two days earlier, 280 Filipino guerrillas and a company of U.S. Rangers had knifed through enemy lines near San Jose and

freed nearly 500 hungry American veterans of the Bataan death march from a prisoner-of-war camp. The success of this operation was very much in MacArthur's mind, and it occurred to him that a similar attack on Manila might free the thousands of Allied POWs and civilian internees there. MacArthur found Major General Vernon D. Mudge, commander of the 1st Cavalry Division, and discussed with him a lightning thrust into the capital. "Go to Manila," he urged Mudge. "Go around the Nips, bounce off the Nips, but go to Manila. Free the internees at Santo Tomás"—a university that the Japanese had converted into a prison camp.

The assignment stunned and excited Mudge. His troops were still 70 miles north of the city, and the 37th Division, having taken Calumpit, was much closer. But Mudge immediately acted on his orders and formed two "Flying Columns," each composed of one cavalry squadron (about 700 men), a tank company, a battery of 105mm howitzers and enough vehicles to carry all his soldiers and their supplies. He put Brigadier General William Chase in charge of the two units and sent them on their way. "We're travelling light," a colonel explained to a group of Allied journalists and photographers. "When we hit the enemy we're going to cut right through him and get into Manila before he knows what's happening. The rest of the division will be coming along after us and we'll let them worry about what we leave behind."

The Flying Columns followed Highway 5 from Guimba, roaring along the eastern edge of the Luzon plain, sometimes reaching speeds of 30 miles an hour. Occasionally, the second Flying Column peeled off for a while, rumbling over back roads and through rice paddies to outflank some Japanese force that the first column had encountered. Leapfrogging ahead, the columns raced across bridges before the Japanese could blow them up, and if an occasional bridge had been destroyed, the men forded the rivers, holding their weapons over their heads.

Marine Corps dive bombers watched over the columns from above, scouting and scourging the way ahead. Only once did a column call for air support, but it was so close to the enemy that the Marine pilots did not dare to shoot. Instead, the fliers swooped low in mock strafing runs that drove the Japanese back.

By February 3, the Flying Columns had outsped the 37th Division, whose infantrymen had been slowed by destroyed bridges and deep, unfordable rivers north of Manila Bay. The cavalrymen had one last bridge to cross up ahead at Novaliches, five miles from Manila; a deep gorge there would hold them up for at least a day if the Japanese blew up the single stone bridge that spanned it. That afternoon, Marine pilots radioed that the Novaliches bridge was still standing. But the Japanese had planted dynamite on the span, and when the first column raced up to the bridge, the fuses were already burning and enemy rifle fire from across the gorge kept the cavalrymen away. But the Americans had with them a bomb-disposal expert, Navy Lieutenant James P. Sutton. Reacting quickly, Sutton braved the rifle fire, dashed onto the bridge and cut the sizzling fuses with seconds to spare. The two columns then crossed the bridge and set off on the last leg of the drive to Santo Tomás.

Meanwhile, the Marine planes over Manila were buzzing Santo Tomás, where nearly 4,000 long-suffering Allied civilians were interned. Japanese guards, trying to save face by ignoring the enemy aircraft, failed to notice that one of the planes dropped a small package over the compound. But the prisoners saw it and one of them sneaked out to retrieve it. Attached to a pair of pilot's goggles was a scribbled promise of rescue: "Roll out the barrel. Santa Claus is coming Sunday or Monday."

The prisoners did not have to wait that long. The cavalrymen of the first column roared into Manila at dusk on Saturday, February 3, 1945—the first American troops to enter the Philippine capital since December 1942. Guided by Filipino guerrillas, the tanks sped down Manila's Rizal Avenue to Santo Tomás and crashed through the university's gate. The cavalrymen quickly freed most of the internees. But a band of Japanese defenders was holed up with more than 200 hostages, and it took a day of tense bargaining (pages 122-133) before the complete success of the mission was assured.

Even as the drama of liberation was unfolding at Santo Tomás, the infantrymen of the 37th Division were closing in on Manila from the north. They had been stalled on the outskirts by enemy resistance—and by beer. The troops had met a group of smiling Filipinos who led them to the Balintawak Brewery. The thirsty GIs stayed long enough to

Outlines on an aerial photograph of Manila, taken after the month-long battle for the capital, locate the main zones of action. The U.S. forces fought for and won the ancient walled city of Intramuros, the government center, the northern and southern port areas (separated by the Pasig River) and finally the vital harbor itself, where dozens of American ships are shown landing supplies to be used in future campaigns.

drink copiously and to fill their canteens and five-gallon cans; one soldier reportedly took a beer shower. The brief binge was "like a shot in the arm," said one GI. "Now I'll be able to walk into Manila like I was fresh."

As the infantrymen entered the capital on the 4th of February, they found themselves confronted by a defending force of some 20,000 men, consisting of 16,000 Naval troops under the hard-bitten Rear Admiral Sanji Iwabuchi and 4,000 soldiers who had been trapped by the Allied advance. When General Yamashita had ordered his soldiers to evacuate Manila and head east, Iwabuchi decided that it was his duty to stay there and keep the city's harbor installations out of the hands of the Americans for as long as possible. He deployed his local troops for a last-ditch defense and ordered his forces on Corregidor, 25 miles southwest of Manila Harbor, to fight to the death.

Iwabuchi's men had fortified Manila with barbed-wire entanglements and barricades of overturned trucks and trolleys. Houses were converted into machine-gun nests, with their entrances sandbagged, stairways barricaded and walls ripped open for firing slits. Big guns had been removed from Japanese ships in the harbor and were dug in on strategic street corners.

Iwabuchi ordered his men to blow up all of the city's military installations, by which he meant the entire port area and all bridges, as well as the municipal water supply and electric power system. The admiral's forces followed his orders—and more. One group of men dynamited the northern port area and retreated southward across the Pasig River, blowing up all the bridges behind them. The blasts ignited fires, and shifting winds drove the flames into a section of bamboo houses near the harbor. Soon much of the northern half of the city was ablaze.

The flames of burning Manila were visible up to 50 miles away, and dense smoke hampered the 37th Division as its troops fought enemy units from street to street. The GIs demolished buildings to create firebreaks, but not until the wind shifted again did the flames die down. On February 7

the 37th Division troops started crossing the Pasig River on assault boats, and they soon established a bridgehead on the south bank. At the same time, the 1st Cavalry Division, whose two Flying Columns had been kept busy clearing Japanese mines since entering Manila, swept in a wide arc around the city's eastern edge. In the southwestern outskirts the cavalrymen linked up with General Eichelberger's 11th Airborne Division, which had regrouped after its race north from Nasugbu Bay and Tagaytay Ridge.

Admiral Iwabuchi's Naval forces in Manila were now surrounded, but they showed no signs of giving up. As the three U.S. divisions—one infantry, one cavalry, one air-borne—prepared for the final moves in the Manila squeeze play, other American forces were mounting another operation to dislodge Iwabuchi's garrison on Corregidor.

Although the capture of Manila and the opening of its vital port were the ultimate goals of MacArthur's battle for Luzon, Corregidor held even greater emotional significance for the Americans. The tiny island they called "The Rock" was a symbol of American heroism and defeat. It was on Corregidor that U.S. forces under Lieut. General Jonathan Wainwright had held out courageously for a month before surrendering to the Japanese in May 1942. Now Iwabuchi's forces on Corregidor were in the same hopeless position.

Iwabuchi considered Corregidor vital to the defense of Manila because the cannon on the island could interdict shipping bound for the harbor. And Iwabuchi had done all he could to make Corregidor an impregnable fortress. The narrow beaches below and beyond the island's 600-foot-high cliff-sided plateau had been mined, and a mountain of ammunition and supplies had been stuffed into the old storage tunnels in Corregidor's rock. American intelligence officers knew nothing of this build-up. When MacArthur ordered elements of Krueger's Sixth Army to seize Corregidor so that Allied ships could freely enter the bay, he did so on the basis of reports that there were only 850 Japanese on The Rock. Actually, Corregidor was manned by more than 5,000 resolute Japanese—Naval troops and some soldiers left behind by Yamashita.

To crack this bastion, MacArthur and Krueger decided on a combined air and sea attack. Paratroopers were to land on the plateau and capture the artillery batteries there. Then

seaborne troops would land on the south shore of the island. The assault was set for February 16.

At 8:30 that morning, after a withering aerial and naval bombardment, the first wave of airborne troops from the 503rd Parachute Infantry Regiment made difficult jumps from C-47 transports, aiming at two tiny areas flat enough to be designated drop zones. Many paratroopers missed their zones and were killed or injured in falls on rough terrain. But the rest wriggled out of their tangled chutes, got their bearings and scrambled to their appointed assembly areas.

Fortunately for the 503rd, the Japanese had scurried into their underground network when the bombardment began, and few saw the airdrop begin. Their commander, Captain

Touring Corregidor shortly after it was recaptured in February of 1945, General MacArthur leads a group of officers past the Malinta tunnel, where the American garrison had held out for so long in 1942. For his visit to the island, MacArthur had borrowed four PT boats from the Navy and, he said, "we went back to the Rock the same way we had left it."

Akira Itagaki, was taken by surprise when a group of 25 to 30 paratroopers, blown off target, landed directly on his observation post. His startled troops fired on the parachutists, but the Americans quickly attacked the post and killed the Japanese commander and seven of his men. With their leader dead and their communications center knocked out by the preinvasion bombardment, the Japanese had lost their ability to conduct a coordinated defense.

Within two hours the men of the 503rd had cleared the Japanese from the wrecked buildings on the plateau. They nailed an American flag to the top of the highest pole they could find and set up machine guns and 75mm howitzers to cover the seaborne landing. The invasion flotilla consisted of 25 landing craft carrying troops of the 34th Infantry Regiment, 24th Division—veterans of Breakneck Ridge on Leyte and ZigZag Pass at the neck of the Bataan Peninsula.

The infantrymen landed virtually unopposed and dashed about 200 yards inland toward a rocky mass called Malinta Hill. As they scrambled up the hill, several tanks and vehicles struggling ashore behind them were blown up by minefields on the beach. "Pieces of jeeps and tanks and tank-destroyers were flying in the sunshine," wrote the combat reporter Jan Valtin. The infantry companies reached the top of Malinta Hill and felt lucky to find the summit deserted.

However, the hill itself was chock-full of Japanese. They were hiding in the network of American-made tunnels in-

side the hill. The tunnels were packed with Japanese munitions that had been carefully recorded by the supply officer: 35,000 artillery shells, two million rounds of rifle and machine-gun bullets, 80,000 mortar shells, more than 93,000 hand grenades and a ton of TNT.

For nearly a week the men of the 34th Regiment sat atop this powder keg. Their assignment was to keep the Japanese who were inside Malinta or east of it from rushing the paratroopers defending the plateau. The infantrymen were to hold the hill, said one American officer, "until we kill all the Japs or the Japs have killed all of us." Every day, demolition experts using explosive charges would seal off the tunnel exits. Every night, the Japanese would dig their way out and vainly attack the American positions, sometimes in considerable numbers. The Americans repelled each of the charges, inflicting heavy casualties. "It was like a massacre in a lunatic asylum," one man wrote. But the 34th Regiment paid a high price too. Its K Company, which had helped capture the hill initially, was whittled down to 33 men from the original 161.

By February 21, the American forces from the beaches, along with the paratroopers from the plateau, were preparing to attack past Malinta and wipe out pockets of Japanese resistance on the eastern end of the island. There were still about 2,000 Japanese inside the hill, however, and that night they were planning to launch a last escape attempt and attack. They intended to open the blocked tunnel exits and stun the U.S. troops with a small-scale explosion. But at 9:30 p.m., Malinta Hill blew up with a deafening roar. There was too much blasting powder in the tunnels, and what the Japanese had envisioned as a carefully controlled demolition became an inferno.

Flames shot out of tunnel mouths and ventilation shafts, lighting up the darkness. An avalanche of rock slid down the south side of the hill, burying six Americans who had been guarding a cave entrance. Rocks and debris flew in every direction, and cracks opened up all over the hill. On the hilltop men in foxholes were bounced about by the force of the blast. In the aftermath, about 600 Japanese did manage to escape eastward, but the explosion killed or stunned so many others that their planned attacks died a-borning.

For five days the Americans pressed on eastward with mopping-up operations. Then, suddenly, the remaining un-

THE STRUGGLE TO REOPEN MANILA BAY

After winning the battle for Manila, the Americans set out to clear the devastated harbor for cargo ships with urgently needed supplies. It was a herculean task and a dangerous one too. Manila Bay was littered with mines and wrecked ships, many of them partly submerged in the shallow water and defended by fugitive Japanese troops. An even more formidable obstacle was Fort Drum in the center of the harbor entrance. Snipers manned this 40-year-old citadel, whose thick concrete walls were impregnable to bombing attacks.

Commodore William A. Sullivan, a naval salvage expert, ordered 17 ships equipped for minesweeping to clear the bay of Manila. Assault teams hit Fort Drum and 32 battered hulks to eliminate their diehard Japanese defenders. Army engineers and Seabees were called to raise or destroy the rusting ships.

Despite all the obstacles, the complex operation produced results in only nine days. On the 15th of March, the first Liberty ship entered the harbor. Two months later, 90,000 tons of supplies were funneling into Manila every week.

Wielding flamethrowers, GIs flush out grenade-throwing Japanese troops on a half-sunken ship in Manila Harbor. More than 30 starving fugitives managed to hold out inside the wrecks for two weeks and died resisting.

Fort Drum, a concrete blockhouse 350 feet long and 150 feet wide (top right), was attacked by U.S. Army personnel, who used a ramp rigged to an amphibious assault ship and climbed onto the roof in the face of sniper fire. Army engineers pumped 3,000 gallons of oil into the fort's open vents (lower right) and placed 600 pounds of TNT in another opening. The Americans thereupon set a fuse and fled. Burning oil seeped into the fort's magazine, touching off a blast (below) that wrecked the structure. "There was a deafening roar from the fort," recalled an eyewitness; "smoke and flames poured from every vent, gun port, shell hole and sally port."

derground defenders detonated another arsenal. This suicidal explosion was even greater than the Malinta blowup; it shook the entire island and showered the offshore fleet with rocky debris.

The tremendous blast lifted the top off a knoll on the eastern end of Corregidor, and an American officer who had been standing on the knoll when the blast occurred was hurled 30 feet through the air. He only had the wind knocked out of him, but after he came to, he was stunned anew. "I have never seen such a sight in my life," he said. "Utter carnage, bodies laying everywhere, *everywhere*." The tunnel entrance had become a huge crater. A medical officer reported: "As soon as I got all the casualties off, I sat down on a rock and burst out crying. I couldn't stop myself and didn't even want to. I had seen more than a man could stand and still stay normal."

Two hundred Japanese soldiers died in the blast. Their deaths brought Japanese casualties to about 4,500 and ended the fight for the island. In their struggle for The Rock, the Americans suffered 1,200 casualties—more than one quarter of their original 4,560-man assault force.

To the Americans in and around Manila, it seemed that the capital would fall long before Corregidor. Admiral Iwabuchi's troops were isolated on the south side of the Pasig River and apparently could not hold out for long. American spirits soared. Before entering the city on February 7, General MacArthur issued an optimistic communiqué, claiming that "our forces are rapidly clearing the enemy from Manila" and that the "complete destruction" of the Japanese defenders was "imminent." Congratulations poured in from Allied leaders around the world, and MacArthur planned a huge victory parade. But the parade did not take place; the fight for Manila was just beginning.

Iwabuchi had decided to make a last-ditch stand in the buildings south of the Pasig. The core of his defense was Intramuros, the original walled city built by the Spanish in the 16th Century. Intramuros was enclosed by stone walls up to 40 feet thick at the base and averaging 16 feet high, and was guarded on the north side by the Pasig River.

The Americans slowly cleared the southern half of Manila and gradually closed in on Intramuros. The fighting was savage—and was made more difficult by the presence of Manila's 700,000 residents. To protect the civilians, MacArthur prohibited air attacks. At first artillery shelling was also banned, but as U.S. casualties mounted that restriction was removed. "Day and night the shelling goes on," reported Time correspondent William P. Gray. "How many hundreds or thousands of civilians already have died by fire or shelling outside Intramuros, nobody knows. Hundreds of city blocks are burned and flattened. Many unburned buildings are pocked or shattered by gunfire."

The Japanese held on. One of the toughest fights took place at an enemy-held city police station, a two-story concrete structure blocking the way to Intramuros. The Japanese had installed machine guns inside and out, and had surrounded the building with obstacles that GIs of the 129th Regiment—veterans of the vicious fighting on Bougainville—called the most formidable they had ever seen. Howitzers and tanks blasted the building to soften up its defenses. Then the infantrymen rushed in. "Our mistake," wrote one GI, "was in starting at the basement and working up. By the time we reached the first floor, we had a fire fight on our hands. . . . In one room alone, we had to wipe out three machine-gun positions. By the time we had cleared that first floor, the Japanese were on the second floor, destroying the stairway so we couldn't climb up, and then cutting holes in the floor to drop grenades on us."

The Americans withdrew. In a few days they reentered, only to be driven out again. Not until February 20, after eight days of shelling and fighting had reduced the police station to rubble, were the Japanese guns silenced.

All the while, similar fights were going on at most of Manila's landmark buildings—the City Hall, the Post Office, the Manila Club, the University of the Philippines and the Manila Hotel, formerly the residence of General MacArthur. At the hotel, MacArthur watched as the Japanese set his prewar penthouse suite ablaze. Then the general entered the hotel with a patrol. "Every landing was a fight," he later wrote. "Of the penthouse, nothing was left but ashes. It had evidently been the command post of a rearguard action. We left its colonel dead on the smoldering threshold."

Flushed from their warrens a few at a time, the Japanese fell back toward Intramuros. As they retreated, they went on a rampage. The American soldiers advancing through the wreckage found mounds of Filipinos dead—all deliberately shot. Other Filipinos had been bayoneted or burned to death, many with their hands tied behind their backs.

By February 17, American troops had reached the 150-acre enclave of Intramuros. Holed up inside were hundreds of Iwabuchi's men. They were holding as hostages some 4,000 Filipino civilians.

General Griswold, who had arrived from the north to direct the last stages of the battle for Manila, tried to save the hostages. Repeatedly, loudspeakers boomed out his pleas in Japanese to the enemy. "Your situation is hopeless—your defeat inevitable," said one message. "I offer you honorable surrender. If you decide to accept, raise a large Filipino flag . . . and send an unarmed emissary with a white flag to our lines. In the event that you do not accept my offer, I exhort you that true to the spirit of the Bushido and the Code of the Samurai you permit all civilians to evacuate the Intramuros by the Victoria Gate without delay in order that no innocent blood be shed."

No Philippine flag was raised; no hostages were released. Griswold decided to blast his way into Intramuros.

For six days the ancient citadel was subjected to a massive bombardment by 78 howitzers, a dozen 76mm guns, 24 heavy mortars and six tank guns. Some of the howitzers were brought up close and fired point-blank at the fortress to blast open holes in the thick walls. Others lobbed shells over the walls and pulverized the buildings within. In all, nearly 8,000 artillery shells exploded on Intramuros.

On the morning of February 23, the shelling was stopped and the 37th Division assaulted Intramuros from two sides. A battalion of the 129th Regiment crossed the Pasig River in assault boats and entered the ancient city from the north. On the east, the 145th Regiment sent one battalion through a breach that had been blasted in the wall and another battalion stormed through a gate.

Hundreds of Japanese had been killed in the long bombardment, but the survivors fought on with skill and unshakable resolve. They made good use of an extensive tunnel system they had dug and made strong stands in old dungeons built by the Spanish. These underground hide-outs became death traps as the Americans tossed in hand grenades, turned on flamethrowers, or poured gasoline down the air holes and ignited it. At this point, the Japanese gained a short breathing spell by releasing 3,000 civilian hostages from two churches within Intramuros; the attack was halted until the frightened Filipinos, mostly women and children, were escorted from the battle scene. Most of the male hostages had been executed; their bodies were later found stacked up in the dungeons.

On the afternoon of February 24, a company of the 145th Regiment advanced through an underground tunnel, using grenades and bazookas to eliminate the last pocket of resistance. Well over 1,000 Japanese had died defending Intramuros. Because artillery fire had taken such a heavy toll of Japanese, only 25 Americans were killed in the assault. But the old walled city—and everything in it—was in ruins.

Even after the capture of Intramuros, the battle for Manila raged on. Several hundred Japanese, including Admiral Iwabuchi, were still holding out near Intramuros in the large, modern government buildings: the Legislative Building, the Finance Building, the Bureau of Agriculture and Commerce. The American commanders first considered starving out the defenders, but captured Japanese soldiers and Filipino hostages who managed to escape reported that the Japanese had enough supplies to hold out indefinitely. So the GIs dragged up their howitzers, fired away point-blank and systematically destroyed the buildings. When the troops moved in, they were met by a few defiant Japanese machine gunners who fired until they were killed. Not until March 3, one month after the siege of Manila had begun, did the Americans silence the last holdouts in the Finance Building.

The liberation of Manila had been a brutal, costly affair. Between the landing at Lingayen Gulf and the capture of Manila, the Americans had suffered almost 25,000 casualties; in Manila itself the U.S. lost more than 1,000 killed and 5,500 wounded. By March 3, 1945, Japanese casualties on Luzon were estimated at 124,000, including more than 16,000 dead in Manila alone. And Manila itself had almost died in the process of liberation. In its sprawling ruins lay the bodies of more than 100,000 Filipinos who had perished during the battle for the city—at least six civilians for every fighting man killed on both sides.

The Americans had not seen the last of the fighting on Luzon. General Yamashita was still at large with his main force in his mountain strongholds up north. But more pressing business awaited the Americans: the invasion of the islands to the south.

DELIVERANCE AT SANTO TOMAS

Liberated but still unfree, internees in Santo Tomás prison camp are restrained by U.S. cavalrymen to protect them from Japanese troops at large in Manila.

"THE LIBERATION OF MY OWN PRISON CAMP"

As the main body of the U.S. Sixth Army battled its way southward toward Manila, armored "Flying Columns" of the 1st Cavalry Division raced on ahead through enemy lines into the Philippine capital to free some 3,700 Allied civilians who had been imprisoned since 1942 in the buildings of Santo Tomás University.

The mission had special significance for one accompanying newsman, LIFE photographer Carl Mydans, whose pictures appear on these pages. Mydans, who had been captured in Manila by the Japanese at the outbreak of the war, had himself spent more than eight months interned in Santo Tomás before being sent to another camp and finally released in a prisoner exchange. He was returning, Mydans said, for the "liberation of my own prison camp."

At about 9:00 p.m. on Saturday, February 3, 1945, Mydans rolled up to the university with the armored vanguard and watched the lead tank, named Battling Basic, crash through the campus gate. "I remember," he wrote, "how astonished I was to see that gate, which had stood so long between me and freedom, fall over like a painted illusion."

The Japanese inside were quickly put to flight, and the internees swarmed joyfully around the liberators. "A woman threw her arms about me," recalled Mydans. "Hands grabbed me and lifted me and carried me, equipment and all, onto the stairs" of the Administration Building. Mydans saw many familiar people, including two former prison-camp roommates (left), wasted by three years of hunger.

Then alarming news spread through the crowd at the Administration Building. Cavalrymen had discovered that desperate Japanese troops were holding many internees hostage in another campus building. The liberated prisoners were sent back to their quarters, and for 36 tense hours the lives of the hostages hung by a slender thread.

It was not until Monday, February 5, 1945, that the people of Santo Tomás could celebrate with confidence. Though their repatriation was still a long way off, the men, women and children joined together (right) and thankfully sang "God Bless America."

Lee Rogers (left), a retired naval-yard worker, and miner John C. Todd show the results of their long captivity. Rogers had lost 55 pounds, Todd 76.

Free at last, jubilant internees cheer and wave as the American flag is unfurled from the balcony of the Administration Building at Santo Tomás University.

Just after daybreak on February 5, Colonel Brady (left) and interpreter Stanley (in white shirt) lead Hayashi (center) and his Japanese troops out of Santo Tomás.

NEGOTIATIONS TO FREE CAPTIVES AND CAPTORS

Soon after breaking into Santo Tomás, U.S. cavalrymen heard cries for help coming from the Education Building, where 65 Japanese soldiers, led by the camp commandant, Lieut. Colonel Toshio Hayashi, held some 220 internees as hostages on the upper floors. "Let us out!" shouted the prisoners. "The Japs won't let us out! They're holding us in here! Let us out!"

Brigadier General William Chase, commander of the rescue operation, decided to negotiate. "Our mission," he said, "is to save these prisoners, not get them killed."

Throughout the day, Chase exchanged messages with Hayashi through prisoner

intermediaries. Then he sent in as his negotiator Lieut. Colonel Charles E. Brady, a trusted officer with a famous mustache, which he trimmed meticulously and waxed to sharp points.

Brady went into the Education Building and came face to face with the burly Japanese commander. Hayashi stood with his feet spread apart, repeatedly lifting two pistols out of his hip holsters and dropping them back in again. "My hand twitched so, watching that son-of-a-bitch," recalled Brady, "that I had to twirl my mustache to keep it steady." Hayashi insisted on "safe conduct with honor"—which meant that he would release the hostages only if his men could come out with full arms and ammunition. Brady said no. Slowly a compromise was hammered out: the Japanese

could keep their personal weapons, but no grenades or machine guns.

At daybreak on Monday, a tense parade marched across the campus and out the main gate. In the lead were Brady, Hayashi and Ernest Stanley, an interned Canadian missionary who served as their interpreter. They were followed by the Japanese soldiers, marching three abreast, shouting in cadence to their stride. Along each flank walked a line of Brady's men, their rifles and submachine guns at the ready.

When the procession got to within just a few blocks of the Japanese lines in Manila, Brady released Hayashi and his men. The freed soldiers were afraid that the Americans would shoot them and, wrote eyewitness Mydans, they "broke ranks and scrambled in terror."

Pleading for their release, hostages line the windows of the Education Building while their Japanese captors hide in back of them and on the floor below.

In a shanty-filled courtyard, freed prisoners follow the drab old routine of camp life. Their quarters were considered better than the packed dormitories.

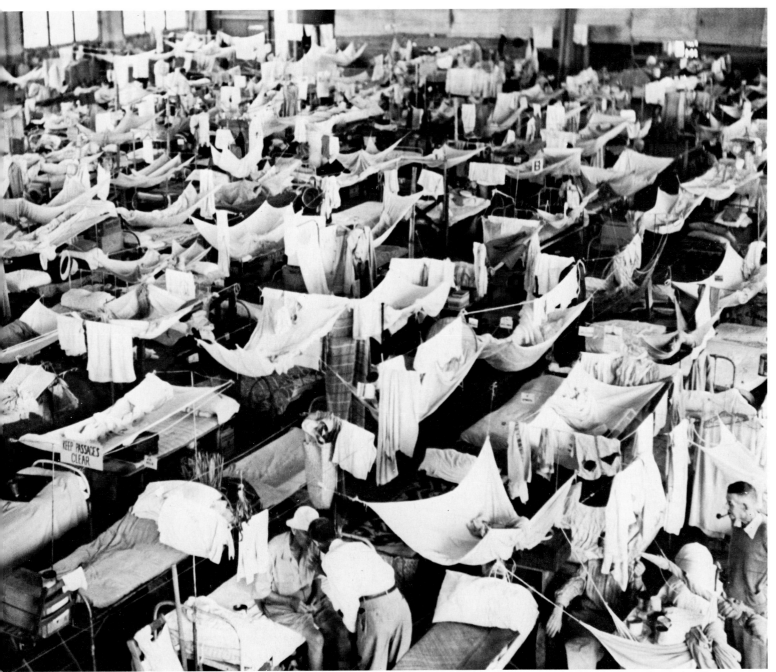

Hundreds of cots crowd the gymnasium. In these cramped quarters, internees often stashed their personal possessions on the mosquito netting above the cots.

SHOCKING GLIMPSES OF THE PRISONERS' LIVES

When the American forces began exploring Santo Tomás, they were shocked by the internees' miserable living conditions. Not so Carl Mydans. The photographer remembered his months of imprisonment so vividly that he fell into the old regimen almost without thought. "I queued up in the same food line," he wrote, "shared the same mirror with the same men in my old room, saw the same people sitting in the same chairs in the same corridors." Mydans was possessed by the "uncanny feeling that nothing at all had changed and that I was still a prisoner."

The university gymnasium—"the horror spot of the camp," as Mydans called it—housed 400 single men, most of them sick or elderly, who spent their days and nights on cots crammed head to foot and side by side. In the courtyards, interned families lived in small shanties they made of assorted refuse—scraps of tin, wood, corrugated metal, bamboo, matting and blankets.

Everywhere Mydans looked he saw the grim signs of hunger and malnutrition—pallid skin stretched tight over fleshless bones, with legs and ankles swollen from beriberi. At the time of the liberation, the average adult male weighed 112 pounds and women weighed 100 pounds—an average loss of 27 per cent of body weight during imprisonment. Only the children were in fair condition, and that was because their parents fed them part of their own meager rations.

An emaciated father holds a can of army food for his son. But the food came too late for 23 internees who died of malnutrition and related diseases in the first 15 days of February.

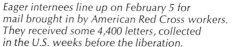

Eager internees line up on February 5 for mail brought in by American Red Cross workers. They received some 4,400 letters, collected in the U.S. weeks before the liberation.

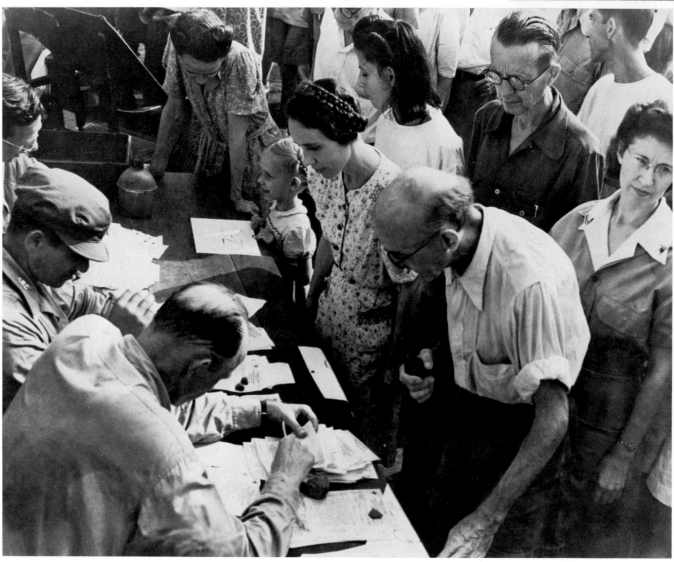

GAINING STRENGTH FOR THE HOMEWARD JOURNEY

The living conditions at Santo Tomás improved slowly after February 5, when the U.S. Sixth Army opened supply routes to the camp. Army food began arriving regularly and hearty meals were served. The internees, who were accustomed to only one handful of rice per day under the Japa- nese, soon were feasting on GI fare—pork with gravy, mashed potatoes, beans, corn- beef hash, fruit cocktail and milk. Some internees gained a pound a day.

The internees received a different kind of sustenance from American Red Cross workers who arrived in camp shortly after the liberation with letters from relatives and friends. For many inmates, the mail was the first news from home since 1942. Yet the letters also increased the internees' impatience to go home, and nothing could speed the complex repatriation process. The Allied officials would not release in- mates until their well-being in the outside world was assured, and the arrangements meant a long delay for internees who had lived in the Philippines before the War and had lost their money, homes and families. The last inmates did not leave Santo Tomás until July 31, 1945, six months after the prison was liberated.

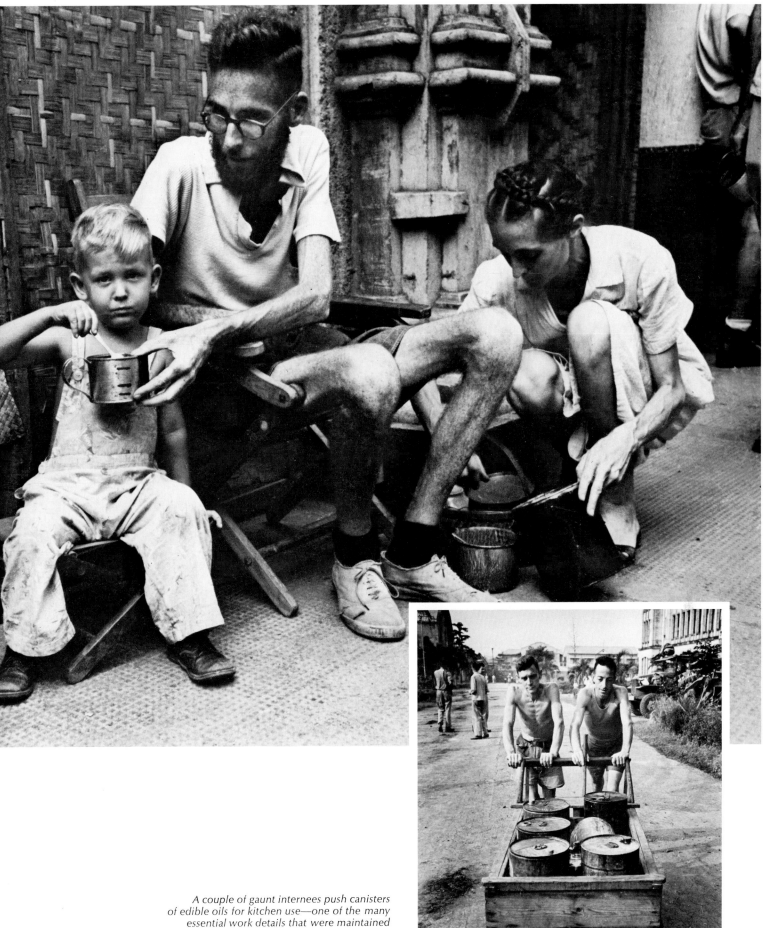

A couple of gaunt internees push canisters of edible oils for kitchen use—one of the many essential work details that were maintained until the last inmates were repatriated.

In the entrance hall of the Administration Building, freed internees crowd around their liberator, General MacArthur, during his February 7 visit. The general had

known a number of the inmates in prewar Manila and now greeted them by name. "It was wonderful," said MacArthur, "to be a life-saver, not a life-taker."

A CITY THAT DIED IN BATTLE

Early in the long, devastating battle for Manila, U.S. troops in an amphibious vehicle fire at Japanese machine-gun positions on the far bank of the Pasig River.

"MANILA HAS CEASED TO EXIST"

Between February 3 and March 3, 1945, Manila was laid waste and bled white by the fighting between some 16,000 diehard Japanese defenders and a large part of the U.S. Sixth Army. But the ruination of Manila began even before the fighting. As the Americans approached the city, the Japanese began destroying power plants and military installations, and igniting fires that consumed hundreds of homes and shops. On February 2 a citizen wrote: "The flames that can be seen daily . . . the explosions that every moment hurt our ears, the dynamite that the soldiers bury in the streets, the barbed wire that blocks the passageway . . . have filled us with anguish. Where am I going? And my children? . . . Everything is an uncertainty of terror."

With the arrival of the Americans, the destruction escalated and innocent citizens became the victims of the fighting. Hundreds of people were cut down by the small-arms cross fire, and many hundreds more were killed and maimed when the American commanders, alarmed by their mounting casualties, ordered their artillery and mortars to bombard the Japanese positions. "Dead and more dead lay sprawled and scattered on both sides of the thoroughfares," reported one survivor, "and the atmosphere was filled with such nauseating odor as to cause people to vomit out what little they had in their stomachs."

The retreating Japanese, seething with frustration and enraged by the loyalty of the Filipinos to the United States, looted houses, raped, tortured and murdered, especially in Intramuros, Manila's ancient walled city, where nearly 1,000 Filipinos died.

When the battle finally ended, the city was a great sprawl of debris. "Manila," said U.S. General Eichelberger, "has ceased to exist except for some places that the Japanese thought were not worth defending or where our American troops got in by surprise." Close to 100,000 of the 700,000 people living in Manila had perished. Carlos Romulo, the noted Manila editor, walked among the corpses and the ruins, and "wherever I went," he said, "I felt like a ghost in a dead city."

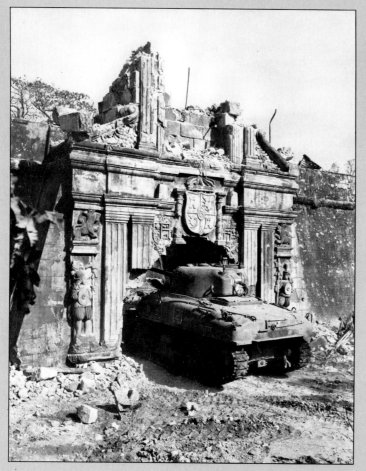

A U.S. tank batters its way into the old city of Intramuros through a historic stone gate, one of many Manila monuments destroyed in the battle.

A Filipino nun smiles in spite of her painful burns. American troops had just freed her and thousands of other civilians who had been trapped in Intramuros.

A residential street becomes a battlefield as Americans fire at enemy machine gunners. The Japanese gave ground slowly, in some places forcing the Americans

SLAUGHTER IN THE STREETS

The American troops moved in, the Japanese fought back, the civilians fled their homes. So it went in one section of the city after another as the battle raged through Manila. Many citizens ran blindly into the line of fire and were hit by shrapnel or bullets. Others were deliberately mowed down by vindictive Japanese soldiers. "On the streets, people were running away terrified," one Filipino recalled. "Women and children cried to heaven . . . wounded persons lay on the streets, some of them

to fight for each house.

Bearing whatever possessions they could carry or tug along, some civilians flee the blazing fires in a Chinese quarter of the city.

abandoned by their families, while others were there in the throes of agony. We lost sight of our neighbors, and we did not know where to go."

No place held by the Japanese was safe for the civilians. Many people thought they would find refuge within the reinforced concrete walls of the Philippine General Hospital, and nearly 7,000 men, women and children crowded inside. But the Japanese turned the hospital into a fortress, and the Americans shelled it.

Lucky Filipinos managed to reach American lines. Many of them arrived wounded, some on all fours. "Mutilated, their wounds wrapped in rags full of blood, they come down the streets of the liberated zone in macabre processions of death," one citizen wrote, "and arrive at the hospital in numbers too great to attend to." Another civilian watched the processions in horrified disbelief. "I never realized," he said, "how much punishment the human body could endure."

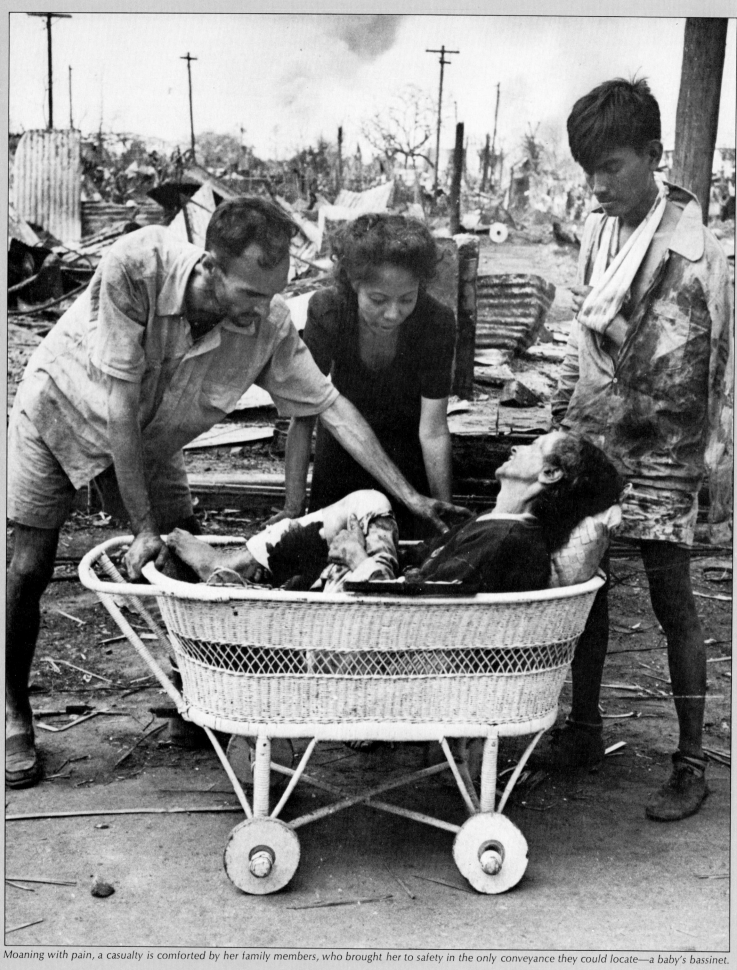

Moaning with pain, a casualty is comforted by her family members, who brought her to safety in the only conveyance they could locate—a baby's bassinet.

On a jeep ride to an aid station, a woman with a shrapnel wound in her leg lies on a stretcher of bamboo fencing. She is attended by her husband, a European.

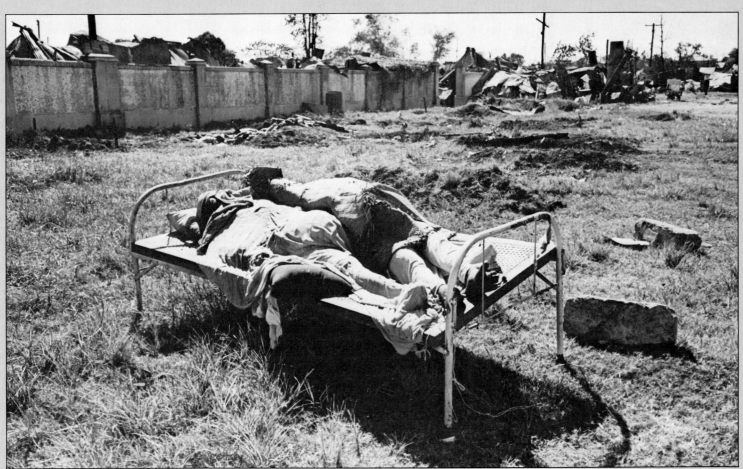

Two dead civilians lie on a bed on the south bank of the Pasig. They had been carried to the field mortally wounded and then were abandoned after they died.

Attacking Intramuros, GIs swarm ashore near the walled city just before civilian hostages were released by the Japanese.

During a break in the fighting, freed hostages wait to be ferried across the Pasig to the liberated zone (background).

Shell-shocked and wounded women receive a helping hand from GIs after release from a church in Intramuros. Most of those freed were women and children.

SHELL-SHOCKED CAPTIVES OF INTRAMUROS

In early February, about 4,000 residents of Intramuros were taken hostage by the Japanese. The men were locked up in Fort Santiago; the women and children were herded into two churches. They had practically no water, and the food they brought with them was soon exhausted.

The Americans began shelling the city on February 17. Shell fragments showered down on the churches. In one, more than 300 people died; said Mrs. Trinidad Mendoza, a hostage whose 15-year-old daughter was killed: "Dreadful darkness filled the interior of the church. We trampled on the dead bodies lying everywhere."

On February 23 the shelling ended, and as the Americans stormed Intramuros, the Japanese released a flood of civilians. But only 3,000 people were freed of the original 4,000; the rest had been killed.

Stealthily advancing through the ruins of Intramuros, American infantrymen conduct a thorough house-to-house search for enemy soldiers. The Japanese refused

Hands tied behind his back, a slaughtered Filipino hostage lies in the debris of a fallen roof.

A little boy—murdered by the Japanese—sprawls beside another victim in the wreckage of Intramuros.

to surrender and fought stubbornly to the death.

DEATH AMONG
THE RUINS

Soon after the civilian hostages had been released from Intramuros, the Americans completed the capture of the old walled city. Here they found the remains of the missing hostages: priests who had been buried alive inside underground shelters, women and infants who had been mutilat-ed with bayonets and sabers, men who had died in torture and flames. "Manila was a charnel house of the dead," wrote Car-los Romulo. "These were my neighbors and my friends whose tortured bodies I saw . . . their heads shaved, their hands tied behind their backs, and bayonet stabs running them through and through. This girl who looked up at me wordlessly, her young breasts crisscrossed with bayonet strokes, had been in school with my son."

Manila landmarks that were ravaged during the month-long battle for the city include (clockwise from left): the Post Office; the Roman Catholic Cathedral of

Manila; the Legislative Building; the City Hall, where exhausted American soldiers take a breather after fighting their way inside; and a section of Intramuros.

Survivors in the liberated zones take shelter inside crude shanties that they constructed of debris. Tens of thousands of homeless refugees lived in squalor, hungry, destitute and suffering from diseases and malnutrition.

Manila after the battle stretches away in an endless vista of devastated buildings. Around the battered walls of Intramuros stand the tents of GIs, who soon went to work to clear the wreckage they had helped to create.

5

Early in February 1945, while the U.S. Sixth Army was fighting to take Manila, General MacArthur prepared to launch an ambitious operation aimed at recapturing not just a single island but every major bypassed island in the southern Philippines.

MacArthur's plan was eminently feasible. Leyte had been seized, Luzon had been invaded, air bases had been set up on Mindoro, and the enemy's air and naval power had virtually been destroyed. It was impossible for the Japanese to reinforce or rescue their isolated garrisons on the southern islands. But by the same token, MacArthur could have let the Japanese in the south "wither on the vine," a tactic he had used in previous Pacific campaigns. But he had returned to liberate all of the islands; anything less, he had often said, would be a breach of his promise to the Filipinos. And there was danger in bypassing islands and leaving their populations—and any American prisoners of war—to the dubious mercy of frustrated Japanese troops.

Moreover, some of the islands that MacArthur intended to liberate had strategic value, especially as sites for air bases from which planes could interdict Japanese shipping and support an invasion of Borneo *(pages 164-175)* by Mac-Arthur's Australian troops.

MacArthur wanted to get his southern operation under way in a hurry, before the monsoon season bogged down troop movements and delayed construction of airfields. So, on February 5 he told General Krueger, the Sixth Army commander, that some of his units were needed for the new campaign, and that his remaining troops were merely to drive the Japanese into the mountains of Luzon and wear them down by attrition. On the following day, MacArthur issued the first in a series of orders for the operation, code-named *Victor,* directing General Eichelberger, commander of the Eighth Army, to invade and capture the central and southern Philippines.

At this point, the Eighth Army consisted mainly of the Americal and the 31st Divisions and part of the 24th Division. MacArthur promptly added to it. In rapid succession he stripped the Sixth Army of the 40th and the 41st Divisions and the remainder of the 24th Division, and gave them to Eichelberger. Through the next two weeks, the multiple invasion—which was to be one of the most complex amphibious operations ever undertaken—quickly took shape.

INVASIONS BY THE DOZEN

The campaign was planned to unfold in overlapping stages, with each of the various landings on separate island groups to get under way before the previous phase was completed.

From its base in Leyte the beefed-up Eighth Army began moving in mid-February, and it did not stop moving for the next two months. "There has never been another army just like it," General Eichelberger later wrote. "In one 44-day period alone these troops conducted 14 major landings and 24 minor ones, thus rolling up an average of a landing every day and a half. There was never a time, during this action-packed interlude, when some task force of my command was not fighting a battle. And most of the time, hundreds of miles apart, separate task forces were fighting separate battles simultaneously."

The Eighth Army's first task was to capture islands that dominated the Visayan Passages south of Luzon. Japanese guns on these islands endangered the Americans using the waterways, forcing supply convoys plying between Leyte and Luzon to take much longer routes than necessary.

The Visayan operation kicked off on February 19. As elements of the Eighth Army carried out their landings, they found the going easier than expected. Some islands had already been taken over by Filipino guerrillas. Preliminary naval bombardments proved unnecessary for other islands; the defenders had already retreated inland to strong positions in mountainous terrain. This Japanese tactic was part of General Yamashita's plan to tie up American troops in bitter rear-guard actions. But it failed here; after a few days on each island the GIs would board their landing craft again and move on to their next target, leaving guerrilla units to eliminate or bottle up the Japanese. During these assaults along the Visayan Passages, the PT boats of the U.S. Seventh Fleet scurried around the islands, preventing the escape of Japanese troops and keeping a lookout for seaborne counterattacks that never materialized.

Before the Visayan Islands had been completely cleared, the Eighth Army turned its attention to Palawan, a long, rugged, heavily forested island stretching southwestward from American-held Mindoro almost to Borneo. MacArthur wanted Palawan, the westernmost major island of the Philippines, as a base that would allow him to extend the range of his air power over the South China Sea and the Dutch East Indies. On February 28, after half an hour of naval bombardment, the 41st Division's 186th Regimental Combat Team swept ashore at Puerto Princesa on Palawan and quickly discovered that the Japanese troops had already vacated the port area.

Close to the town they found the remains of some 150 American prisoners in two burned air-raid shelters. It turned out that the men had been killed by the Japanese in December. At that time the captives were being forced to work as laborers on an airstrip. When their captors spotted the U.S. invasion fleet bound for Mindoro on December 14, they panicked, thinking that Palawan was about to be attacked. The men were taken from their stockade, herded into the shelters, doused with gasoline and set afire. Machine guns mowed down those who tried to climb out of the inferno, but three escaped through a tunnel. Rescued and hidden by guerrillas, the survivors emerged from the jungle to recount the atrocity.

U.S. engineers hurried to repair and improve the runway, but they were slowed by soggy terrain and bomb craters, and it was not until the end of March that planes from the strip would begin ranging over the South China Sea.

The delay prompted the Thirteenth Air Force, which was responsible for supporting Eichelberger's southern Philippines campaign, to use a novel and somewhat risky expedient in preparation for the March 10 invasion of Zamboanga City, at the tip of the Zamboanga peninsula in western Mindanao. A squadron of Marine Corsair fighters was sent to a strip about 150 miles north of Zamboanga City, at the town of Dipolog. The strip was held by a large guerrilla force led by Colonel Fertig and had already been used by American cargo planes supplying the guerrillas and by a number of pilots on combat missions who had made emergency landings there. On March 8, two days before the Zamboanga landings, C-47 cargo planes flew in two companies of the 24th Division to reinforce the guerrillas; they were followed by 16 Corsair fighters. A close-support air base had been obtained without firing a shot.

Fertig informed Eighth Army headquarters that the landing areas would not be defended and that the 8,900 Japanese had moved out of the city. Even so, Zamboanga and the beaches flanking it were pounded by two cruisers, six destroyers, B-24 bombers from Morotai and the Marine fighters from Dipolog over the course of two days. Then, after the bombardment ended on March 10, the 41st Division's 162nd Infantry Regiment began landing in amtracs. The troops, virtually unopposed, swarmed inland and took possession of an abandoned prewar airstrip.

The 163rd Infantry Regiment followed the assault troops ashore, and on the next day pushed into the rubble of Zamboanga City and occupied a second airfield that was in better condition. Engineers immediately began to expand this field to a 5,000-foot-long strip. Four days later, Marine fliers brought in their planes from Dipolog and began operating from the forward strip.

The Japanese were playing a waiting game. The Japanese 54th Independent Mixed Brigade, along with other Army and Navy troops, had retreated into an elaborate series of defense works on high ground two or three miles inland, where they held a commanding view of the forward strip and the U.S. positions around the town. Their defenses

extended across a five-mile-wide front and were three miles deep in places. All positions were protected by barbed wire, booby traps and minefields.

To root out the Japanese, the two American infantry regiments, attacking abreast and backed up by heavy artillery fire and Marine air support, moved into the foothills. The terrain was so rugged and overgrown that the men often had to pace their advance to the crawl of bulldozers gouging supply roads out of the jungle.

For the Marine pilots, the struggle for Zamboanga was easier or, as one of them put it, "an intimate war." With the Japanese so close by, the Marines could look over the target area from their briefing tent. And in the air they could strafe and drop their bombs without losing sight of their base. When they landed, the ground controller would be there to tell them how they had done.

Every time the infantrymen encountered a stubborn Japanese position, they called for fast strafing missions by the

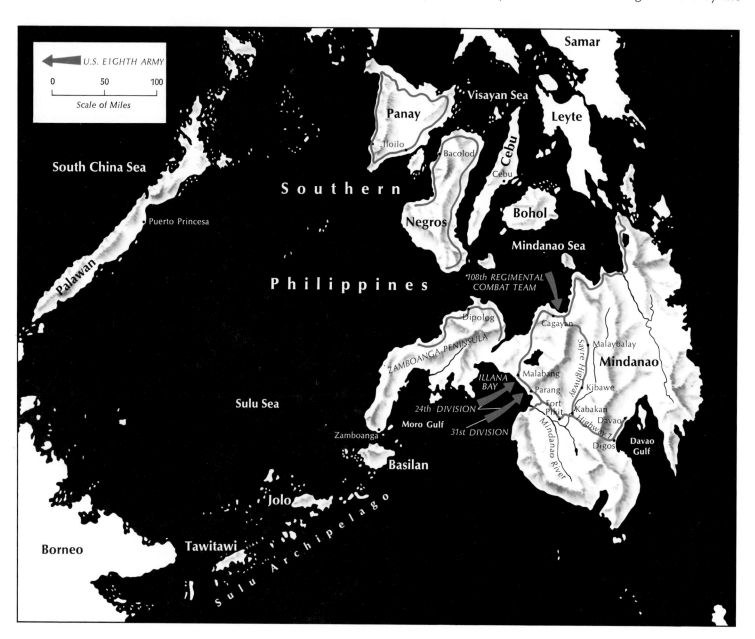

Marine Corsairs or for some Dauntlesses to deliver 500-pound bombs. The bomb runs were uncannily accurate. Before long, GIs of the 41st Division were saying the Marine fliers could "drive tacks with their bombs."

The Marine pilots were also adept at improvisation. At Dipolog there was no ground-air radio network or any accurate maps to lead the planes to targets. When a column of 150 well-armed Japanese approached to within 10 miles of the Dipolog airstrip, U.S. Army Major Donald H. Wills, who was attached to the guerrilla group there, found himself unable to pinpoint the enemy's location for the pilots. But he was familiar with the area and knew exactly where the Japanese were, and he decided to act as tour guide. He climbed into the single-seat cockpit of a Corsair fighter and then had the smallest of the Marine pilots at the strip, First Lieutenant Winfield S. Sharpe, squeeze in after him and sit on his lap. Wills navigated and pointed out the targets to Sharpe; the pint-sized pilot then led three planes in six effective strafing runs on the enemy positions. The Japanese withdrew, and the threat to the Dipolog airstrip evaporated.

To the south, the Japanese defense position above Zamboanga City began to crack after a week of steady pressure from air and ground. At the end of the month, the Japanese commander, realizing that further resistance was futile, ordered his 5,000 survivors to retreat. Blocked by guerrillas, chased through the wild and largely unexplored hinterland of the peninsula, they suffered terrible losses. Only about 1,400 came out alive. The 41st Division lost some 220 men killed and 665 wounded.

While heavy fighting was going on in Zamboanga, smaller elements of the 41st Division went into action to the south and seized control of the Sulu archipelago, obtaining air bases closer to Borneo. At the same time, sizable forces of two other divisions began a campaign to liberate the four major central Visayan Islands: Panay, Negros, Cebu and Bohol. This island group, situated at the waist of the Philippine archipelago, was already surrounded by American-controlled islands and thus had no pressing military value. But the four principal islands were all heavily populated, and the general, adhering to his belief, refused to leave them in enemy hands.

The invasion of Panay was a walkover. The guerrilla lead-er there, Colonel Macario Peralta, had long since taken control of most of the island. Peralta had been one of the first guerrilla leaders to contact MacArthur's headquarters in November 1942, and his 20,000 men had received whatever arms and supplies the Americans could spare. As the men of the Eighth Army's 40th Division came ashore on March 18, twelve miles from Iloilo, the capital, they were met not by Japanese but by Colonel Peralta and an honor guard of guerrillas lined up smartly on the beach, all dressed in starched khaki uniforms and wearing polished decorations.

The Japanese commander had moved all his troops to the Iloilo area, intending to defend the harbor and airfield there for as long as possible. But as the 185th Infantry Regiment of the 40th Division rapidly expanded its beachhead, the Japanese realized that they would not be able to hold the city. In a concerted effort, they broke through a thin guerrilla blocking line and escaped into the mountains of the interior.

On the afternoon of March 20, U.S. tanks nosed into Iloilo, followed by jeeps loaded with brass: General Eichelberger; Rear Admiral Arthur D. Struble, the amphibious commander; Major General Rapp Brush, the commander of the 40th Division; and Colonel Peralta. "I suggested that Struble, Brush and I take part in the advance and see how far we could get," Eichelberger wrote. "Our jeeps pushed forward with the tank spearhead in the early afternoon. A half hour later, to our astonishment, we found ourselves in the center of Iloilo and surrounded by a laughing, cheering, flower-throwing city population which seemed to have gone crazy with joy."

Allied air raids had ruined two thirds of the city, but the docks were intact and the harbor was clear. Late that afternoon, in a formal ceremony at Colonel Peralta's headquarters, General Eichelberger pinned the Distinguished Service Cross on the guerrilla chief, while a guerrilla brass band played the proper martial music. Assuming the Japanese contingent on Panay was too small to cause serious trouble, neither the guerrillas nor the Americans pursued the enemy into the mountains. The entire Panay operation cost the U.S. only 20 men killed and 50 wounded.

On Cebu, the next central Visayan island on the schedule, Major General William H. Arnold's Americal Division, understrength after mopping up on Leyte, encountered a

The Americans' sweep through the southern Philippines was the most complex single campaign of the Pacific war. Between mid-February and late June of 1945, the U.S. Eighth Army made dozens of amphibious landings to liberate the Visayan Islands, Palawan and the Sulu archipelago. The largest assault, on Mindanao, began on April 17, after preliminary attacks had secured the island's Zamboanga peninsula. The bulk of the U.S. 24th Division landed at Parang, while one battalion came ashore at Malabang. The 24th Division, later reinforced by the 31st Division, was to fight across the island along Highway 1 and capture the primary port of Davao. The 108th Regimental Combat Team of the 40th Division landed at Macajalar Bay on May 10. It was to drive south along Sayre Highway and join elements of the 31st, striking north from the road junction at Kabakan.

much more difficult situation. Some 14,500 Japanese troops, commanded by Major General Takeo Manjome, had been constructing a series of defense lines in the hills north of Cebu City, the second largest Philippine urban center and a major commercial port. Machine guns were concealed in caves and situated in pillboxes, bunkers and tunnels. Anti-aircraft guns and light artillery pieces were dispersed in positions overlooking the city and the coastal plain. And, as the Americans found out at their cost, Manjome had sown extensive minefields and dug tank traps at all the probable landing beaches.

When the leading amtracs of the 132nd and 182nd Infantry Regiments trundled ashore five miles southwest of Cebu City on the morning of March 26, the minefields stopped them cold. Ten of the first 15 amtracs were knocked out within a few feet of the waterline, and the landing area soon jammed up as subsequent waves reached the shore but could not move inland. The advance was stalled for an hour and a half while a lane was cleared through the minefields. If the Japanese had struck during the confusion, they could have inflicted heavy losses. But as on Panay and Zamboanga, the defenders followed their tactic of quick withdrawal to inland positions. The following day the men of the Americal Division probed cautiously through the abandoned Japanese defenses and entered Cebu City.

As the GIs advanced into the countryside, they ran into enemy forces positioned in the hills above the city. The Japanese suffered heavy casualties but held their ground. The American advance was further delayed when the Japanese blew up an ammunition cache that had been hidden in caves. The explosion knocked out three American tanks, and killed or wounded 50 men in one infantry company.

A week after entering Cebu City, General Arnold's forces were still battering at Manjome's main defense line; their air raids, and artillery and naval fire were killing Japanese in great numbers, but the infantry still could not break through. At this point, Arnold asked Eichelberger to give him the 164th Regimental Combat Team, which had been held in reserve, and on April 9 the 164th arrived on Cebu.

Marching at night with guerrilla guides and staying under cover during the day, the 164th Regimental Combat Team moved up a river valley and encircled the Japanese position in a 27-mile sweep. On April 13 it attacked the Japanese flank while the other two infantry regiments of the division launched a frontal assault. Five days later, organized resistance on Cebu came to an end. In all, 5,500 Japanese died on Cebu; the Americans lost 410 men.

While the fighting for Cebu was still going on, elements of the 40th Division from Panay had jumped across the narrow Guimaras Strait to attack the northwestern part of the island of Negros, between Panay and Cebu. Negros, a rich island of sugar plantations, had been the Japanese Fourth Air Army's most important base south of Luzon, but now there were no functioning planes on the eight airfields. Guerrilla forces controlled most of the island, and, in the usual pattern, the 14,000 Japanese defenders had pulled back to the mountains to make their stand, leaving behind only enough soldiers to blow up bridges and delay the Americans' advance.

The Americans knew that at all costs they must save the modern, 650-foot-long steel bridge across the deep ravine of the Bago River, between the landing beaches and their

On board the command ship U.S.S. Rocky Mount, Lieut. General Robert Eichelberger (left) and his subordinates stolidly await the first reports of the landings of his U.S. Eighth Army troops at Zamboanga in Mindanao. Long convinced that "calm leaders allay the hysterias which are both endemic and epidemic to battle," Eichelberger made a point of displaying his composure at such times of high tension.

objective, Bacolod, the largest city of north Negros. The Japanese had already mined the bridge for demolition, and if they destroyed it, there would be no quick and easy way to replace it. Such were the stakes when the Americans launched a preinvasion raid to prevent the bridge from being blown up.

Before dawn on March 29, a reinforced platoon commanded by Second Lieutenant Aaron A. Hanson sneaked ashore a mile and a half away from the beaches where the rest of the 185th Regimental Combat Team was scheduled to land later that morning. Hanson and his 62 men groped through the darkness toward the bridge. A guerrilla was waiting for them with the news that nine Japanese with three oxcarts were approaching along a paved highway. Just as dawn began to break, Hanson saw the Japanese and the Japanese spotted the Americans. Not daring to fire for fear of alerting the bridge guards, Hanson and his men raced for the bridge. A fight broke out immediately. Even though Hanson's men managed to disperse the Japanese and start across the bridge, they were immediately pinned down by heavy fire from the other side.

Two 1,000-pound aerial bombs had been strapped to the underside of the bridge, and in the middle stood an electric detonator. Suddenly, a Japanese soldier ran out. As he knelt to push the plunger, an American shot him dead.

After trading fire with the Americans for a few minutes, the guards on the other end of the bridge abandoned their post, and Hanson set up defenses to protect the span. An hour later 60 more Japanese, unaware that the Americans had captured the bridge, arrived at the span and were dispersed by Hanson's machine guns and bazookas. Bacolod was taken easily the next day.

Reconnaissance patrols of the 40th Division swept around the island and quickly surrounded the Japanese in the central mountains. More substantial forces followed to bolster the American cordon. Although the Japanese were to hold out in the mountains for two months, the Americans had won effective control of northern Negros and were prepared to move on.

The last significant target island in the Visayas, Bohol, was invaded from Cebu on April 11 by elements of the Americal Division. Only 330 Japanese were on the island, and they could do little but annoy and harass the American force.

Other elements of the division on Cebu then crossed a strait to destroy a small Japanese garrison at the southern end of Negros. By the end of April, scattered American units were fighting or mopping up surrounded Japanese units on Negros, Cebu, Bohol, Panay, Palawan, the Sulu Islands and the Zamboanga peninsula. But the Eighth Army's job in the southern Philippines was far from over.

On April 17, the Eighth launched the biggest and bloodiest operation of its campaign—the battle for Mindanao. Actually, Mindanao had already been attacked; the Zamboanga peninsula was part of it. But the peninsula was connected to the island only by a narrow, mountainous isthmus impassable to large, mechanized bodies of troops. So the invasion of the main body of the island was planned and executed as an entirely separate operation. Once again, although there were 43,000 Japanese troops on Mindanao, they were completely isolated and did not pose a threat to the progress of the war. In accordance with MacArthur's policy, the operation was designed simply to liberate Filipinos and destroy Japanese troops.

The primary target was the populous area around the southeastern port of Davao, where the main Japanese bases and forces were located. Before the War, the Japanese had established large commercial interests in Davao and had developed extensive hemp plantations around the shores of Davao Gulf. About 13,000 Japanese civilians lived in the area, protected by naval and air bases, extensive fortifications and the Japanese 100th Division.

In the north-central part of the island, another large force of Japanese, composed of the 30th Division and assorted units, was strung out below Macajalar Bay on the Sayre Highway, which led south from the bay to connect with Mindanao's single east-west highway. Since the two highways linked, troops from the north could theoretically come to the assistance of the Japanese at Davao. But the roads in the interior were so primitive, and the guerrillas there so adept at ambush and harassment, that the Japanese found it impossible to move large forces quickly from place to place. Therefore, the two Japanese concentrations, one in Davao and the other in north-central Mindanao, were effectively cut off from each other.

The commanders of both forces thought that the most

likely avenue of American attack would be an amphibious landing near Davao. Consequently, the 100th Division had built extensive fortifications on Davao Gulf, with most of the artillery and machine-gun-fire lanes pointing toward the sea. The rear was left undefended on the assumption that the rugged hinterland to the west of Davao would discourage an assault from that direction.

The idea of landing at Davao appealed to Eichelberger; it would have been the quickest way to capture the area and destroy the Japanese 100th Division. But huge American forces had just invaded Okinawa, and the U.S. Navy could not spare the ships required. Eichelberger decided that General Sibert's X Corps would land instead at Illana Bay, on Mindanao's west coast, and then move east over 110 miles of primitive country to fall upon Davao from the rear. Illana Bay was lightly defended, and the wide Mindanao River, which emptied there, promised waterborne access to the interior. An airstrip near the beach would provide a forward base for planes supporting the assault.

Sibert's plan called for the 24th Infantry Division to make the main assault at the port of Malabang and seize the airstrip. Then it was to proceed down the coast to the port of Parang and the mouth of the Mindanao River, where the inland trek would begin. This plan was altered, however, because of a guerrilla coup. For several weeks prior to the April 17 invasion date, a unit of Colonel Fertig's guerrillas had been fighting toward the Malabang airstrip. With the assistance of air strikes by Marine planes based at Zamboanga, the guerrillas captured the airport two weeks before the invasion and the pilots immediately began using the airstrip as a forward base. Indeed, most of the Marine fliers who took part in the preinvasion bombardment of the Illana Bay area touched down at the strip, conferred with the guerrillas and then took off again to strafe and bombard the Japanese positions that the guerrillas had pointed out.

On April 11, the guerrillas made a mistake that turned out to be a blessing in disguise: they allowed 100 Japanese whom they had trapped in the Malabang area to break through their lines and flee south. The bright side of the breakthrough was immediately apparent to the guerrillas: they promptly radioed the Americans that Malabang was undefended and could be taken without assault by troops of the 24th Division.

The detailed plans for the landings were immediately

changed. A reduced force of just one battalion landed at Malabang to guard the airstrip, while on the morning of April 17, after a two-hour naval bombardment, the bulk of the 24th Division stormed ashore 17 miles down the coast at the town of Parang, on Mindanao's east-west highway. Even at Parang the troops met little opposition. They found evidence that the defenders had been surprised and driven off by the preinvasion bombardment. Poking through the ruins of the Japanese command post at Parang, a lieutenant discovered five dead or injured carrier pigeons, each with the same message strapped to one of its legs: "The Americans are here." Because the pigeons had remained grounded, and because the Japanese lacked adequate radio equipment, the commander at Davao did not learn of the landings at Parang for five days.

By the afternoon of April 17, men of the 24th Division had secured the entire area and had started moving inland, down the east-west highway, on what would turn out to be the longest sustained overland march by any American unit in the entire Pacific war. More than 100 miles of steaming wilderness separated the 24th Division troops from Davao Gulf. The rainy season was expected to begin any day, and the American commanders were not optimistic about beating the monsoon to Davao. Their route, grandly named Highway 1, was of little help; neglected by the Japanese during the occupation, the roadway in some places had been reduced to a narrow, tangled trail through the encroaching jungle.

On the first leg of the trek, some of the troops took the less difficult route inland, the broad Mindanao River. On April 18, while the 19th Infantry Regiment struggled along the highway, the 21st boarded a makeshift fleet of shallow-draft vessels and moved up the waterway. They were followed by four 110-foot Navy subchasers that had been armed with rocket launchers and other heavy weapons. General Eichelberger said of the strange advance: "There hadn't been a military adventure quite like it since Federal gunboats operated on the lower Mississippi during the Civil War. These were, literally, gunboats; even captured Japanese barges were manned and gunned and pressed into the ferry service. The river runs roughly parallel to Highway 1 so with the advantage of walkie-talkie radio contact, the water transported combat units were able to make shore landings and drive Japanese troops to the woods."

By the evening of the 19th, the waterborne troops had advanced 26 miles, but Major General Roscoe B. Woodruff, the 24th Division's commander, ordered them to pull back because the 19th Infantry Regiment, moving along the jungle highway, could not maintain the pace. The 19th was forced to halt at every ravine while engineers constructed Bailey bridges to replace spans burned or blown up by the Japanese. Enemy machine guns, emplaced in the jungle at hairpin turns in the road, often delayed the advance for an hour or two. Sometimes the Japanese merely waited unseen in the jungle a few yards away and then at night crept out to bayonet sleeping GIs or blow up an artillery piece. One dark night a grenade exploded near a corporal who was guarding a rebuilt bridge. Taking no chances, he spent the hours until dawn shooting at random into the darkness. In the morning he found a dead Japanese soldier just three yards from his foxhole.

Meanwhile, the waterborne troops sailed smoothly inland. As the flotilla chugged along, small detachments of the 21st were put ashore at intervals to guard the approaches to the river and prevent ambushes. Soon the 34th Infantry Regiment, which had been following, took over as vanguard of the waterborne advance. By April 21 the soldiers had reached a point almost 35 miles inland, where the road crossed a branch of the Mindanao River at Fort Pikit, an old U.S. Army post. Here they expected trouble. Guerrillas had said that the Japanese had destroyed the steel bridge spanning the river downstream from Fort Pikit, and they had warned that about 800 Japanese with two cannon were dug in around a ferry crossing near the wrecked bridge.

In midafternoon on April 21, the subchasers steaming toward Fort Pikit encountered the wreckage of the bridge, and the Japanese, as expected. The gunners opened up on the enemy positions at the ferry crossing, and the Japanese, startled by the sudden appearance of a river navy, fled at once. Some LCMs (Landing Craft, Mechanized) scooted around the twisted girders of the wrecked bridge and made their way farther upstream to Fort Pikit, which they attacked at close range with automatic-weapons fire and rockets. By the time 34th Infantry Regiment troops went ashore at Fort Pikit in the evening, the Japanese had abandoned it.

Launching the invasion of Cebu, destroyers of the U.S. Seventh Fleet bombard the narrow beach front while amtracs head toward the shore with assault teams of the Americal Division. The landing was for the most part unopposed, but an intricate pattern of land mines planted by the Japanese destroyed or damaged half of the U.S. amphibious vehicles.

The 34th forged ahead, continuing the advance from Fort Pikit by water and also along the highway on the south bank of the river. On April 22, advance elements of the 34th reached Kabakan, a vital road junction near the center of Mindanao. On the next day, as the footsore 19th Infantry Regiment on Highway 1 trailed behind, the main body of the 34th entered Kabakan and, against sporadic opposition, took control of the junction.

It was a major accomplishment. Extending from east-west Highway 1 at Kabakan was Mindanao's other major road, the Sayre Highway, which ran north toward Macajalar Bay. In capturing the junction, the 24th Division had driven a wedge between the Japanese forces in Davao and those on the Sayre Highway.

But the Americans could not afford to slow down. Sibert's X Corps was still racing against the onset of the monsoon season, and the general knew that the first day of rain could dissolve his hard-won gains in mud. To take full advantage of his early progress, Sibert decided to divide his forces. Another division, the 31st, had landed at Parang five days after the 24th. Sibert ordered two regimental combat teams of the 31st to come upriver to Kabakan; one of them was directed to defend the junction and the other was ordered to attack north along the Sayre Highway toward Macajalar Bay. At the same time, Sibert ordered the 24th Division, under General Woodruff, to continue rapidly eastward toward Davao on Highway 1. By now, the Americans had a strong supply line to support their advance; the LCM armada had turned the Mindanao River into an efficient cargo route, and both of the divisions were moving large quantities of supplies into the interior.

Faulty Japanese communications also aided the Americans. The Japanese at Davao learned of the invasion at just about the time that Kabakan was captured. Lieut. General Jiro Harada, commander of the 100th Division, believed that only a small diversionary force had landed at Illana Bay. He remained convinced that the major U.S. assault would come from the sea at Davao Gulf; consequently, he failed to send troops west to intercept the Americans or to set up defensive positions facing westward along the highway.

However, the Americans' drive east was turning into a struggle. Beyond Kabakan there was no smooth river for the 24th Division to ride on; the men had to slog along on foot over the miserable highway. They soon outdistanced their supporting artillery and vehicles and had to carry many of their supplies on their backs. They were forced to take wide detours around burning bridges, and they skirmished again and again with small units of Japanese retreating from the center of the island. And to make their trek even more frustrating, they had to plow through swarms of locusts and endure the perfidy of local inhabitants.

Much of Mindanao was populated by Muslim Moros, the most colorful and perhaps the most independent of the Filipinos. Many of them had cast their lot with Colonel Fertig's guerrillas, and in their tiny fishing vessels, they had carried messages and supplies and agents around the island. To ensure the allegiance of these fierce warriors, Fertig paid them 20 centavos and one bullet for each pair of Japanese ears they brought in. By early 1945, the Moros were delivering Japanese ears by the jar. But some of the Moros proved to be untrustworthy.

On the night of April 24, a Moro tribesman wearing a red turban and carrying a gold and ivory dagger strolled into a 24th Division bivouac and told the company commander that 75 Japanese soldiers were cooking rice or sleeping in a bamboo grove 2,000 yards ahead. The company was alerted; the men pushed stealthily into the bamboo. Suddenly dozens of mortar shells rained in on the GIs. As the Americans withdrew from the trap, a company of Japanese dashed out of a nearby field of grass in a flanking attack. With grenades, spears and fixed bayonets, they routed the surprised GIs, who retreated in disorder.

This piece of Moro treachery made the Americans distinctly leery of the Filipinos they encountered on their march toward Davao. But most of the local inhabitants welcomed them and helped them. Lieutenant Robert Drennan of the 19th Infantry Regiment was passing through a mountain village with his platoon when he was accosted by a shaggy middle-aged man who waved a piece of paper and asked him in English, "Are you from the 19th Infantry?"

"How do you know?" Drennan asked suspiciously.

"Please read the paper, sir," the Filipino said.

The document, dated 1924, granted an honorable discharge from the 19th Regiment in Hawaii to Private Maximo Cabayan. "I am Maximo Cabayan," the veteran proudly

To gain time in their advance toward the Japanese entrenched at the key port of Davao, troops of the U.S. 24th Division avoid a tangled stretch of jungle road by taking to the Mindanao River in Army landing craft. Intended primarily for ship-to-shore use, these shallow-draft craft could travel parts of the river that were impassable to conventional vessels.

declared. "I wish to serve my old outfit." Drennan immediately appointed Cabayan interpreter and scout for the platoon for the duration of the march to Davao.

As the Americans pressed on, they discovered that the Japanese had prepared some unpleasant surprises for them. Besides strewing the roadway with mines, the defenders had made ingenious use of a large stockpile of bombs, otherwise useless to them since they had no planes left. They planted hundreds of the bombs along the highway, burying each one vertically with only an inch of its nose poking above the ground, and strung wires to foxholes in the jungle near the road. Japanese soldiers in the foxholes would wait until the Americans came by, and then pull on the wires and explode the bombs.

As a countermeasure, the Americans brought up mortars and blasted the Japanese on both sides of the roadway before they could trigger the bombs. The buried bombs were then marked with sticks and paper, and the 24th Division troops moved on.

The retreating Japanese used other deadly tricks, as Private Joseph Turner discovered. Turner was walking along a road with a mine-disposal crew when suddenly, as he later recalled, "a 250-pound aerial bomb dropped in front of us. The Japs had rigged up a block and tackle in a tree along the road, hoisted the bomb to the top, and then waited a safe distance away with the end of the rope that held up the bomb." The bomb failed to explode, but to the consternation of the GIs, the Japanese kept tugging on the rope and bouncing the bomb around. A GI shot through the rope with his Tommy gun. Not all the disposal crews were so lucky. While one squad was working to disarm a bomb, it exploded and, said Turner, "nothing was left of the squad except a blackish smear on the tree trunks."

By April 26 the Americans were approaching the town of Digos, where Highway 1 reached the Davao Gulf coast, 20 miles south of Davao City. With only a few days' warning of the American advance, the 3,350 Japanese troops at Digos had little time to turn their eastward-facing coastal defenses around to greet the enemy coming in from the west. After putting up scattered resistance, they withdrew into the foothills 17 miles north of the city. On April 27, advance patrols of the 34th Infantry Regiment swept down Highway 1 into Digos and halted on the shore of Davao Gulf. They had traversed the island in just 10 days.

As the 24th Division poured into Digos and headed north toward Davao along the coastal road, General Harada finally realized that the main American attack was upon him and that he had no hope of holding Davao, which was already a shambles from weeks of American bombing. Harada had one last recourse. West of the city, three or four miles inland from the coastal road, the Japanese had constructed an extensive series of defense works, complete with heavy artillery. Ordering his troops that were falling back from Digos to delay the Americans' progress for as long as possible, Harada and his entire force abandoned Davao and took up positions in the fortifications in the western hills. All of the 13,000 Japanese civilians in Davao fled with them.

Harada's rear guard did their work well. Burned bridges, snipers, roadblocks and hundreds of buried mines slowed the 24th Division's progress northward along the coast. The Japanese had also mined the routes around the demolished bridges. Japanese artillery and mortars hidden in the hills fired on the advancing troops from the flank, and when the Americans moved inland off the road to silence those guns, they ran up against scores of pillboxes, caves and tunnels full of Japanese.

But the obstacles were overcome one by one, and on May 3 the 19th Infantry Regiment gazed across the Davao River at the ruined city. The bridge had been blown out in the center, and both ends were mined. The Americans were stymied, but only temporarily. Under rifle cover, an engineer sergeant named Alfred Sousa swam to the far bank and cut the wires leading to the mines and then defused them. The two ends of the blasted bridge were connected by a makeshift span of logs, ladders, tree trunks and ropes, and infantrymen walked unopposed into the city, Japan's last urban stronghold in the Philippines.

The 24th Division's agonizing march and swift seizure of Davao was a remarkable military achievement. It had been "a gambler's game," General Eichelberger wrote. "We were determined to improvise until enlightening events made the picture clearer. . . . There are times for caution, and there are times for audacity. If the 24th had been cautious, it would not have beaten the rainy season to Davao." Even so, the division still faced heavy fighting: Harada's hill defenses had yet to be breached.

Meanwhile, to the northwest, the U.S. 31st Division had barely begun to tangle with a sizable Japanese contingent holed up along the Sayre Highway. The 31st had waited at the central road junction at Kabakan until the 24th had safely reached the shores of Davao Gulf. Then, on April 27, General Sibert gave the word to go, and the 124th Regimental Combat Team of the 31st Division began its advance north up the Sayre Highway. A few miles beyond the Kabakan road junction, the highway crossed the Pulangi River, a tributary of the Mindanao River. The bridge there was out, but three landing craft of the river fleet had maneuvered up to the crossing, and they ferried the units across.

The advance got under way again just in time. Several

days earlier, the commander of the Japanese 30th Division, Lieut. General Gyosaku Morozumi, had withdrawn his forward forces back toward Macajalar Bay after the fall of Fort Pikit. When no further American advance developed northward for a few days, Morozumi dispatched the 1st Battalion of his 74th Infantry Regiment southward again and ordered it to hold the Pulangi River crossing. At 10 p.m. on April 27, the forward elements of the Japanese battalion ran headlong into the vanguard of the American 124th Regimental Combat Team nine miles north of the crossing.

The unsuspecting Americans were weary, sullen and interested mainly in where they would bivouac for the night. The Japanese soldiers were alert and aggressive—and their automatic-weapons fire almost annihilated the American advance patrol. What followed was a confused battle that raged throughout the night on and around the highway. The Americans managed to hold their ground, and in the morning the Japanese battalion commander was found dead within American lines. The rest of the battalion, its morale apparently shattered, vanished into the underbrush.

Although the clash had involved no more than a few hundred men on each side (10 Americans and 50 Japanese were killed), its significance was great. Had the Americans allowed the Japanese to reach the Pulangi crossing, the Japanese would have been able to hold the river's north bank and cause a dangerous delay in the American advance. As Eichelberger later declared, "Certainly a stalemate at the river would have given Morozumi plenty of time to deploy his troops intelligently and to strengthen his defenses. Undoubtedly, he could have made our progress cruel and costly." Instead, the Americans were safely across the river and moving north toward the town of Kibawe. For several days, all that delayed them was the lengthening of their supply lines and the condition of the highway.

"Sayre Highway was something of a fraud," Eichelberger wrote. "A stretch of 30 miles had never been completed. For ten miles the road proceeded through flat, black river-bottom soil, which baked hard in dry weather and became quagmire in wet weather. This section had been corduroyed, but after three years of neglect the logs had rotted to a pulp. . . . The first one-quarter-ton truck which essayed the journey bogged down of its own weight."

The road—what there was of it—twisted through deep

gorges toward Macajalar Bay. There were 70 bridges in the first 25 miles north of Kabakan, and none of them was intact. Again and again the infantrymen had to slide down one side of a ravine and scramble up the other steep, muddy slope, sometimes in the face of Japanese snipers. One enemy position on the far side of a gorge was taken by surprise simply because the Japanese did not believe that the Americans could make the climb.

Despite the difficult terrain and the scattered opposition, the advance battalion moved so fast that it soon was out of range of supporting artillery and had to be supplied by airdrops. On May 3 the GIs captured the town of Kibawe and a small airstrip where cargo planes could land. There they held up the march until the engineers to the south could improve the road and build the bridges that were needed to bring artillery and heavy equipment forward.

Sometimes, in order to move howitzers or trucks across the yawning gorges, engineers stretched steel cables between huge trees on either side of the ravine. The heavy equipment was hung on the cables with a pulley arrangement and then winched over.

Until bridges could be built, wounded men on stretchers were also hauled across the dizzying ravines on these primitive cable spans. At one ravine that could not be connected by a prefabricated Bailey bridge, engineers using bull-

dozers simply rearranged the landscape. In less than three days they shoved 20,000 cubic yards of fill into the ravine and then built a road across it; the 31st Division's commander claimed that his 106th Engineer Combat Battalion moved more dirt in a shorter amount of time than any other battalion in the War. They also managed to set up 16 Bailey bridges, 65 wooden bridges and hundreds of smaller bypasses—and all of this while fighting periodic skirmishes to beat off Japanese raids.

During the engineers' struggle to bring in heavy equipment, the advance elements of the 124th, probing north on the Sayre Highway, were halted by a series of determined Japanese attacks about 15 miles north of Kibawe. General Morozumi had decided to send the bulk of his forces eastward, into easily defensible mountain terrain. In a last-ditch effort to gain time for the retreat, he launched a series of stabbing attacks that thwarted the American spearhead for six days. Not until May 12, when U.S. artillery arrived at the front and swung into action, did the Americans succeed in shoving the stubborn Japanese off the highway. By this time, additional U.S. forces had arrived on Mindanao, enabling General Sibert to bring even greater pressure to bear. On the 10th of May, the 108th Regimental Combat Team of the 40th Division had landed unopposed on Macajalar Bay on the north coast and pushed southward down the Sayre

Captured Japanese Lieutenant Minoru Wada guides U.S. Marine Corps Mitchell bombers and their Corsair fighter escorts to his division's headquarters on Mindanao. Wada agreed to betray his comrades because they already judged him a traitor for not fighting to the death.

Highway toward a linkup with troops of the 31st Division.

Morozumi's last attempt to hold part of the Sayre Highway came on May 20. Realizing that he could not haul his cumbersome artillery into the difficult terrain to the east, he left all his field guns at the town of Malaybalay. As he and his forces retreated into the mountains, the rear-guard artillerymen made a valiant last stand. They succeeded in stopping the 31st Division—but only for a day. On May 21 the Americans overran the Japanese positions and entered Malaybalay. Two days later, 12 miles to the north of town, patrols from the 31st Division shook hands with men of the 108th Regimental Combat Team who had turned south from Macajalar Bay. All of the Sayre Highway was now in American hands.

The American forces now wheeled eastward in pursuit of Morozumi's retreating troops. Chased by the Americans, hounded by guerrillas, the Japanese units split up and fled deeper and deeper into the rugged rain forests of central Mindanao, where they no longer posed a threat.

In early May, when Davao fell, General MacArthur had announced victory in Mindanao. Tactically he was correct, but as General Eichelberger later observed with a tinge of sarcasm, "there were many hard weeks ahead for the GIs who had no newspapers to tell them that everything was well in hand." Although the 24th Division held Davao port and the adjoining coastline and therefore could bring in supplies and reinforcements at will, the Japanese 100th Division was far from defeated. Despite their lack of air power and supplies, the Japanese managed to establish a formidable defense in the hills northwest of the ruined city. General Harada had skillfully deployed his nine infantry battalions on a defense line approximately 25 miles long, running roughly parallel to the coast about two miles inland. His artillery, machine guns, rockets and mortars were cleverly emplaced.

To get at the Japanese positions, GIs of the 24th had to struggle through abandoned fields of abaca, the source of Manila hemp. The abaca had originally been planted 10 feet apart, but new shoots had filled in the space between plants. The GIs found it harder to wriggle through the abacas than to hack through jungle vines. Combat reporter Jan Valtin wrote that the abacas' "long, lush, leaves are interwoven in a welter of green so dense that a strong man must fight with the whole weight of his body for each foot of progress through this ocean of verdure. In the abaca fields, visibility was rarely more than ten feet. No breeze ever reached through the gloomy expanse of green, and more men—American and Japanese—fell prostrate from the overpowering heat than from bullets. The common way for scouts to locate an enemy position in abaca fighting was to advance until they received machine gun fire at a range of three to five yards. One rifle platoon lost fourteen scouts in the course of the 'abaca campaign.'"

Throughout this weird battlefield, the Japanese had built an intricate network of pillboxes, which, said a 24th Division sergeant, "follow the contour of the ground so that there is absolutely no sign of their presence except the two-inch-wide firing slits. You could walk by one each day for a year and never know it was there unless someone shot at you." The only two ways for a GI to eliminate a pillbox was to toss a grenade into the narrow firing slit or to use a flamethrower. Either way it took an extra measure of courage and a bit of luck.

Sergeant Fred Dalessio had both. He was crawling uphill through an abaca field with a message to his company commander when, he recalled, "I hit a little path and then I looked into the eyes of a Jap two feet away. The Jap was in a pillbox commanding the trail and he was sitting behind a machine gun. I took one big jump and got on top of the position. I thought I'd be pretty safe there until I thought out what I could do. I couldn't lean over and shoot into the opening and I didn't have any grenades. So I hollered to my buddies to throw me a couple of phosphorus grenades. The Jap in the pillbox was firing like mad, but he couldn't get out of it. I tossed the grenades and fried him to a crisp."

By day, the Americans north of Davao inched forward, slowly slashing their way through the abaca fields, dropping mortar and artillery shells on the Japanese emplacements. At night they dug in, strung barbed wire and planted booby traps in front of their lines, and did their best to defend themselves against Japanese infiltrators and occasional nighttime banzai attacks. American patrols found themselves cut off and lost in enemy territory; many men spent days wandering through the bush before finding their lines—and some never got back at all. There was heroism on both sides: lone Japanese standing off whole platoons; lone GIs rushing machine guns. In fighting of this sort a single soldier could make a big difference.

On May 8, Private First Class James H. Diamond and his Company D, part of the 21st Infantry Regiment, crossed to the east bank of the Talomo River to aid in an attack on a formidable Japanese defense line north of Davao. Suddenly, three hidden Japanese pillboxes and a nest of snipers opened up on Company D, hitting some men and knocking them into the stream, and pinning down everyone else on the riverbank. Diamond refused to stay put. He got up, killed the nearest sniper and then, standing in sight of the Japanese, directed artillery fire on the pillboxes.

"He just stood there in the open and pointed his arm at the spots he wanted the armor to hit," said Private First Class Abel Souza, one of Diamond's buddies. "This gave us others a chance to put one of our machine guns into action and Jim came back to us and grinned." And Diamond's heroics were just beginning.

A little later the Japanese knocked out the American machine gun and charged. Said Souza, "Jim Diamond was on his feet again faster than I can say it. He sprayed the Japs with his submachine gun and forced them down until we were set up again for action. After that he called for the tank destroyers to come forward but they wouldn't come. So Jim went back and climbed on the turret of one and showed them where the Japs were dug in, and pretty soon some more pillboxes were knocked out."

On the next morning Diamond's battalion was still hard-pressed. The wounded were piling up and there was no way to transport the casualties across the river to the relative safety of the west bank; Japanese artillery had smashed a temporary bridge. Diamond stood up again and volunteered to carry the wounded across the swift, shoulder-high stream. The other men thought Diamond would never be able to make it across with the first casualty. But he did, and then the others pitched in and helped.

That afternoon Diamond was hit by shell fragments, but still he continued to assist the other wounded men across the river. On the west bank Diamond discovered an abandoned jeep. He put two of the wounded soldiers inside and drove off through a Japanese mortar barrage. Four times Diamond ran the mortar gauntlet and returned, carrying out eight wounded men. Before he was finished, the tires on the jeep were so mangled from shell fragments that the vehicle was riding on its rims.

On the third day of the ordeal on the Talomo, Diamond's battalion was ordered to withdraw across the river to the west bank. A squad was assigned to repair the little wooden bridge, but a sudden and steady Japanese shelling pinned down the repair crew. Once more Diamond volunteered. Souza went with him and the two men, braving the enemy artillery, used broken timbers, rope and a roll of telephone wire to make the bridge passable for one man at a time. That night, the battalion safely crossed the river on the hastily repaired bridge.

A few days later, after the battalion was cut off in another sector, Jim Diamond volunteered to lead a small patrol through 500 yards of bush to evacuate casualties. Halfway to their destination, the GIs were spotted by a Japanese machine gunner and pinned down in what seemed to be a hopeless position. Then Diamond noticed an abandoned machine gun with an ammunition box next to it 50 yards away. He dashed for the gun, apparently intending to turn it on the Japanese and draw their fire so that the rest of the patrol could escape the trap. He had almost reached the gun when a bullet tore into him and he fell to the ground. But his final dash accomplished his purpose. "Though mortally wounded as he reached the gun," said his posthumous Medal of Honor citation, "he succeeded in drawing sufficient fire upon himself so that the remaining members of the patrol could reach safety."

It took nearly five weeks for the Americans to crack General Harada's defenses; not until June 10 did the last organized resistance in the Davao area come to an end. On June 30, General Eichelberger informed MacArthur that operations had concluded everywhere on Mindanao, but the mop-up continued for another six weeks.

The campaign cost the U.S. Army 820 men killed and nearly 3,000 wounded. The Japanese casualties were shocking. Fighting heroically, the Japanese had lost approximately 13,000 men in their futile defense of Mindanao. And it was just this kind of desperate, futile courage that thousands of Japanese were showing in their last major fight in the Philippines—in the jungled mountains of northern Luzon.

THUNDER OVER BORNEO

Huge fires light the sky over an oil field in northwestern Borneo. The retreating Japanese had set fire to the wells in a vain attempt to deny oil to the Allies.

HEAVY FIREPOWER FOR MAKE-WORK ATTACKS

Australian Major-General George Wootten (left) coordinates plans for the assault on Brunei Bay with the U.S. Navy's Rear Admiral Forrest Royal.

In February 1945, General MacArthur decided to liberate the Texas-sized island of Borneo, a British and Dutch possession that had supplied the Japanese with 40 per cent of their fuel oil since they seized it in 1942. MacArthur realized that the U.S. invasion of the Philippines had turned Borneo into just another bypassed Japanese outpost, with both its oil and its 30,000 defenders cut off from Japan. But he reasoned that Borneo would provide new Allied airfields and an ideal Pacific base for Britain's Royal Navy. Of more immediate importance, the invasion would occupy the currently inactive Australian 7th and 9th Infantry Divisions.

Not everyone shared MacArthur's enthusiasm. The British considered Brunei Bay on the northwestern coast too remote for a Naval base and declined to participate. Australia's Army commander, General Sir Thomas A. Blamey, was reluctant to risk his men's lives on such a questionable enterprise and tried to persuade MacArthur to drop or scale down the invasion. But MacArthur had his way.

MacArthur's battle plan called for three separate landings, each preceded by a massive bombardment. Tarakan Island on Borneo's northeastern coast was shelled for four days, and the bombardment of Brunei Bay was three times heavier. Then Balikpapan on the southeastern coast was devastated by the longest bombardment of the War, lasting 20 days. Allied planes dropped 3,000 tons of bombs on the town, and warships of the U.S. Seventh Fleet fired 38,000 shells, 7,300 rockets and some 114,000 small-caliber rounds.

A number of Australians later complained that the bombardments were excessive; one commander observed correctly that "much of the destruction served no military purpose." But there was no disputing the results. The terrific poundings drove the Japanese back from the shore, and the Australian troops—landing at Tarakan on May 1, at Brunei Bay on June 10 and at Balikpapan on July 1—captured all their objectives with minimal fighting. Allied firepower was largely responsible for a startling disproportion in the casualty figures for the campaign: the Japanese dead numbered 5,700—10 times more than the Australians.

A U.S. B-24 completes a bombing run over smoke-shrouded Balikpapan, while landing craft (lower left) carry Australian invasion troops toward the beaches.

Soaked and exhausted, Australian sappers (right) watch from a ship as
their explosive charges blow gaps in Japanese beach obstacles at Tarakan.
In spite of enemy mortar and machine-gun fire, the sappers managed
to clear the beach for the foot soldiers without suffering a single casualty.

A B-25 bomber lays a smoke screen along Tarakan's beach to blind
Japanese gunners. Meanwhile (bottom) Australian engineers wade through
shoulder-deep water and plant demolition charges on steel rails. A
machine gunner on a U.S. Navy gunboat stands by to provide covering fire.

An Australian tank rolls off a cavernous landing ship onto a pontoon
pier laid over the muddy beach. Upon reaching solid ground, another tank
hit a 350-pound Japanese mine and was blown 18 feet into the air.

TARAKAN: OVERCOMING A LETHAL OBSTACLE COURSE

Before the 26th Brigade could go ashore on oil-rich Tarakan Island, Allied engineers had to clear a path through three tiers of barriers. U.S. minesweepers first swept the approach channels of mines. Next, sappers of the Royal Australian Engineers breached four offshore rows of steel rails *(opposite)* laced with booby traps and barbed wire. Finally, American Seabees laid pontoons and causeways across the beaches to keep vehicles from bogging down in the mud.

Then, the Australian infantrymen went ashore—into a series of bitter little battles. The 2,300-man Japanese garrison trapped on the island resisted fiercely, sometimes charging the invaders with bayonets that were tied to the ends of bamboo poles. The Australians lost 225 men killed to win a worthless prize. The island's airfield— the main objective of the landing—was so heavily damaged by Allied bombs that it could not be used to support the later Borneo operations.

Buildings in Brunei Town burn fiercely following a U.S. fire-bomb raid in support of nearby Australian landings in Brunei Bay. Numerous nonmilitary targets

BRUNEI BAY: BATTLES FOR OIL WELLS

Following a day of shelling and saturation bombing, 14,000 troops of the Australian 9th Division poured ashore in Brunei Bay on June 10, landing simultaneously on Labuan Island at the mouth of the bay and near Brunei Town on the mainland. The bombardment had driven the 3,000 Japanese back into the jungle, and not a single Australian casualty was sustained on the beaches. After a visit ashore, MacArthur exulted: "Rarely is such a great strategic prize obtained at such low cost."

Infantry units advanced overland to capture two major oil fields at Seria and Miri. Here, the retreating Japanese had ignited more than 300 oil wells, and the Australians turned to fire fighting. It took all of their equipment, plus the ingenious use of artillery and bulldozers, to extinguish the oil-fueled infernos.

An American patrol boat searches for Japanese targets as smoke plumes rise 7,000 feet from the burning oil field at Seria. Australian engineers labored for three months to put out the fires in the oil wells.

Invading an island in Brunei Bay, 9th Division troops take cover from snipers fighting a rear-guard action. But the Australians' main opposition was swamps of gluelike mud, which trapped both men and vehicles.

were destroyed, including Brunei's cinema and marketplace.

Sustaining the massive shelling at Balikpapan, Australian signalmen (top left) radio the map coordinates of enemy positions to their comrades. Crewmen (bottom left) cover their ears as a shell hurtles from the tube of their 4.2-inch mortar. At right, shirtless artillerymen fire their 25-pounder at Japanese targets shrouded in smoke from burning oil tanks.

BALIKPAPAN: RAGING SHEETS OF FIRE

As 21,000 men of the Australian 7th Division prepared for an assault on Balikpapan, a phalanx of Allied commanders—including General MacArthur—assembled to ob-

serve the landing. One reason for their interest was the possibility that the 4,000 Japanese in the garrison would try out new tactics they were believed to be preparing for the expected invasion of Japan.

But the defenders did not have a chance to try anything. The long Allied bombardment had leveled the port area, and when the slouch-hatted Australians came ashore they found only 10 live defenders, lying dazed or wounded on the beach. Nearby, the bodies of 460 Japanese soldiers lay next to wrecked pillboxes and caved-in trenches. Many of the Japanese had died in a strange fire storm: burning oil from bombed storage tanks had flooded streets and blown up ammunition dumps, and the explosions had driven flaming sheets of oil into Japanese positions.

The battered survivors fell back into the hills beyond Balikpapan. Eventually they were routed out with 42,000 rounds of 25-pound artillery and 14,000 shells from off-shore cruisers and destroyers.

A 7th Division infantryman fires into a Japanese trench system guarding damaged oil tanks near Balikpapan. The Japanese lost roughly 1,800 men killed in the Balikpapan invasion, compared with 229 Australian dead.

Emerging effortlessly from an antitank ditch near Balikpapan, an Australian Matilda tank pushes inland in pursuit of retreating Japanese. The defenders had planned to fill the 14-foot-wide ditches with burning oil, but Allied bombers destroyed the oil tanks in the 20-day preliminary bombardment.

6

In February 1945, when the U.S. Eighth Army launched its great sweep through the southern Philippines, General Yamashita and his remaining forces on Luzon were bracing to meet an assault by the Sixth Army under the command of General Krueger. Yamashita had no hope for victory and was fighting for only one objective—time. His aim was to tie up American troops—as many as possible for as long as possible—and thereby give Japan breathing space to prepare for invasions ever closer to the home islands.

The old warrior had skillfully organized his last-ditch stand. He had started work back in November of 1944. In December he moved his headquarters and José Laurel's puppet government from Manila to the mountain resort of Baguio in north-central Luzon. During the U.S. invasion of Luzon in January, he completed the evacuation of Manila, having deployed some 275,000 troops in mountain strongholds. Under his personal command was a force named the *Shobu* Group (the name celebrates the military art), numbering about 152,000 men.

Although he lacked sufficient ammunition and supplies, his mountain defenses were strong enough to withstand a long, large-scale assault, and behind them lay the fertile Cagayan Valley, whose crops could feed his troops for months. Yamashita settled back and waited for the enemy to launch an attack.

Yamashita's plan for a protracted resistance in northern Luzon received invaluable help from an unexpected quarter, his enemy. Even as MacArthur ordered the Sixth Army to eliminate Japanese resistance on Luzon, he prolonged that effort by transferring the equivalent of three divisions from the Sixth Army to the Eighth Army for the southern Philippines operation. Consequently, General Krueger lacked the manpower to do his job promptly. And Krueger knew that each day of delay was another day for the Japanese to solidify their defenses.

Krueger's toughest job was to destroy Yamashita's big *Shobu* Group in the north. But a smaller group, known as the *Shimbu* (for martial spirit), presented a more immediate threat. Its forward line lay less than 15 miles east of Manila, close enough for a Japanese counterattack or a long-range artillery barrage on the capital. More important, the *Shimbu* forces, which controlled vital dams and aqueducts, had cut

YAMASHITA'S LAST STAND

off much of Manila's water supply, leaving the capital vulnerable to epidemics. To eliminate these dangers, Krueger on February 15 ordered an offensive to capture the dams and push back the *Shimbu* forces.

The operation was misguided and prolonged by two U.S. intelligence failures. Sixth Army intelligence estimated that the *Shimbu* Group numbered only 20,000 soldiers; its actual strength was about 50,000. As a result of this error, only two divisions of the XIV Corps were sent against the Japanese. Secondly, the Americans attacked the wrong dam. Of the two major dams in river valleys behind the Japanese lines, only one, the Ipo Dam on the Angat River, supplied water to the capital. The other, the Wawa Dam on the Marikina River, had been abandoned as a supplier to the capital in 1938. Intelligence officers, misled by out-of-date information, believed that pipelines still connected the Wawa Dam to the city and thus considered it an essential target; because it was closer to Manila than the Ipo, Krueger decided to capture it first.

The Wawa Dam blocked the twisting Marikina River in the Sierra Madre, a mountain range approximately 12 miles northeast of Manila. On the western slopes of the Sierra Madre, at the edge of Luzon's central plain, Japanese units of the *Shimbu* Group held a line 30 miles long. In order to get at the Japanese positions, the XIV Corps troops would have to advance eastward from Manila across an expanse of valley riceland completely exposed to Japanese in the heights. The only cover for the Americans was a line of low hills in the valley, and there the troops assembled, out of sight of the enemy.

"From the crest of the ridge the infantry and cavalry could look across the hot, dry, rice paddies to the Sierra Madre," the U.S. Army history of the campaign said. "The mountains looked ominous—you knew the Japanese were in them, but you couldn't see them: you knew on the other hand that they'd be able to see you all too well as you started across the valley. The prospects were thoroughly unpleasant."

On the U.S. right flank, two regiments of the 2nd Cavalry Brigade crossed over the hills on February 20 and, to their surprise, traversed the exposed valley against little opposition. But the Japanese were merely waiting until the Americans came within close range of their formidable mountain defenses. And three days later, when the cavalrymen moved up the slopes of the Sierra Madre, their rapid advance ground to a halt against the Japanese main line of resistance. From then on, for nearly two weeks, the cavalrymen measured their daily advance in feet.

The Japanese had devoted months to preparing these mountain defenses—which were as formidable a series of obstacles as any in the Philippine campaign. They consisted primarily of deep caves in the hillsides with man-made tunnels leading from a main shaft to numerous exits on the slopes. The Japanese fought with rifles and machine guns and sometimes mortars at the mouths of these horizontal tunnels, and then, when attacked, scurried back to the main shaft to pop up at another exit.

It took time and daring to eliminate each position. Bombs and artillery barely damaged the caves—unless a lucky direct hit could be made on a tunnel entrance—but a heavy barrage would keep the Japanese underground. The moment the shelling or bombing stopped, demolition men would sneak up to one of the entrances and toss in searing white phosphorus grenades or roast the aperture with flamethrowers to make sure no Japanese would poke his head out. Then they would ignite several hundred pounds of TNT at the opening. One by one they blew up and sealed off the tunnels and then detonated explosives in the main shaft, suffocating the Japanese inside. During one 48-hour period, the cavalrymen sealed off 137 cave complexes.

To the north of the cavalrymen's advance, the American 6th Infantry Division, which crossed the valley on February 22, was encountering similar problems. Steep mountains blocked its way. In addition to cave defenses, the Japanese troops on the mountains had plenty of artillery, including 75mm and 105mm pieces as well as naval guns and rockets. Concentrated Japanese fire brought the American advance to a standstill. An American infantry battalion, supported by the massed firepower of five U.S. artillery battalions, repeatedly forced its way up the slope of a mountain during the day, only to be pushed back to the valley at night when the Japanese fire intensified.

One evening the Japanese gunners spotted an American artillery position and opened fire on it. The Japanese shells hit the American gasoline dump, and the resulting fire not only threatened a battery but also gave the Japanese observers a brightly illuminated target for them to shoot at.

Two bulldozer drivers, ignoring the flying shrapnel and the threat of explosions, managed to extinguish the blaze by heaping dirt on it. But by then the Japanese guns were zeroed in, and their shells continued to fall in and around the battalion's position. Under cover of darkness the battalion moved its guns to a new position, leaving behind a battery of dummy weapons of wood and canvas. To complete the deception, a wiring device was rigged up to detonate powder flashes in the dummy positions. For several days the Japanese wasted their ammunition trying to knock out the wooden guns.

By March 22, a month after the campaign had begun, the Americans had penetrated only a few miles into the Sierra Madre, and the Japanese still controlled the Wawa Dam. By then, the 43rd Division had replaced the weary calvary on the *Shimbu* front and General Hall's XI Corps had taken over command of the campaign to capture the dam.

There was a brief, heady moment when Hall thought that the opposition was collapsing. Lieut. General Shizuo Yokoyama, the commander of the *Shimbu* Group, decided to strengthen his positions near the Wawa Dam by sacrificing his left, or southern, flank, which he believed was dangerously vulnerable. He ordered the troops in the southern segment of the *Shimbu* line to withdraw to new positions around the Wawa. As they did so, one hill after another fell to the surprised Americans.

General Hall, encouraged, pressed his men on, but their quick gains ceased as they came up against the strengthened Japanese positions around the dam. Compressed in an area less than three miles wide, the Japanese fought more stubbornly and effectively than ever.

Again and again the Americans hurled themselves against these defenses. Three regiments attacked from the south and the west, but the Japanese moved swiftly to meet each threat. Some of the toughest battles were fought on a hill that GIs called Woodpecker Ridge because of the incessant chatter of the scores of Japanese machine guns deployed there. The front line seesawed back and forth, and an advance of a half mile in a week was considered progress.

As the battle raged on into mid-April, General Krueger somehow discovered, finally, that the Wawa Dam was not a source of water for Manila and that he had expended all this time and manpower attacking the wrong target. He broke the news to MacArthur, whose headquarters then checked with Manila city engineers; they confirmed the mistake. On April 22, two months after the attack on the Wawa Dam had started, General MacArthur radioed Krueger that the Ipo Dam was "the preferred objective" and that its capture

Luzon guerrilla leader Marcos "Marking" Agustín (left) issues orders to his men for the taking of Japanese-held Ipo Dam (right), the most important of Manila's water sources. The guerrillas, operating as a regiment in conjunction with the U.S. 43rd Division, were originally assigned only a diversionary role in the attack. But Marking moved against the main Japanese force, in keeping with his dictum, "Nobody has to give me permission to fight."

would solve Manila's water shortage. The 43rd Division was immediately transferred from its positions south of the Wawa Dam and dispatched to launch a new attack on the Ipo Dam, 12 miles north of the Wawa. Since the American units were already spread too thinly, this promised even greater problems for the men on the front.

The shift of emphasis left the battered 6th Division alone in the struggle to eliminate the Japanese force around the Wawa Dam. It was not until the 30th of April that the weary division was taken from the line and replaced by the 38th Division. In the two months and 10 days since the attack on the *Shimbu* had begun, the 6th Division had lost 335 men killed and 1,000 wounded, and three times as many as that had been evacuated from the front with injuries, illnesses and combat fatigue. The 38th took up the fight—not for water but to destroy the Japanese. More than three weeks of grinding combat remained before the last of the Japanese finally loosed their grip on the hills around the Wawa Dam. By then, another savage struggle was under way for "the preferred objective," the Ipo Dam.

The Ipo Dam lies on the winding Angat River in the rugged Sierra Madre about seven miles east of Luzon's central plain. From the edge of the plain, the Japanese defense line swung in a rough arc through hills southwest of the dam; the strongest fortifications straddled Highway 52, the main road northeast from Manila to Ipo, which twisted along an easily defended corridor in the rocky hills.

Since the highway seemed too risky as an avenue of attack, Major General Leonard F. Wing, the 43rd Division's commander, chose a rough overland approach from the south, where Japanese defenses appeared to be the weakest and where he hoped he could achieve the greatest surprise. To avoid tipping off the Japanese, he decided against sending reconnaissance patrols into the area, even though the terrain was unknown and the attack was scheduled for the middle of the night. The 103rd Infantry and 172nd Infantry, attacking abreast from the south, would be guided only by the flare of white phosphorus artillery shells fired on their initial objectives. At the same time, the 169th Infantry would "demonstrate" along Highway 52, not with the hope of breaking through the heavy defenses but merely to keep the Japanese guessing about what direction the main attack was coming from.

General Wing also had at his disposal the crack guerrilla regiment led by Colonel Marcos "Marking" Agustín. Wing ordered Marking's guerrillas to make a sweep through the mountains north of the Ipo Dam as a feint to further con-

fuse the Japanese. Wing expected no significant results from the guerrilla operation and therefore provided it with little artillery or air support.

Guided by the eerie flashes of the white phosphorus shells, the men of the 103rd and 172nd jumped off at 10 p.m. on May 6 and made good progress through the night and the next day. Only a few scattered and surprised Japanese outposts offered any resistance, and they were quickly overrun. By dusk of May 7 the men of the two regiments found themselves advancing rapidly over a strange, seemingly uninhabited landscape. "Even on the brightest days," the official history related, "the entire region bore an oppressive, weird aspect. Wildly tossed rock outcroppings were the pervading feature. Some stretching horizontally across the land, some pyramiding dizzily to sudden, jumbled heights, these dark grayish outcroppings and sharp pinnacles looked like the product of a fantastic nightmare."

The Japanese were caught off balance by the attack. General Yokoyama was trying to mount a counterattack in the Wawa Dam area, and some of the troops in the Ipo vicinity were on their way south to join this assault when the 43rd Division struck toward the Ipo Dam. The Japanese fell back, and by the evening of May 7 the 103rd Infantry Regiment had reached the main Japanese line south of Ipo. Meanwhile, Marking's guerrillas had swiftly traversed seven miles of mountains on the north of the Angat to come within two miles of the dam. The Japanese main defense line—and the beginning of the monsoon rains—slowed the advance somewhat, but by May 11 the 103rd as well was within two miles of the Ipo Dam.

At this point, General Wing suddenly took note of the guerrillas' progress. As the Army history put it: "What had started out as a feint, from which no significant results were necessarily expected, now bid fair to become as much a part of the main effort as the 103rd Infantry's drive north. The attack toward Ipo Dam had developed into a full-fledged double envelopment. Indeed, a race for the dam was on between the Marking Regiment and the 103rd Infantry."

On May 12, for the first time, General Wing assigned a normal measure of artillery support to the guerrilla regiment. The guerrillas, less hampered by the torrential rains than the more heavily laden and mechanized Americans, promptly broke through the Japanese defense line north of

the river and reached a hill just a mile north of the Ipo Dam. That in itself would not have decided the battle, but on the same day Major General Osamu Kawashima, the local commander at Ipo, received a set of disastrous orders from Yokoyama. Owing to poor communications, General Yokoyama did not know that a reinforced U.S. division was attacking Ipo Dam, and when his counterattack against the 38th Division collapsed on May 12, he ordered Kawashima to send a battalion south again for another assault against U.S. forces in the Wawa Dam area. Kawashima, his defenses at the Ipo Dam in danger, tried to persuade Yokoyama to change his mind, but the *Shimbu* Group commander refused to rescind the order. Reluctantly, Kawashima ordered a battalion to withdraw from the front and move east to assemble for the new counterattack in the Wawa area.

The redeployment of the Japanese battalion proved to be just as disastrous as General Kawashima had feared. As his line began to crumble, Kawashima, defying Yokoyama's orders, commanded the battalion to return to its original place in the line. But it was too late: the 103rd Infantry Regiment had swept over the battalion's positions and occupied a hill less than three quarters of a mile south of the Ipo Dam. The men of the Japanese battalion fought courageously to regain their hill, but the Americans held firm.

On the night of May 13, Marking and his guerrillas won the race for Ipo Dam. With Japanese attention riveted to the south, a guerrilla patrol slipped down the mountain from the north and crossed the dam. The patrol was too small to hold the position, however, so the guerrillas returned to the hill above the Ipo.

For the next three days, while heavy rain grounded air strikes and air supply missions for the American regiments, artillery took over the task of blasting the Japanese. Between May 15 and 17, more than 9,500 shells slammed into the tightening circle of Japanese positions around Ipo Dam. On the 16th the weather cleared slightly and Fifth Air Force fighter-bombers roared in over the jumbled hills in the biggest raid yet on the *Shimbu* positions. First, 185 fighter-bombers dropped 50,000 gallons of napalm on the Japanese lines overlooking Highway 52. Then more planes bombed and strafed artillery batteries farther up the highway and nearer the dam. On the following morning 240 fighter-

To burn Japanese defenders out of the caves surrounding the Ipo Dam, low-flying Fifth Air Force P-38s drop bombs containing napalm—a highly incendiary gasoline gel. Each napalm fire bomb ravaged a 70-by-150-foot area and sent up a column of smoke more than half a mile high. In order to be able to see their targets, successive pilots had to make an upwind approach and drop their bombs on the near side.

bombers spread another 62,500 gallons of napalm on the approaches to the dam.

The devastating air strikes enabled the 169th Infantry to step up its diversionary actions to a full-scale assault along the highway on May 17. The 103rd and the 172nd Infantry Regiments and the guerrillas also attacked, driving steadily through the mud past piles of burned Japanese corpses. General Kawashima, realizing that he could no longer hold the dam, ordered his troops to retreat to the east. They left so quickly that they failed to set off the demolition charges that had been prepared at the dam.

In midmorning of May 17 a patrol of the 103rd slithered down the slopes to the southern end of the dam, only to withdraw on finding no friendly forces in the area. A few hours later, from the other side, guerrillas reached the dam for the second time, waded across the river and raised an American flag above the power station on the south bank. Spotting the flag, another 103rd Infantry unit went down to the dam and found the guerrillas in firm control of both sides. Manila's water crisis was finally ended.

In the meantime, the Japanese defenses were collapsing on the Wawa front. Engineers of the 38th Division managed at last to bulldoze new roads that enabled medium tanks, flamethrower tanks and half-tracks with multiple .50-caliber machine guns to join in the assault. The large mobile flame-throwers burned out the remaining Japanese caves, and on May 21 enemy resistance began to crumble. By May 27, General Yokoyama realized that with Ipo gone he could not hold Wawa either, and he ordered the remnants of his *Shimbu* force to melt away to the mountains to the east. There, in the weeks that followed, they were contained and slowly worn down.

In northern Luzon, meanwhile, General Swift's I Corps had been engaged in a long series of grinding battles against General Yamashita's main *Shobu* Group. The terrain in the north was even more rugged than the mountains east of Manila, the enemy was just as determined and the short-age of American troops was even more pronounced. After Krueger had lost three divisions to the Eighth Army in February and reshuffled the remainder, General Swift was left with only three divisions plus a guerrilla equivalent of one division—a total combat force of about 70,000 men,

wholly inadequate for dealing a prompt and decisive defeat to the 140,000-man *Shobu* Group.

The Japanese forces were facing Innis with their backs to their Cagayan Valley food supply. The valley, 40 miles wide and about 150 miles long, lay open to the sea on Luzon's north coast, but on the west and south it was separated from the central plain by some of the steepest and highest mountains of the Philippines, the Central Cordillera and the Caraballo range. General Yamashita prepared his main defenses in these mountains, taking great pains to guard the passes that the Americans would have to break through in order to reach the valley. The most sensible approach for the Americans would have been an amphibious landing on the north coast, but ships necessary for that task could not be spared from the campaign in the southern Philippines. Krueger's Sixth Army would have to take the valley the hard way—over the mountains.

Late in February, the I Corps launched a three-pronged attack against the *Shobu* mountain stronghold. On the left

Recently outfitted in new U.S. uniforms, a group of Filipino guerrillas from Colonel Russell W. Volckmann's force pause for a meal of GI rations during their drive toward Baguio with the American 33rd Division. The guerrillas protected U.S. supply lines and also secured the coastline around the strategic port town of San Fernando. "With very limited means at their disposal," said the Sixth Army's commander, General Krueger, "the gallant Filipino forces rendered invaluable support to our operations."

flank the 33rd Division began probing attacks northeast toward Baguio, the resort town where Yamashita had established his headquarters. In the middle, the 32nd Division struck northward along the Villa Verde trail, a dusty, narrow track leading to the passes guarding the Cagayan Valley. And on the right flank the 25th Division started a major push, also to the north, along Highway 5, the main road through the passes to the valley.

It fell to the 33rd Division to take Highway 11, a paved roadway hugging the sides of spectacular gorges and leading to Baguio. The Japanese expected a major American effort to be made on the highway, and their artillery and mortars were zeroed in on every turn of the road. American artillery and planes found it almost impossible to get at the Japanese guns, for they were well concealed in caves 200 to 500 feet above the highway. Observation planes flew constant patrols, looking for Japanese artillery flashes, but the Japanese gunners merely waited until the planes were gone, then wheeled their fieldpieces out of a cave, fired a few rounds and rolled the guns back in again before the pilots could locate them.

Most of the fighting took place on the steep, wooded hills on both sides of the road, which had to be scaled to knock out concealed Japanese machine guns and artillery positions that stopped the GIs' progress along the road.

One of the hills that blocked the route to Baguio was named Question Mark Hill after its shape, and it was an unforgettable place for the men of I Company of the 130th Infantry, 33rd Division. As Item Company (i.e., I Company) moved out to attack, its commanding officer, Captain Alan J. Kennedy, discovered that his men were down to about a third of a canteen of water each. Since his map showed a stream ahead, he was not too concerned. But the stream turned out to be dry—and by then it was too late to go back, for another company, also advancing, was depending on Item Company's support. Kennedy's men had nearly reached the crest of Question Mark Hill when the Japanese spotted them and pinned them down with heavy fire. Ken-

nedy was ordered by radio to hold fast until ammunition—and water—could be sent up in the morning.

That night, the Japanese on the crest again opened fire with machine guns and mortars, and attacked down the hill. American artillery fire, called in by Kennedy, stalled the Japanese attack. As Kennedy returned to his command post, said the division's battle report, "every man he passed enroute offered some evidence of the torture caused by the lack of water. Some lay in their foxholes and sucked in huge gulps of air to ease the pain of their aching throats. Others attempted to keep up their strength by downing a D-ration, but the sounds of their retching and vomiting was sickening as the rich chocolate clogged their parched throats. The sporadic moans of the wounded only added to the general hellishness of the situation."

Kennedy radioed battalion headquarters that his company could not function unless it got water, but carrying parties were unable to get through. An airdrop of water was promised for early in the morning, but at dawn Kennedy found that the Japanese had infiltrated machine guns between his two lines and threatened to decimate his company if the men so much as budged.

At 8:30 a C-47 zoomed across Item Company's hillside position dropping crates and containers. "Half crazed riflemen braved enemy fire to sprint out and recover the precious supplies," the battle report continued. "As the last piece was carried to the CP, a collective cry of sorrow escaped every man's lips. Not a drop of water had been kicked out of the plane." Kennedy demanded another airdrop and the C-47 returned. This time the parched troops could see the five-gallon cans dangling under the parachutes—all of which landed in Japanese positions. The men of Item Company, now without water for 20 hours, wept.

All day, Able Company, leading a water-carrying party, tried to break through to Item's position. A Japanese machine gun killed the sergeant in charge of Able's lead platoon, and the noncom who took over was gunned down a few minutes later. A lieutenant from a reserve platoon rushed up to take command. Then the Japanese on Question Mark Hill started lobbing mortar shells on Able Company, and the company commander decided that, despite the risk to the men of Item near the crest, he would have to call in howit-

zer fire to silence the mortars. While Kennedy's men huddled in agony in their foxholes, the artillerymen in the rear carefully computed the angles and ranges and managed to knock out several of the Japanese mortars.

Late in the afternoon the relief company finally broke through the Japanese lines and converged on Item's perimeter. "A pitiful sight greeted them there," reported the division history. "Several men were delirious. . . . Others lay unconscious in their holes. The Engineer carrying party came up in a few minutes and gave Item all the water it could drink." Leaving Able Company on the hill, Kennedy's men picked up their wounded and returned to the rear.

After two weeks of this agonizing progress, the 33rd Division troops were completely exhausted. Said the battle report: "Daily spanning of one steep mountain after another lowered the body resistance—to the point where simple fevers removed a large number from the battle. . . . Salt tablets were lifesavers. It took only three or four minutes of steady climbing in the overpowering tropical heat to drench a man in his own perspiration. Sweat seeped through web equipment and leather boots, and sometimes actually bleached M-1 stocks. It was pitiful to see these infantrymen madly rip their clothes with sweat-drenched hands in order to capture an eddy of cool air."

When the wind was in the right direction, the Japanese sometimes sprayed the tall cogon grass with gasoline and set it afire, and choking black smoke was blown into the American lines. In the nearly perpendicular terrain, litter bearers who were bringing the wounded men to an aid station had to struggle up and down slopes for a full day to cover a distance that appeared as only 400 yards on the map. In six weeks of fighting, one regiment of the 33rd Division advanced only 12 miles; then, on April 16, it was hit by a Japanese counterattack.

"For sheer desperation this counterattack was unmatched in the fighting," stated the battle report. "Machine gunners and automatic riflemen cut down the swarms of frenzied enemy as they heedlessly rushed into final protective lines. The shrill battle cries of the Nips and the moans of their wounded could be heard above the roar of battle."

At the height of the attack, one man's reckless bravery turned the tide for the Americans. Private First Class Burton J. Lee emerged from his foxhole with his Browning automatic rifle and walked out to meet the Japanese. "Pausing only to press his magazine release and insert a fresh ammunition load, Lee threw round after round into the tightly packed Japanese ranks, causing the enemy to hesitate and then hit the ground. Lee continued to advance, his weapon active every step of the way." The other GIs "saw Lee suddenly stagger as several puffs of dust showed on the back of his fatigue blouse." He had been hit by light machine-gun fire. "Almost cut in half, Lee didn't fall. Those watching him could see him try to hold his feet with his BAR still spitting fire! Four, five, six yards, firing all the time. Then Lee abruptly dropped his rifle and pitched to the grass, dead." But Lee's reckless last stand served to rally the Americans, and they repelled the enemy counterattack.

As the 33rd Division was pressing its battle up Highway 11, units of the relatively fresh 37th arrived on the scene and launched an attack along Highway 9, which ran from the coast due east to Baguio. This paved road traversed easier, thinly defended terrain, and the men of the 37th Division made good progress.

By the 17th of April, their advance along Highway 9 had reached Irisan Gorge, only three miles from Baguio, where the road, winding along the slopes of steep, rugged ridges, crossed the Irisan River. Because of a twist in the river, five hills overlooked a demolished bridge at the river crossing, and all of the hills would have to be taken before the bridge could be repaired and the main force of the division could cross. Irisan Gorge was the last defensible spot before Baguio, and the Japanese dispatched all their remaining able-bodied troops in the town to hold it.

At this point, Yamashita's position in Baguio was deteriorating fast. Guerrilla harassment of his supply lines and heavy air strikes by U.S. planes had severely reduced the southward flow of food and medicines to his mountain headquarters. Rations for his troops had been cut to less than one quarter of a pound of rice per day, and hospitals had run out of antimalaria drugs. In order to relieve the food shortage, Yamashita had allowed thousands of civilians to leave town; with the help of guerrilla guides, they made their way to the American lines. Yamashita had already sent José Laurel and most of the Philippine collaborationist government to Tokyo, and he now prepared to pull out himself and retreat northward.

On the morning of April 17, the Americans tried to bull their way across Irisan Gorge and race into nearby Baguio. As American tanks nosed around the edge of a ridge, approaching the crossing over the gorge, two of them were knocked out by Japanese antitank guns. The advancing troops were repulsed by machine-gun and small-arms fire from three of the ridges overlooking the gorge. Obviously, a direct assault along the road would not be successful. That afternoon the 37th Division troops began attacking the Japanese-held ridges one by one. For four days they fought and scrambled in a confused and jumbled battle. Troops assaulting one ridge would suddenly come under fire from Japanese positions on a second hill. But the superior American firepower, and the 37th Division's ability to throw fresh troops into the battle, eventually turned the tide. By dusk on the 20th, most of the Japanese in the area had withdrawn to their last ridgeline, which was pounded by air strikes and artillery the next morning. When the GIs moved up the ridge later the same day, they found that the Japanese had fled. The gorge was clear.

With the fall of Irisan, the Japanese withdrew from Baguio, leaving only a delaying force to cover the retreat.

Mustachioed Colonel Russell Volckmann, the often-pursued leader of a Luzon guerrilla group, confers with a high-ranking Filipino officer, Basilio Valdes, during their pursuit of General Yamashita in July 1945. Volckmann was legendary for his hairbreadth escapes. There was a guerrilla saying, "God walks with Volckmann," to which Volckmann once responded, "I hope He doesn't stumble!"

Servicemen queue up to buy a distillery's raw liquor. Two sailors have already drunk too much.

In an old movie theater, an audience of GIs and

LIVING IT UP IN A RESURGENT CAPITAL

While the fighting went on to the north, thousands of servicemen on leave or doing relief work in devastated Manila were having a rousing good time. All sorts of

Americans and their Filipino dates dance to the rhythms of a local band in a crowded nightclub.

WACs enjoys the music of the Manila Symphony Orchestra, conducted by Herbert Zipper. The U.S. Army sponsored such concerts several times a week.

Philippine businesses mushroomed to cater to the soldiers and sailors.

"The impact of the liberators upon the city was simply tremendous," wrote Herbert Zipper, an Austrian who had worked in the capital since 1939 as the conductor of the Manila Symphony and whose Viennese wife, Trudl, painted the watercolors shown on these pages. The servicemen spent fortunes at souvenir shops on "enormous quantities of what was often plain junk," Zipper said, and they patronized the local distillery "any time of the day, any day of the week, rain or shine." By evening, an "ever increasing stream of eager servicemen" was pouring into nightclubs to dance with the local women, who, to the GIs' delight, could jitterbug—even in wooden clogs.

Between the relief work and the prodigal merrymaking, the Americans gave a big boost to the spirits of the war-ravaged citizens. "Manila lived in a fever," Zipper said, "at times in hysterical relief."

General Swift, however, did not know this. Fearing a counterattack on his forces, who were vulnerable because of their long supply lines, Swift ordered both the 37th and the 33rd Divisions to halt. For several days the Americans waited—while approximately 10,000 Japanese troops escaped northward from the city. On April 26, an American patrol finally entered Baguio. Yamashita had lost a sizable link in his mountain defense chain—but still he had managed to tie up the Americans for nearly 10 weeks.

Southeast of Baguio, in the meantime, the two other wings of the I Corps's attack were pushing northward through the mountains toward the Cagayan Valley—the 32nd Division on the Villa Verde trail and, farther to the east, the 25th Division on the main highway, Route 5. General Swift of the I Corps had expected that Route 5 would be the most difficult approach to the valley. The Japanese were known to be defending it in strength, and it led over Balete Pass, one of the best defensive positions in the region. As it turned out, Swift was incorrect.

The Villa Verde trail proved to be much harder. It was merely an ancient footpath over craggy, waterless heights, and its twists and turns were often three to five times longer than a straight-line distance between two points. Furthermore, there were not enough 32nd troops available to do the job. Still, the 32nd Division troops initially moved along at a brisk clip. Meeting only light resistance on the lower reaches of the trail, they approached within 10 miles of the village of Santa Fe, where the trail converged with Route 5, by the first week of March.

The rapid American advance alarmed the regional commandant, Major General Haruo Konuma, and he rushed in reinforcements. At first he could round up only a few miscellaneous companies and understrength artillery units, about 1,000 soldiers in all, but they did manage to delay the 32nd Division until Konuma could bring down the 2nd Armored Division from 15 miles north of Santa Fe. The Japanese division's tanks had been lost during the U.S. drive toward Manila, and the tankmen were being retrained to fight as infantry. Although they were not considered ready for combat, they were heavily armed with automatic weapons and artillery, and they were just as willing as any of their compatriots to die in battle. On March 5, Konuma threw

them into the line on the Villa Verde trail in an area known as the Salacsac passes, and ordered them to hold at all costs. They obeyed their orders well. It ultimately took the 32nd Division more than two months to cross the five miles of the Salacsac passes on the Villa Verde trail.

The terrain of Salacsac was heavily forested, but there were enough open areas to give the Japanese a good view of just about every turn of the trail. On each knoll and hill the troops of the 2nd Armored Division set up at least one machine gun, and every wooded draw through which the Americans might outflank these emplacements was zeroed in for artillery or mortars. Natural and man-made caves dotted the area.

The Salacsac fighting kept repeating a bloody sequence of events. First the Americans would make a frontal assault on a Japanese hill position. If it failed, the GIs would wait for air strikes and artillery fire to soften up the Japanese. Then companies and battalions would attempt to outflank the Japanese, sometimes successfully, sometimes disastrously. This went on, said the official report, "day after dreary day, either in heat enervating to the extreme on clear days, or in cloud bursts, fog and mud. The spectacular could hardly happen—there wasn't enough room—and never did. Troops would become tired and dispirited: nonbattle casualties would exceed those injured in combat. . . . This was combined mountain and tropical warfare at its worst."

The hardships were as great or greater for the Japanese of the 2nd Armored. Tetsuro Ogawa, a Japanese civilian caught up in the Salacsac fighting after retreating from Manila with the troops, reported that "each soldier of this division fought like a wild beast, hiding in a foxhole or cave that was scarcely large enough for one man, eating berries and moss when there was no rice, and being rationed to one canteen of water every three days. When a staff officer of General Yamashita's headquarters visited the front, he saw many soldiers without an eye or an arm. They had been wounded trying to throw back enemy hand grenades, which exploded while still in their hands. The severity of the battle did not permit these wounded soldiers to retreat to field hospitals unless their wounds were 'serious.' "

With its regiments alternating—one of them resting in the rear while the other two were struggling on the trail—the 32nd Division slowly pushed its way across the blasted

THE CAPTURE OF BAGUIO: A NEW BEGINNING AMID THE RUINS

Smiling citizens of Baguio greet a tankload of U.S. infantrymen as the vehicle rumbles through the town's bombed-out, fire-blackened ruins.

Baguio, the mile-high resort town where General Yamashita had his headquarters, fell to the U.S. 33rd and 37th Divisions on April 27, 1945, after a lengthy, grueling campaign. The actual capture of the town was an easy matter, for unbeknown to the Americans, the bulk of Japanese soldiers had already retreated to the north. In fact, the GIs could have marched into Baguio the day before, but their corps commander, knowing that Emperor Hirohito's birthday was April 27, had postponed the takeover in order—as he said—to give Hirohito some bad news as a gift.

On the outskirts of town the GIs found a tunnel that led to Yamashita's abandoned headquarters, an underground complex of more than 40 rooms, decorated with fine furniture and Oriental rugs looted from the nearby summer homes of rich Manila families. But on entering Baguio proper, the soldiers came upon little more than ruins. Persistent U.S. bombing, climaxed by intense shelling, had leveled or gutted most of the elegant villas. Many citizens were homeless and needed medical care.

While the GIs pressed through Baguio in pursuit of the Japanese, U.S. Civil Affairs personnel moved into town and began restoring normal services to the 30,000 inhabitants. Fallen power lines and broken water mains were repaired. The local hospital was stocked with Army medicines, and the jobless were offered work carrying supplies or building roads for the Army.

As a semblance of order started to appear, the U.S. administrator applied a final touch to the liberation. He sought out former mayor Vicsio Valderassa, who had been ousted from office by the Japanese, and turned over to him the reins of municipal government.

landscape. Not until the 28th of May, nearly three months after the drive started, did the depleted regiments of the division push through the Salacsac passes and make contact, close to the junction village of Santa Fe, with friendly forces advancing up Route 5.

By that time, many 32nd Division troops were suffering from combat fatigue and battle neuroses. Morale had plummeted. Replacements were slow to arrive, and many new company-grade and noncommissioned officers were barely qualified for combat command. Frontline veterans, hoping to be rotated back to the U.S., hung back to avoid risking themselves. A number of men deliberately wounded themselves to escape combat. Still the division fought on; in all, 825 men were killed and more than 2,100 wounded on the Villa Verde trail. The Japanese paid a much higher price, losing approximately 5,750 men killed.

The 25th Division, the third arm of the I Corps's three-part assault, was meanwhile nudging its way up Route 5, the main highway from the central plain north to Cagayan Valley. Like the 32nd a few miles to the west, the 25th got off to a rapid and easy start, thanks to the enemy's failure.

The Japanese were so concerned with the movement of one regiment on Highway 5 that they failed to block a flanking maneuver carried out by another regiment, the 35th Infantry. The 35th moved swiftly over a narrow dirt trail in the mountains just to the east of the highway, then turned westward on a side road and attacked the hamlet of Digdig, the 25th Division's first objective along Route 5. The garrison, not prepared for an attack from that quarter, fled to the north, and the Americans occupied the town on March 3. The capture of Digdig put the 25th Division far ahead of schedule.

But the swift gains were deceptive; north of Digdig the Japanese were more dangerous—as General Swift himself found out. The I Corps commander was driving up Highway 5 toward division headquarters above Digdig when a roving group of Japanese opened fire on his staff car from the jungle. Swift and his driver leaped from the car and dived into a ditch. Then the general rounded up half a dozen men and organized a patrol to eliminate the snipers. The GIs were stunned at the spectacle of a two-star general leading a patrol, but they followed Swift into the dense under-

growth. The general's men flushed out and killed three Japanese soldiers, and Swift resumed his trip delighted with his frontline stint.

At about the same time, a sizable battle was raging well beyond Digdig. Colonel Harold Riegelman, a corps staff officer, went forward, up a steep, crooked trail, to observe the performance of the corps mortar battalions. "They were firing at 1,500 yards, alternatively white phosphorus and high explosive. The men were stripped to the waist, their bodies dripping and their trousers soaked with sweat. Each gun was going five to the minute."

Riegelman kept moving ahead to see where the shells were landing, and he quickly drew up at a point where a ridge fell away abruptly to the north. "Before us the tide of battle flowed," Riegelman said. "At our feet the spitting of rifle and machine guns told of infantry storming the heavily jungled slope immediately ahead. The deep pocket beyond the near spur was drenched with howitzer and mortar shells. Howitzers searched the bottom of the pocket and the farther slope; mortars dropped their high explosive and phosphorus shells onto the reverse slope. The phosphorus plumes blended with the darker high explosive smoke. It was hard to believe that life could survive the rain of steel and fire. The reverberations of the guns down the valley and the crump-crump of the explosions up ahead re-echoed from the hills."

Then there was a pause in the din. "The small arms fire was no longer at our feet. The troops had topped the near spur and were down into the purged pocket beyond. The heavy fires lifted into the next pocket. And now I noted that heavier calibers were bursting in the more distant folds and at the tops of farther spurs to rout and blind enemy observation. And so the battle went on—spur after spur, pocket after pocket. Slowly ever nearer to coveted, well defended Balete Pass."

Balete Pass was a saddle 3,000 feet high on the long and jumbled complex of ridges that divided the Cagayan watershed from that of the central plain. The terrain was part of the same ridge system that formed the nearby Salacsac passes on the Villa Verde trail, but the peaks surrounding Balete Pass on Highway 5 were steeper and more thoroughly honeycombed with Japanese artillery caves. Balete Pass was the main gateway to the Cagayan Valley, and the Japa-

A Japanese prisoner stands in humiliation beside the American soldiers who captured him near Baguio in north-central Luzon. Enemy troops who surrendered were usually the wounded, sick or starving who had been left behind by their fleeing comrades. Some bedridden Japanese patients in Baguio and nearby Bayombong were killed by their own doctors to prevent them from falling into the hands of the Americans.

nese had made extensive preparations to hold it. By March 10 the 25th Division was less than five miles from the pass. But it would take two months to cover that distance.

General Charles L. Mullins Jr., the 25th Division commander, tried every possible tactic to bludgeon his way through Balete Pass. Direct assaults on the highway were stopped cold by the Japanese on the craggy ridges overlooking the pass. Flanking maneuvers, successful earlier, came to little avail.

It was not until April 15 that one of Mullins' units accomplished a seemingly minor gain that later proved significant. On the right side of the division line, the 27th Infantry Regiment managed to maneuver three medium tanks onto a Japanese-held hill called Myoko Ridge. The track on the razor-back crest was so narrow that the tank treads sometimes hung over into thin air, but the tanks eventually moved forward, spitting gouts of napalm from their flamethrowers. The Japanese, unequipped to fight tanks on such mountainous terrain, fled as the armored vehicles loomed up out of the forest and bore down on them. Still, this

American success produced an advance of only a few hundred yards in several days.

Late in April, with his forces still more than two miles from Balete Pass, General Mullins was beginning to look for yet another plan of attack when the 27th Infantry suddenly achieved a major breakthrough in the gap opened by the three tanks. While the bulk of the regiment was still attacking Myoko Ridge, Colonel Philip F. Lindeman, the 27th's commander, sent a reinforced platoon through a precipitous ravine between Myoko Ridge and Highway 5. The GIs advanced 2,500 yards without being detected by the Japanese; they had discovered the gap in the Japanese lines and within hours an entire battalion poured through it. The following day the battalion attacked the surprised Japanese on a knob named Lone Tree Hill. Many of the Japanese died in their foxholes without firing a shot; others abandoned their field guns and fled.

Though less than one mile from the pass, the GIs on Lone Tree Hill could not be supplied over the route they had taken, and they had to wait two weeks while the other

regiments caught up to them. In the meantime, the generals on both sides made momentous decisions. General Yamashita, arriving on the Balete front after evacuating Baguio, decided that he had sacrificed enough of his troops in the defense of the pass: of the 12,000 Japanese who had been committed at Balete, only 3,000 troops were left. On May 5, Yamashita ordered the survivors to begin withdrawing northward. At the same time, General Krueger realized that neither the 25th Division nor the 32nd Division on the Villa Verde trail was in shape to exploit the seemingly imminent breakthrough at the pass. So Krueger sent Mullins a regiment of the 37th Division, which had taken part in the capture of Baguio.

Thus reinforced, the 25th Division concentrated its forces for the final push to Balete Pass. On May 9 a patrol from the 27th Infantry, coming up from Lone Tree Hill, reached the highway at the pass, found no Japanese there and soon

made contact with the other regiments. By May 13 the last Japanese in the area had been accounted for and General Mullins declared the pass secured.

From there the advance should have been all downhill, militarily as well as topographically, because the Japanese 10th Division was almost finished as a combat unit. Yet it took two more weeks before the 25th Division reached Santa Fe, the village at the junction of Route 5 and the Villa Verde trail. On May 29, the 25th Division troops finally made contact with the main body of the 32nd Division near Santa Fe, and the battle for the gateway to the Cagayan Valley was over. It had cost the 25th and 32nd Divisions 1,510 infantrymen killed and 4,250 men wounded.

As his defenses crumbled, General Yamashita made desperate attempts to reorganize his forces for flank attacks on the American column that he knew would soon be storming down into the Cagayan Valley. But the Americans moved

General Tomoyuki Yamashita, commander of the Japanese Fourteenth Area Army, leads his faithful staff officers out of the Luzon mountains to surrender on September 2, 1945, the same day Japan itself surrendered. Yamashita abjured the traditional samurai ceremony of hara-kiri in the belief that he had a higher responsibility. "If I kill myself," the general explained, "someone else will have to take the blame."

too fast. The depleted 25th and 32nd Divisions were yanked from the line, and the 37th Division, which had made the fast thrust into Baguio a month earlier, was dispatched to seize the Cagayan Valley. With its regiments taking turns in the lead, the 37th Division dashed north on Highway 5 in a movement reminiscent of the 1st Cavalry Division's "Flying Column" attack on Manila in early February. Within two weeks, brushing off a few antitank charges by suicidal Japanese demolition men, elements of the division reached the flatlands of the Cagayan Valley itself, 75 highway miles beyond Santa Fe.

They found much of the valley already controlled by the 11th Infantry, a unit of Colonel Russell Volckmann's guerrilla force in northern Luzon. Major Don Blackburn, the 11th's leader, had several thousand well-armed men in his command, and he controlled the entire west bank of the Cagayan River running through the valley, except for a small Japanese enclave near Aparri, at the river's mouth. Blackburn had even repaired an old airstrip in the center of the valley so that C-47 cargo planes could supply his forces. American fighter and bomber pilots often landed there, too, to refuel—or to pick up war souvenirs. Volckmann, who flew to the strip frequently while the Japanese were still active a few miles away, later recalled: "On several of my visits I was quite concerned to find as many as 10 to 15 planes parked along the runway. The lure of souvenirs such as Japanese Samurai swords, flags, and other items, as well as the unusual surroundings and the different food, were welcome changes in the boring routine of these combat airmen." The guerrillas did a lively business in trophies, which Blackburn discreetly put thus: "The 11th, of course, benefitted in terms of special supplies and equipment that they could not get through regular channels."

In mid-June, Blackburn's guerrillas found themselves at the center of the action. From the south, the 37th Division continued its dash down the valley. In the north, a U.S. Ranger task force that had swept all around Luzon's west and north coasts joined with one of Blackburn's battalions for an assault on the Japanese base at Aparri. And on June 21, Krueger, mistakenly believing that the Japanese were congregating at Aparri, ordered an airborne assault on the town in order, as he put it, "to close the trap and prevent the enemy from all possibilities of escaping from Aparri."

The Japanese, retreating northward to the mountains, had no intention of getting caught in the cul de sac of Aparri. There were just a few Japanese there, and on the day that Krueger ordered the airborne attack, Blackburn's guerrillas and the Ranger task force wiped them out. On June 23, when a battalion combat team of the 11th Airborne Division parachuted into the area, it was greeted by Rangers and guerrillas. Blackburn considered the airborne operation a public-relations show and grudgingly played along with it. "The guerrillas," Blackburn said later, "cleaned up the airstrip they had captured and ruffled up the cogon grass they had trampled to make it look nice and fresh for the photographers. Then they took up positions from which they could defend the airstrip just in case any Japs returned. These positions were carefully concealed so that the paratroops, who had not been informed that they were capturing a town that had been taken, would not mistake the guerrillas for Japs."

On June 26, elements of the 37th Division linked up with paratroop patrols. The Cagayan Valley was won, and General MacArthur, as he had with the southern campaign, announced, somewhat prematurely, the end of the northern Luzon campaign. There were still six weeks of fighting ahead, for Yamashita and the survivors of his *Shobu* force had simply retreated into the high Central Cordillera west of the Cagayan Valley. All through the summer guerrilla units and three American divisions, having surrounded the last Japanese pocket, kept attacking, slicing up the Japanese stronghold and forcing Yamashita to move his headquarters.

Yamashita and his ragged troops were growing desperate. Their food and medical supplies were running out; they had little ammunition left. But they marshaled their meager resources and continued to fight bitterly for every ravine and ridge. Even though their cause was lost, they struggled on to fulfill their final mission—pinning down American troops who they feared might otherwise walk the streets of a conquered Tokyo.

Elsewhere in the Philippines thousands of other isolated Japanese troops found themselves in the same situation as Yamashita and his men on Luzon—starving, hunted and with little hope of survival. For all their courage and tenacity, the Japanese had suffered, in the words of MacArthur, "an unbroken series of crushing defeats."

THE MAKESHIFT ARMY

Mindanao guerrillas look up to their leader, Captain Donald LeCouvre, mounted on their only horse. He was an Army officer who refused to surrender in 1942.

ELUSIVE LEGIONS OF BAREFOOT FIGHTERS

When the fighting in the Philippines was over, the United States owed a large debt to the guerrillas throughout the islands who had resisted the Japanese during the years of occupation and fought with the Americans after the invasion. "If we have to die, let us die fighting," was the sentiment that had united tens of thousands of them after the fall of Corregidor. People of every background—Catholics, Muslim Moros, pagan tribesmen—joined forces with fugitive American and Filipino officers to form a barefoot army that eventually controlled more Philippine territory than the Japanese. Most Filipinos who did not join the fight supported the guerrillas in every way they could. A U.S.

intelligence report said of one island's guerrilla leader: "All Cebu is behind him. All the Japs in Cebu are after him."

Before the invasion, guns were hard to come by—in many guerrilla groups only one man in five had a rifle. One outfit ingeniously fashioned .30-caliber bullets by cutting up brass curtain rods, filing the ends to a solid point, then filling the cartridges with gunpowder filched from Japanese mines and priming them with a homemade mixture of sulfur and the carbon from coconut shells. Unfortunately, these bullets took so long to manufacture that 60 men could turn out only about 160 a day.

Until American aid arrived, most guerrillas had to make do with the islands' traditional weapons: bolos, and bows and arrows—sometimes with arrowheads dipped in poison. But right up to the end of the fighting the guerrillas' best weapons remained, as one of them put it, "silence, invisibility, and speed."

Former enemies, a couple of Muslim Moros wearing turbans stand united with Catholic members of a guerrilla group on Mindanao. Thanks to the Philippines' rich ethnic mixture, one guerrilla outfit was composed of Chinese, while other groups had primitive tribesmen serving as bearers.

Using a native outrigger as a dock for an American landing craft, a chain of Filipinos unloads guns and ammunition that are earmarked for the guerrillas. Before the U.S. invasion, submarines smuggled in more than 1,600 tons of supplies to support clandestine Filipino guerrilla activities.

Practicing parries with razor-sharp bolos, two guerrillas attract an audience of comrades on Leyte. The Japanese had ordered the surrender of all deadly weapons.

Guerrillas on Leyte inspect American firearms that will be ferried to a resistance group fighting on Luzon.

Planning an attack, barefoot guerrillas and their booted officer locate Japanese positions on a captured map.

Backing the invasion of Leyte, guerrillas in search of Japanese fugitives close in on a suspicious house. The photographer was later killed by a Japanese sniper.

A Luzon guerrilla hauls supplies behind a woman comrade credited with killing seven Japanese.

JUNGLE SPECIALISTS IN HIT-AND-RUN ATTACKS

Though many guerrilla groups undertook joint operations with the GI invaders, most were essentially hit-and-run freelancers, relying on guile and speed to make up for their lack of conventional military training. Lieut. Commander Charles "Chick" Parsons, MacArthur's chief liaison officer to the resistance movement, called the typical guerrilla "a jungle fighter, pure and simple," but added, "he is a specialist in his own line and as a guerrilla he is, in my opinion, the best in the world."

Operating in small units, the guerrillas would strike from ambush, pick up the dead enemy's guns and ammunition, and be gone before Japanese reinforcements could arrive. In a standard ambush, the guerrillas would take cover on both sides of a trail, often at a narrow defile, and hit a patrol as it passed below them. They would attack truck convoys in much the same manner. When the men on one side of the road fired a few shots, the Japanese would pile out of the trucks and into the ditch on the far side of the road. There the other guerrillas would dispatch them, often with their bolos.

Such attacks by many units confused the local Japanese garrisons. One small guerrilla force, the Headhunters, was so active and elusive that its headquarters was never attacked even though the Japanese knew the location. "Too many guerrillas," said a Japanese officer. "Ten thousand of them."

On every island, the guerrilla groups put out a maximum effort to coincide with the American invasion. Their all-out attacks—the bridges they blew up, the communications lines they cut and the airfields they seized—did more than just help the GIs. "Beyond the shadow of a doubt," said the official Army history of the Philippine campaign, "the guerrillas saved many thousands of American lives."

Meeting with two guerrilla chieftains to thank them for their help, General Douglas MacArthur is introduced by the pistol-packing Governor of Jolo to the venerable Sultan of Sulu, the spiritual leader of 300,000 Muslims. The Sultan's remote headquarters had kept the Stars and Stripes flying throughout the period of Japanese occupation of the Philippines.

Unfurling American and Philippine flags for the first time in three years, Luzon guerrillas parade triumphantly through the newly liberated town of San Fernando. To the guerrillas, the liberation confirmed a credo adopted by one group after the fall of Bataan: "We believe that God is with us all the while we do right, and that victory shall be ours in the end."

ACKNOWLEDGMENTS

For help given in preparing this book the editors are especially grateful to His Excellency Alejandro Melchor, Ambassador at Large of the Republic of the Philippines. The editors also wish to express their gratitude to General Marcos Agustin, Armed Forces of the Philippines (Ret.), Manila; Desiderio Anolín, Manila; Colonel Uldarico S. Baclagon, Armed Forces of the Philippines (Ret.), Manila; Lounsbury D. Bates, Library, Harvard Club of New York City, New York; Dana Bell, U.S. Air Force Still Photo Depository, Arlington, Virginia; Ambassador Roberto S. Benedicto, Manila; Edward J. Boone Jr., Acting Chief Administrator, MacArthur Memorial, Norfolk, Virginia; Carole Boutté, Senior Researcher, U.S. Army Audio-Visual Activity, Pentagon, Arlington, Virginia; Esteban Cabaños, President, Philippine Veterans Bank, Manila; Sally Cochran, Library, Harvard Club of New York City, New York; V. M. Destefano, Chief, Reference Library, U.S. Army Audio-Visual Activity, Pentagon, Arlington, Virginia; Commissioner Venancio Duque, Philippine Commission of Elections, Manila; Major Gaetano Faillace, USAR (Ret.), Sherman Oaks, California; Charles B. Ferguson, Farmington, Connecticut; Frauke Geilhof, Mondadori Press, Milan, Italy; Charles R. Haberlein Jr., Photographic Section, Curator Branch, Naval History Division, Department of the Navy, Washington, D.C.; Gina Hankin, Library, U.S. Military Academy, West Point, New York; Agnes F. Hoover, Photographic Section, Curator Branch, Naval History Division, Department of the Navy, Washington, D.C.; Jiro Kimata, Tokyo; William H. Leary, National Archives and Records Service, Audio-Visual Division, Washington, D.C.; Sarah Lewis, New York, New York; Patty Maddocks, Director, Photographic Services, U.S. Naval Institute, Annapolis, Maryland; Mrs. Ramón (Luz) Magsaysay, Manila; Colonel Gamaliel Manikan, Armed Forces of the Philippines (Ret.), Manila; Ferdinand E. Marcos, President, Republic of the Philippines, Manila; Pacifico Marcos, M.D., Manila; Colonel Melanio Milán, Armed Forces of the Philippines, Manila; Colonel Primitivo Milán, Armed Forces of the Philippines, Chief of Office of Historical Activities, Manila; Military History Department, National Defense College, Japan; Carl Mydans, TIME Inc., New York, New York; Shelley Mydans, Larchmont, New York; Commander Leonardo Q. Nuval, Philippine Navy (Ret.), Manila; Commodore Santiago Nuval, Philippine Navy (Ret.), Manila; Commander Charles Parsons, USN (Ret.), Manila; General Vicente Raval, Armed Forces of the Philippines (Ret.), Manila; Mary Richie Smith, New York, New York; Summer Steinberg, New York, New York; Charlotte Snyder, Library, U.S. Military Academy, West Point, New York; General Alejo S. Santos, Armed Forces of the Philippines (Ret.), Manila; Brigadier General Edwin H. Simmons, USMC (Ret.), Director, Marine Corps History and Museums, Washington, D.C.; Jim Trimble, National Archives and Records Service, Audio-Visual Division, Washington, D.C.; Makoto Ukuta, War History Department, Japan Defense Agency, Tokyo; Charles M. Vinch, Photo Researcher, Office of the Chief of Public Affairs, U.S. Army, Pentagon, Arlington, Virginia; Mrs. Jesús A. Villamor, Columbia, Maryland; Egon Weiss, Library, U.S. Military Academy, West Point, New York; Marie Yates, U.S. Army Audio-Visual Activity, Pentagon, Arlington, Virginia; Professor Herbert Zipper, University of Southern California, Los Angeles, California.

The index for this book was prepared by Mel Ingber.

BIBLIOGRAPHY

Abaya, Hernando J., *Betrayal in the Philippines*. A. A. Wyn, Inc., 1946.

Adams, Henry H., *Years to Victory*. David McKay Co., Inc., 1973.

Agoncillo, Teodoro A., *The Fateful Years: Japan's Adventure in the Philippines, 1941-45*, Vols. 1 and 2. R. P. Garcia Publishing Co., 1965.

Baclagon, Colonel Uldarico S., *The Philippine Resistance Movement Against Japan, 10 December 1941-14 June 1945*. Veterans Federation of the Philippines, 1965.

Barker, A. J.:
  Suicide Weapon. Ballantine Books Inc., 1971.
  Yamashita. Ballantine Books Inc., 1973.

Belote, James H. and William M., *Corregidor: The Saga of a Fortress*. Harper & Row, 1967.

Boggs, Major Charles W., Jr., USMC, *Marine Aviation in the Philippines*. Historical Division, Headquarters, U.S. Marine Corps, 1951.

Buggy, Hugh, *Pacific Victory*. Issued by the Australian Minister for Information, the Hon. A. A. Calwell, M.H.R., (no date).

Cannon, M. Hamlin, *United States Army in World War II, The War in the Pacific, Leyte: The Return to the Philippines*. Office of the Chief of Military History, Department of the Army, 1954.

Craig, William, *The Fall of Japan*. Dell, 1967.

Craven, Wesley Frank, and James Lea Cate, eds., *The Army Air Forces in World War II, Vol. V, The Pacific: Matterhorn to Nagasaki (June 1944 to August 1945)*. The University of Chicago Press, 1953.

Cronin, Captain Francis D., *Under the Southern Cross, The Saga of the Americal Division*. Combat Forces Press, 1951.

Day, Beth, *Manila Hotel: The Heart and Memory of a City*. National Media Production Center, 1978.

Dissette, Edward, and H. C. Adamson, *Guerrilla Submarines*. Ballantine Books Inc., 1972.

Division Public Relations Section, *The 6th Infantry Division in World War II 1939-1945*. Infantry Journal Press, 1947.

Eichelberger, Robert L., *Our Jungle Road to Tokyo*. The Viking Press, 1950.

Eisenhower, Dwight D., *At Ease: Stories I Tell to Friends*. Doubleday & Co., Inc., 1967.

Fahey, James J., *Pacific War Diary 1942-1945*. Houghton Mifflin Co., 1963.

Falk, Stanley L., *Decision at Leyte*. W. W. Norton & Co., Inc., 1966.

Ferguson, Charles B., *Philippines Guerrilla Communications Report, 1942-1945*. Unpublished, 1945.

Field, James A., Jr., *The Japanese at Leyte Gulf: The Sho Operation*. Princeton University Press, 1947.

Flanagan, Major Edward M., Jr., *The Angels: A History of the 11th Airborne Division 1943-1946*. Infantry Journal Press, 1948.

Fortier, Colonel Malcolm Vaughn, *The Life of a P.O.W. under the Japanese: In Caricature*. C. W. Hill Printing Co., 1946.

Haggerty, Edward, *Guerrilla Padre in Mindanao*. Longmans, Green and Co., 1946.

Halsey, Fleet Admiral William F., USN, and Lieutenant Commander J. Bryan II, USNR, *Admiral Halsey's Story*. McGraw-Hill Book Co., Inc., 1947.

Harkins, Philip, *Blackburn's Headhunters*. W. W. Norton & Co., Inc., 1955.

Hayes, Lieutenant Grace P., *The History of the Joint Chiefs of Staff in World War II*, Vol. II; *The Advance to Victory*. Historical Section, Joint Chiefs of Staff.

Hoyt, Edwin P., *The Battle of Leyte Gulf: The Death Knell of the Japanese Fleet*. Weybright and Talley, 1972.

Ienaga, Saburó, *The Pacific War: World War II and the Japanese, 1931-1945*. Pantheon Books, 1968.

Impact, Vol. III, August 1945. Office of the Assistant Chief of Air Staff Intelligence, Washington, D.C., 1945.

Ind, Colonel Allison, USA, *Allied Intelligence Bureau: Our Secret Weapon in the War Against Japan*. David McKay Co., Inc., 1958.

Ingham, Travis, *Rendezvous by Submarine*. Doubleday, Doran and Co., Inc., 1945.

Inoguchi, Captain Rikhei, and Commander Tadashi Nakajima, *The Divine Wind: Japan's Kamikaze Force in World War II*. Bantam Books, 1958.

Ito, Masanori, *The End of the Imperial Japanese Navy*. Weidenfeld and Nicolson, 1956.

James, D. Clayton:
  The Years of MacArthur, Vol. I, 1880-1941. Houghton Mifflin Co., 1970.
  The Years of MacArthur, Vol. II, 1941-1945. Houghton Mifflin Co., 1975.
  The Japanese Navy in World War II. U.S. Naval Institute, 1971.

Jones, F. C., *Japan's New Order in East Asia: Its Rise and Fall 1937-45*. Oxford University Press, 1954.

Karig, Captain Walter, USNR, Lieutenant Commander Russell L. Harris, USNR, and Lieutenant Commander Frank A. Manson, USN, *Battle Report: The End of an Empire*. Rinehart and Co., Inc., 1948.

Karolevitz, Captain Robert F., ed., *The 25th Division and World War 2*. The Army and Navy Publishing Co., 1946.

Keats, John, *They Fought Alone*. J. B. Lippincott Co., 1963.

Kenney, George C., *General Kenney Reports: A Personal History of the Pacific War*. Duell, Sloan and Pearce, 1949.

Krueger, General Walter, USA (Ret.), *From Down Under to Nippon: The Story of Sixth Army in World War II*. Combat Forces Press, 1953.

Lichauco, Marcial P., *"Dear Mother Putnam."* Marcial P. Lichauco, Publisher, 1949.

Lockwood, Vice Admiral Charles A., USN (Ret.), and Colonel Hans Christian Adamson, USAF (Ret.), *Battles of the Philippine Sea*. Thomas & Crowell Co., 1967.

Long, Gavin, *The Final Campaigns*. Australian War Memorial, 1963.

MacArthur, Douglas, *Reminiscences*. McGraw-Hill Book Co., 1964.

MacIntyre, Donald, *Leyte Gulf: Armada in the Pacific*. Ballantine Books Inc., 1970.

McCartney, William F., Jr., *The Junglers, A History of the 41st Infantry Division*. Washington Infantry Journal Press, 1948.

Madval, Por, *Las Estrellas Dencen al Sol*. National Printing, Manila, 1946.

Manchester, William, *American Caesar: Douglas MacArthur 1880-1964*. Little, Brown and Co., 1978.

Manikan, Colonel Gamaliel L., Armed Forces of the Philippines (Ret.), *Guerrilla Warfare on Panay Island in the Philippines*. Sixth Military District Veterans Foundation, Inc., 1977.

Mayer, Sydney L., *MacArthur*. Ballantine Books Inc., 1971.

Mellnik, Brigadier General Steve, USA (Ret.), *Philippine Diary 1939-1945*. Van Nostrand Reinhold Co., 1969.

Miller, Nathan, *The U.S. Navy—An Illustrated History*. American Heritage and U.S. Naval Institute, 1977.

Millot, Bernard, *Divine Thunder: The Life and Death of the Kamikazes*. The McCall Publishing Co., 1970.

Morison, Samuel Eliot:
   History of United States Naval Operations in World War II. Little, Brown and Co.
      Vol. XII, *Leyte June 1944—January 1945,* 1970.
      Vol. XIII, *The Liberation of the Philippines: Luzon, Mindanao, the Visayas 1944-1945,* 1975.
   The Two-Ocean War: A Short History of the United States Navy in the Second World War. Little, Brown and Co., 1963.
Morton, Louis, *United States Army in World War II: The War in the Pacific, The Fall of the Philippines.* Office of the Chief of Military History, United States Army, 1953.
Mydans, Carl. *More Than Meets the Eye.* Greenwood Press, Publishers, 1974.
Ogawa, Tetsuro, *Terraced Hell.* Charles E. Tuttle Co., 1972.
Okumiya, Masatake, *Zero!* E. P. Dutton & Co., Inc., 1956.
The 129th Infantry in World War II by the regimental staff. Infantry Journal Press, 1947.
Ours to Hold It High: The History of the 77th Infantry Division in World War II. Infantry Journal Press, 1947.
Potter, E. B., *Nimitz.* Naval Institute Press, 1976.
Potter, John Deane, *A Soldier Must Hang.* Frederick Muller Limited, 1963.
Report on the Destruction of Manila and Japanese Atrocities. Office of the Resident Commissioner of the Philippines to the United States, 1945.
Reports of General MacArthur:
   The Campaigns of MacArthur in the Pacific. Vol. I. U.S. Government Printing Office, 1966.
   Japanese Operations in the Southwest Pacific Area. Vol. II, Part II, compiled from Japanese Demobilization Bureaux Records. U.S. Government Printing Office, 1966.
Reyes, Jose G., *Terrorism and Redemption: Japanese Atrocities in the Philippines.* Manila, Philippines, 1947.
Riegelman, Harold, *Caves of Biak.* The Dial Press, 1955.
Romulo, Carlos P., *I See the Philippines Rise.* Doubleday & Co., Inc., 1946.
Sack of Manila. (Based on affidavits of victims and eyewitnesses of Japanese atrocities and collected by U.S. forces that liberated Manila.) U.S. Government Printing Office, 1945.
Sherrod, Robert, *History of Marine Corps Aviation in World War II.* Combat Forces Press, 1952.
Smith, Robert Ross, *United States Army in World War II, The War in the Pacific, Triumph in the Philippines.* Office of the Chief of Military History, Department of the Army, 1963.
Smith, S. E., ed., *The United States Navy in World War II.* William Morrow & Co., Inc., 1966.

Special Historical Collection, Supporting Documents to General Douglas MacArthur's Historical Report on Allied Operations in the Southwest Pacific Area (Item 30, SWPA Series, Vol. II), *The Kamikaze Special Attack Corps* (no date).
Spence, Hartzell, *For Every Tear a Victory: The Story of Ferdinand E. Marcos.* McGraw-Hill Book Co., 1964.
Stafford, Commander Edward P., USN, *The Big E: The Story of the USS Enterprise.* Random House, 1962.
Steinberg, David Joel, *Philippine Collaboration in World War II.* The University of Michigan Press, 1967.
Strong, Herman E., *A Ringside Seat to War.* Vantage Press, © 1965.
Sulzberger, C. L., and the Editors of American Heritage, *The American Heritage Picture History of World War II.* American Heritage Publishing Co., Inc., 1966.
Taylor, Theodore, *The Magnificent Mitscher.* W. W. Norton & Co., Inc., 1954.
33d Infantry Division Historical Committee, *The Golden Cross: A History of the 33d Infantry Division in World War II.* Infantry Journal Press, 1948.
Toland, John, *The Rising Sun (The Decline & Fall of the Japanese Empire) 1936-1945.* Random House, 1970.
Tregonning, K. G., *Under Chartered Company Rule (North Borneo 1881-1946).* University of Malaya Press, 1958.
United States Strategic Bombing Survey (Pacific)—Interrogations of Japanese Officials, Vol. II, Naval Analysis Division. U.S. Government Printing Office, 1946.
Valtin, Jan, *Children of Yesterday.* Readers' Press, 1946.
Volckmann, R. W., *We Remained.* W. W. Norton & Co., Inc., 1954.
Whitney, Major General Courtney, *MacArthur: His Rendezvous with History.* Alfred A. Knopf, 1956.
Willoughby, Major General Charles A., USA (Ret.), *The Guerrilla Resistance Movement in the Philippines: 1941-1945.* Vantage Press, 1972.
Willoughby, Major General Charles A., and John Chamberlain, *MacArthur 1941-1951.* McGraw-Hill Book Co., 1954.
Wolfert, Ira, *American Guerrilla in the Philippines.* Simon and Schuster, 1945.
Woodmansee, Major J. W., Jr., ed., *HM 381 Revolutionary Warfare,* Vol. VI, *Three Experiences Since World War II: Greece, the Philippines, and Cuba.* U.S. Military Academy, (no date).
Woodward, C. Vann, *The Battle for Leyte Gulf.* W. W. Norton & Co., Inc. 1947.
Wright, Major B. C., Division Historian, *The 1st Cavalry Division in World War II.* Toppan Printing Company Ltd., 1947.
"Yay, Colonel," *The Crucible: an Autobiography.* The MacMillan Company, 1950.
Zipper, Herbert (unpublished manuscripts), (no date).

PICTURE CREDITS

Credits from left to right are separated by semicolons, from top to bottom by dashes.

INDEX

*Numerals in italics indicate an illustration
of the subject mentioned*

Field, *44-45*, 107, 108, 111; guerrillas, 18-19, *201, 202-203*; invasion planned, 49; Irisan Gorge, 185; Japanese defense plans, 50, 51, 176; Question Mark Hill, 183-184; Salacsac passes, 188, 190; San Jose, 113; the Sierra Madre, 177-180, 182; Top of the World, 111; U.S. invasion of, 48-49, 106, 107-121. *See also* Manila

M

MacArthur, Arthur, *36*

MacArthur, Douglas, *cover, 1, 31, 34-35, 36, 37, 38-39,* 40-41, *42-43, 44,* 45, *46-47;* and advance on Manila, 110, 111, 113-114; announces end of northern Luzon campaign, 193; approves early invasion of Leyte, 49; argues for recapture of the Philippines, 48-49; career advancement, 38-39; on Corregidor, *116-117;* driven from the Philippines, 46; and Eisenhower, *34-35;* and elimination of threat to Manila, 176, 178; family, 36, 42; and Fertig, 24; Filipino trust of, 19; on Japanese defeat on Leyte, 91; knowledge of guerrillas, 22; Luzon invasion plan, 106; as military adviser, *40-43, 44;* and Nimitz, 48; pledge to return, 19, 31; postpones invasion of Mindoro, 90; and recapture of Borneo, 166, 171, 172-173; and recapture of southern Philippines, 150, 155, 162; reduces forces on Luzon, 176; returns to the Philippines, 78; at Santo Tomás, *132-133;* sets date for Luzon invasion, 49; and Sultan of Sulu, *203;* ties to the Philippines, 36

McClintock, David, 53

McLaughlin, William, 21

Magsaysay, Raymon, 23

Makino, Shiro, 80, 85, 88

Manila: aerial photograph, *115;* civilian casualties, 136, 138-139, *140-141;* clearing harbor, *118-119;* destruction of, *134-149;* Fort Drum, 118, *119;* Intramuros, 120-121, *136, 142-145, 146-147, 148-149;* Japanese occupation, *6-17;* Santo Tomás, 114, *122-133;* the Sierra Madre, 177-180, 182; soldiers on leave in, *186-187;* U.S. advance on, 110-116, 120; water supply, 176-177, *179*, 180, *181,* 182

Manjome, Takeo, 154

Marcos, Ferdinand, *23,* 30

Marking. *See* Agustín, Marcos

Maryland, 57

Matsuo, Isao, 98

Mindanao, *map, 152;* Davao, 155, 157-159, 162-163; guerrillas, 19, 21, 22, 24, 27-28, *194-196;* invasion, 49; invasion at Zamboanga, 151-153; Macajalar Bay, 155, 158, 160, 161; main invasion, 155-163; Sayre Highway, 155, 158, 160-162

Mindoro, air bases, 107; invasion of, 90, 106-107

Mississippi, 57

Mitscher, Marc: air raids on Formosa and Okinawa, 50; air raids on the Philippines, 49; and Battle for Leyte Gulf, 51, 63

Mogami, 70-71

Montgomery, Rodney E., Jr., *86*

Morishita, Nobuei, 73

Moros, 21, 24, 158, *196*

Morozumi, Gyosaku, 160, 161, 162

Mudge, Vernon D., and advance on Manila, 114

Mullins, Charles L., Jr., 191

Musashi, 50-52, *53,* 54-55, *68-69,* 73

Mydans, Carl, 124, 129

Myoko, 54-55

N

Nachi, 70

Nakar, Guillermo, 22, *23*

Nashville, 107

Negros, 18, *101,* 153, 154-155

New Mexico, 108

Nimitz, Chester W.: argues importance of Formosa, 48; disagrees with MacArthur, 48; urges Halsey to assist at Leyte Gulf, 62-63

Nishimura, Shoji, 51, *70;* and Battle for Leyte Gulf, 56-57, 66, *70*

O

Ogawa, Tetsuro, 188

Oldendorf, Jesse B.: at Leyte Gulf, 56, 57; at Luzon, 107

Olsen, Theodore, *87*

Ommaney Bay, 108

Onishi, Takijiro, *94, 96*

Osmeña, Sergio, *38,* 78, 79

Ozawa, Jisaburo, *74;* and Battle for Leyte Gulf, 51, 55, 66, 74

P

Palawan, 151

Panay, 153

Panlilio, Yay, *23*

Parsons, Charles "Chick," 27, 28, 201

Peralta, Macario, Jr., 19, 21, 153

Philippines, *map 20, 67, 152;* Army of, 44; debate over recapture of, 48-49; declared independent by Japan, *8, 10-11;* geography, 19; Japanese conquer, 46; Japanese defense plans, 49-50, 51; money, 8, 21, 24; people aid U.S. wounded, *89;* popular reactions to U.S., 19; puppet government, *6-7,* 11, 176, 185; recapture of southern islands, 150-163; strategic importance of, 21; sympathies of elite, 29, 30; trust of MacArthur, 19; under Japanese occupation, 6-17. *See also* Guerrillas and specific islands

Praeger, Ralph, 22

Princeton, at Battle for Leyte Gulf, 52, *58-59*

Propaganda, using "I shall return," 27, *31*

Q

Quezon, Manuel, 28, 36, *37, 38-39,* 41, *44, 46*

R

Radar: controlled guns, 52, 56; equipped fighters, 86

Raval, Vicente, 19

Remey, 56

Riegelman, Harold, 190

Rogers, Lee, *124*

Romulo, Carlos, 28, 136, 145

Roosevelt, Franklin D., and debate on invasion of the Philippines, 48-49

Roxas, Manuel, 28, 38

Royal, Forrest, *166*

S

St. Lo, 104-105

San Agustín, Primitivo, 30

Sanshiki-don, 52, 54

Santo Tomás, 114, *122-133*

Savo Island, 108

Shima, Kiyohide, *70;* at Leyte Gulf, 51, 59

Sibert, Franklin C., 80, 81, 82, *83,* 156, 158, 160

Smith, Charles, 24, 27, 28

Smith, Daniel F., 54

Smoot, Roland N., 57, 59

Sousa, Alfred, 160

Souza, Abel, 163

Sprague, Clifton A. F., at Leyte Gulf, *60,* 61-62, 163

Stanley, Ernest, *126-127*

Stimson, Henry, *38*

Struble, Arthur D., 153

Sullivan, William A., 118

Sultan of Sulu, *203*

Sulu archipelago, 153

Sutherland, Richard K., *47*

Sutton, James P., 114

Suzuki, Sosaku, 81, 85

Swift, Innis, at Luzon, 109, 110, 113, 182, 188, 190

Swing, Joseph M., 89

T

Talakag, 21

Tanaka, Itsuo, *99*

Tarakan Island, 166, *168-169*

Tennessee, 57

Terauchi, Hisaichi, 51, 85

Thresher, 27, 28

Todd, John C., *124*

Tojo, Hideki, *8*

Tominaga, Kyoji, 79, 85

Toyoda, Soemu, *66;* and Battle for Leyte, 51-52, 66

Turner, Joseph, 159

U

United States, Army of: advance on Baguio, 183-185, 188, *189;* advance on Manila, 110-116, 120-121; at Balete Pass, 190-192; at Breakneck Ridge, 82-84; at Carigara, 80-82; at Clark Field, 111; at Corregidor, 112, 116-118, 120; engineers, 80, 107, 160, 161; at Intramuros, 121, *136, 142-145, 148-149;* invasion of Bohol, 155; invasion of Cebu, 153-154, *156;* invasion of Leyte, 51, 63, 78-85, 88-91; invasion of Luzon, 109-121, 176-193; invasion of Mindanao, 151-153, 155-158, *159,* 160-163; invasion of Negros, 154-155; invasion of Palawan, 151; invasion of Panay, 153; invasion of Sulu archipelago, 153; invasion of Visayan Islands, 151, 153-155; at Ipo Dam, 179-180, 182; lack of air support on Leyte, 79; on leave in Manila, *186-187;* losses on Leyte, 91; losses on Mindanao, 163; at Malinta Hill, 117-118; in north Luzon, 182-185, 188, 190-193; and Operation *Wa,* 85, 88-89; at Ormoc, *84,* 85, 88-89; prisoners of war in the Philippines, *25,* 29; at Question Mark Hill, 183-184; at Salacsac passes, 188, 190; in the Sierra Madre, 177-180, 182; at San Jose, 113; and Wawa Dam, 177-178

United States, Marine Corps of: air forces on Leyte, *86-87;* air forces on Mindanao, 152, 153, 156, *161,* 163; support advance on Manila, 114

United States, Navy of: air raids on Formosa, 50-51; "baby flattops," 60; Battle for Leyte Gulf, 56; forces for Philippine invasion, *50;* losses at Battle for Leyte Gulf, 63; at Luzon, 107-108; supply shipment to guerrillas, 27, 33, 196, *197;* at Tarakan Island, *168,* 169

United States Pacific Ocean Areas forces: advance toward Philippines, 48; air raids on Formosa and Okinawa, 50; air raids on the Philippines, 49; attacks Japanese decoy force, 55-56, 62-63; Battle for Leyte, 51-52, 54-56, 61-63

United States Southwest Pacific Area forces: advance toward the Philippines, 48; air bases on Leyte, 51, 63, 78-85, 88-90; Battle for Leyte Gulf, 51, 56-67, 59, 60-62; at Corregidor, 116-118; invasion of Borneo, *166-175;* invasion of Leyte, 51, 63, 78-85, 88-91; invasion of Luzon, 106, 107-116; invasion of Mindanao, 155-162, *163;* invasion of Palawan, 151; invasion of southern Philippines, 150-151; invasion of Visayan Islands, 151, 153-155; and invasion

Printed in U.S.A.